Palgrave Macmillan Studies in Banking and Financial Institutions

Series Editor
Philip Molyneux
University of Sharjah
Sharjah, United Arab Emirates

The Palgrave Macmillan Studies in Banking and Financial Institutions series is international in orientation and includes studies of banking systems in particular countries or regions as well as contemporary themes such as Islamic Banking, Financial Exclusion, Mergers and Acquisitions, Risk Management, and IT in Banking. The books focus on research and practice and include up to date and innovative studies that cover issues which impact banking systems globally.

More information about this series at
http://www.palgrave.com/gp/series/14678

Caterina Cruciani • Gloria Gardenal
Elisa Cavezzali
Editors

Banking and Beyond

The Evolution of Financing along Traditional and Alternative Avenues

palgrave
macmillan

Editors
Caterina Cruciani
Department of Management
Ca' Foscari University of Venice
Venice, Italy

Gloria Gardenal
Department of Management
Ca' Foscari University of Venice
Venice, Italy

Elisa Cavezzali
Department of Management
Ca' Foscari University of Venice
Venice, Italy

ISSN 2523-336X ISSN 2523-3378 (electronic)
Palgrave Macmillan Studies in Banking and Financial Institutions
ISBN 978-3-030-45751-8 ISBN 978-3-030-45752-5 (eBook)
https://doi.org/10.1007/978-3-030-45752-5

This Palgrave Macmillan imprint is published by the registered company Springer Nature Switzerland AG.
The registered company address is: Gewerbestrasse 11, 6330 Cham, Switzerland

Contents

Notes on Contributors

Giulia Baschieri is Senior Assistant Professor of Corporate Finance at the Department of Management—Alma Mater Studiorum University of Bologna, Italy, where she teaches Corporate Finance. She has a Master in Science in Finance, Intermediary and Markets, and a PhD in Markets and Financial Intermediaries with a thesis on the local home bias in the Italian context. Her research interests refer to asset-pricing dynamics tied to corporate geographic location, and corporate evaluation.

Francesca Battaglia is Associate Professor of Banking and Finance at the University of Naples "Parthenope", Department of Management Studies and Quantitative Methods, where she teaches Risk Management in Banking and Financial Markets and Institutions. She also serves as a member of the teaching board of the Doctorate "Governance, Management and Economics". Her research focuses on risk management, securitization, corporate governance, systemic risk of financial intermediaries and crowdfunding.

Giorgio S. Bertinetti is Full Professor of Corporate Finance and past director at the Department of Management of Ca' Foscari University of Venice, Italy. His research focuses on enterprise risk management, sustainability and corporate performance measures. Recently, he started to investigate the case of the real estate industry.

Francesco Busato is Full Professor of Economics at the University of Naples "Parthenope". He received his BA from University of Rome La Sapienza (summa cum laude), MA from Bocconi University, and PhD in Economics from Columbia University, NY. He served as an assistant professor at the University of Aaarhus Denmark, University of Rome III, as an associate professor and next Full Professor at the University of Naples "Parthenope". He is the head of PhD Program of Economics, Statistics and Sustainability. He teaches classes topics in finance, economics, at bachelor, master and PhD level. He published on peer reviewed international journals in finance, economics (dynamic models) and sustainability.

Marika Carboni is a researcher at the University of Rome III, Italy. Before completing her PhD at the University of Rome "Tor Vergata", Italy, she was a visiting research scholar at Olin Business School, Washington University in St. Louis. Her research has been published in various journals, including *Journal of Banking and Finance.*

Nicola Carta received his Master Degree in Economics and Finance in March 2019 from the Ca' Foscari University of Venice, Italy. Since September 2019, he is a PhD student with a concentration in Finance within the Department of Management of the same university. His research interests broadly concern internal governance, SMEs, entrepreneurial finance and sustainability.

Elisa Cavezzali is Associate Professor of Economics of Financial Intermediaries at the Department of Management where she received her PhD in Business. She achieved a second PhD in Finance from Cass Business School, London. Her main research interests include the security industry, asset allocation and portfolio selection, behavioral finance, corporate financial disclosure, corporate social responsibility and debt restructuring processes. Cavezzali's teaching experience includes financial and banking instruments, commercial banks' management and credit analysis, corporate finance, corporate financial policies, corporate financial disclosure, corporate and investment banking at Bachelor, Master and MBA levels. She was also an "expert" for the European Economic and Social Committee (CESE) about financial markets system and financial derivatives.

Giusy Chesini is Associate Professor of Financial Markets and Institutions at the University of Verona, Italy. She got her PhD in Financial Markets and Institutions at the University of Bergamo, Italy. Her research interests refer to the evolution of financial markets and international stock exchanges, the bank-company relationship, bank regulation, management and performance measurement.

Stefano Cosma is Full Professor of Financial Markets and Institutions at the Department of Communication and Economics, University of Modena and Reggio Emilia, Italy. His research fields are retail banking, consumer credit, households lending and corporate banking. His current research interests include FinTech, open banking and banking platforms.

Caterina Cruciani is Assistant Professor of Financial Markets and Institutions at the Department of Management, Ca' Foscari University of Venice, where she also received a PhD in Economics. She is the operating director of the Center for Experimental Research in Management and Economics (CERME) and a member of the Risk-Lab at Ca' Foscari University of Venice. Cruciani's research interests focus on behavioral finance, financial advisory, and SME financing. She teaches financial and banking instruments, corporate banking and behavioral finance at the University of Venice and has been involved in professional training activities for financial advisors.

Paula Cruz-García holds a PhD in Quantitative Finance and Economy from the University of Valencia. She has been a visiting PhD student at Essex Business School, University of Essex. Her main research interests are banking and financial economics and she has written several papers for specialized journals and book chapters about these topics.

Vincenzo Farina is Associate Professor of Financial Markets and Institutions in the Department of Management and Law at the University of Rome Tor Vergata and Adjunct Professor of Financial Management and Financial Markets in the Department of Finance at Bocconi University. He is member of scientific board of PhD in "Economia Aziendale", University of Rome Tor Vergata.

Andrea Ferrarin is a PhD candidate in Managerial and Actuarial Sciences at the Department of Economic and Statistics of the University of Udine, Italy. His research focuses on the identification of the value drivers of the Italian asset management industry, focusing on the systematic risk determinants.

Josanco Floreani is Associate Professor of Corporate Finance at the Department of Economic and Statistics of the University of Udine, Italy. His research focuses mainly on securities and exchange industry structure, performance measurement and value creation in the exchange industry, credit quality and banks' systematic risk, and SME's capital structure.

Gloria Gardenal is Assistant Professor of Corporate Finance and a member of the Risk-Lab and the Center for Experimental Research in Management and Economics (CERME) at Ca' Foscari University of Venice, where she also received a PhD in Business. Her research focuses on corporate finance, risk management and investment decisions, with a particular interest in behavioral finance. She taught several Bachelor and Master courses including corporate finance, valuation, financial policies and investment strategies and also has been involved in more advanced courses like MBAs in Finance and International Finance.

Elisa Giaretta is Adjunct Professor of Corporate Finance and Research Fellow at the Department of Economics of the University of Verona, Italy. Her research focuses on FinTech innovation and bank digitalization processes, financing firms' networks, firms' longevity and vitality, and firms' dividend policies.

Maria Manganiello received her BSc in "Business Economics" and her MSc in "Economic and Financial Sciences" from the University of Naples "Parthenope" cum laude, respectively. She was awarded at the Chamber of Deputies in Rome as a young merit graduate for the attainment of the first level degree, by obtaining a Master's degree in "Global Marketing, Communication & Made in Italy" at the Italy-USA Foundation, with the adhesion of the Minister of Education, University and Research. She also completed the "Advanced Risk and Portfolio Management Marathon," a master-level program at the University of Rome "Tor Vergata". She is currently a third-year PhD student in the International Program in "Economics, Statistics, and Sustainability" at the Department of Economic and Legal Studies of the University of Naples "Parthenope." Her professional interests include financial economics, quantitative risk management, FinTech, quantitative portfolio management, systemic risk, and real estate.

Ewa Miklaszewska is Professor of Banking and Finance at Cracow University of Economics, where she chairs the Division of Banking and Global Financial System.

Francesco Pattarin is Assistant Professor of Financial Markets and Institutions at the Department of Economics "Marco Biagi", University of Modena and Reggio Emilia, Italy. His research is mainly focused on the mini-bond market, the spending policies of banking foundations, and the psychological determinants of household debt decisions.

Daniela Pennetta is a PhD student in Labour, Development, and Innovation at the "Marco Biagi" Foundation, University of Modena and Reggio Emilia. She is a member of ADEIMF (Italian Association of University Teachers of Financial Intermediaries and Markets). Her research topics include crowdlending, FinTech and digital transformation in financial intermediation.

Maurizio Polato is Full Professor of Financial Markets and Institutions at the Department of Economic and Statistics of the University of Udine, Italy. He holds a PhD in Business from Ca' Foscari University of Venice, Italy. His main research interests include credit quality, bank provisioning and systematic risk in banking business, Islamic versus traditional stock exchanges, financial products and credit lending to SMEs.

Daniele A. Previati is Full Professor of Financial Markets and Institutions at the University of Rome III and Fellow of the SDA Bocconi School of Management, Milan, Italy. He is currently President of ADEIMF, the Italian Association of Scholars in Banking and Finance. His current research interests include FinTech, crowdfunding, alternative finance, banking and central banking communication, sustainability and risk management in financial markets and institutions. With specific reference to the banking sector, he studies stakeholder engagement, HR and intellectual capital management, and operational and reputational risks.

Jan Pys is a PhD student at Cracow University of Economics, having over ten years of practical experience in the banking sector, currently as a head of management accounting for Retail and Consolidation at ING Germany in Frankfurt.

Giulio Velliscig is a PhD student at the Department of Economic and Statistical Sciences of the University of Udine, Italy. His research focuses on bank resolution regulation and explores the impact exerted by the loss-absorbing capacity requirements (TLAC, MREL) on banking business models.

List of Figures

List of Tables

CHAPTER 1

Introduction by the Editors

Caterina Cruciani, Gloria Gardenal, and Elisa Cavezzali

This book presents a selection of original contributions discussed at the 2019 Wolpertinger Conference held in Venice, Italy. The conference represents the annual meeting of the European Association of University Teachers in Banking and Finance and aims at fostering discussions on key topics and areas in the current debate within this field of applied research. The 2019 edition of the conference centred around the future of credit for small and medium enterprises (SMEs) and socially sustainable investing, touching upon the role and the evolution of the banking sector and the financing tools it fosters, while at the same time addressing the impact of new regulations and the ensuing opportunities for financial institutions, firms and individuals.

The book includes two parts. The first part takes on a more marked macroeconomic approach, addressing the impact of policy changes affecting banks and financial institutions. In particular, it deals with the consequences of recent changes in European policy looking both at how policy has been and is communicated and to how it shapes new incentives and

C. Cruciani (✉) • G. Gardenal • E. Cavezzali
Department of Management, Ca' Foscari University of Venice, Venice, Italy
e-mail: cruciani@unive.it; ggardenal@unive.it; elisa.cavezzali@unive.it

C. Cruciani et al. (eds.), *Banking and Beyond*, Palgrave Macmillan Studies in Banking and Financial Institutions,
https://doi.org/10.1007/978-3-030-45752-5_1

challenges for the banking sector and institutional and individual investors. This part touches upon the debate on the "bail-in" versus "bail-out" options and reviews the new opportunities for investors on the covered and subordinated bond markets in Europe, building upon the new regulatory structure provided for by the European authorities. The second part expands the scope of the analysis and explores the role of some of the new financing tools besides the traditional banking sector available to firms and individuals. Specifically, it explores financing options for firms and individuals and describes, for example, which role alternative capital-market tools like mini bonds and crowdfunding are playing in the landscape of SMEs financing, touching upon how financing decisions can affect the survival of start-ups.

Chapter 2 by Marika Carboni, Vincenzo Farina and Daniele A. Previati analyses for the first time central banks' communication strategies, given the increasing role they have been playing in the last decades. In particular, they investigate the differences between the topics contained in European Central Bank (ECB) and Federal Reserve (FED) Governors' speeches over the time span 2007–2019. This contribution finds that both ECB and FED speeches strongly focus on monetary policy issues. However, the United States give emphasis also to two other important issues—financial stability and consumer protection—more than what their European counterpart does.

Chapter 3 by Ewa Miklaszewska and Jan Pys focuses on another relevant issue at the macroeconomic level—the effectiveness of the Single Resolution Mechanism (SRM) and the Bank Recovery and Resolution Directive (BRRD) in Europe—in limiting the use of public spending for the stabilization and restructuring of systemically important banks. Public intervention during the crisis played a fundamental role in stabilizing the banking sector. However, it also produced negative effects such as changes in the market structure, incentives to take risks, variations in the cost of capital and of the competitive conditions. This chapter analyses the implementation of the resolution mechanism for large banks (bail-ins), developed in the post-crisis period, and compares it with bank restructuring programmes based on bail-outs, using the case of two large banks: Deutsche Bank in Germany and ING Group in the Netherlands. The empirical analysis shows how tighter regulation can help shift the perspective towards the longer term and set in motion changes that ultimately lead to improved profitability and cost efficiency.

Chapters 4 and 5 expand the analysis of the impact of policy changes to the ever-evolving bond market. Chapter 4 by Giusy Chesini and Elisa Giaretta focuses on the evolution in the regulation of covered bonds, traditionally left in the hands of Member States. The lack of a harmonized regulation resulted in several national approaches for what concerns key technical issues and posed a challenge to the further development of this financial tool. The European Commission has recently harmonized national rules in the issuance of these securities by providing common definitions, characteristics and regulations with the aim of introducing a European trademark through the "Capital Markets Union Action Plan". In March 2018 the European Commission issued a proposal for a Directive on covered bonds (CBs), laying down the conditions for such bonds to be recognized under EU law and representing an important step forward to strengthen capital markets and investments in the EU. This proposal invigorates investor protection by imposing specific supervisory duties. In this chapter, the authors intend to explore the new European characteristics of these financial instruments and the possibility for banks and investors to take advantage of the new regulation.

Chapter 5 shifts the focus on subordinated bonds. The recent academic literature has started focusing on the evolving role of subordinated debt within the EU resolution framework. The market monitoring function employed by its investors and its crucial role in complying with the Minimum Requirement for Own Funds and Eligible Liabilities (MREL) subordination requirement makes subordinated debt the more affected asset class under the BRRD. In this chapter, the authors (Giulio Velliscig, Josanco Floreani and Maurizio Polato) provide an overview of subordinated debt literature and its evolution within banking regulation with a focus on the BRRD. The chapter explores the different streams of literature that ground both theoretically and empirically future research on the role of subordinated debt within the EU resolution framework.

Chapter 6 provides an empirical test of monetary policy on bank profitability. Paula Cruz-García analyses the effect of monetary policy on the net interest margin and on bank profitability of a panel from 31 OECD countries over the period 2000–2017, focusing specifically on the impact of policy interest rates and the slope of the yield curve. The main results show that expansionary monetary policy measures adopted in numerous economies had a negative impact on net interest margins and, therefore, on bank profitability. The relationship found between interest rates and the slope of the yield curve with both the net interest margin and profitability is non-linear, more specifically concave. This suggests that the negative impact of low interest rates and the flat yield curve is greater the lower and flattened they are, respectively. Therefore, a potential normalization of monetary policy would have highly beneficial effects on restoring margins and profitability.

Moving to the second part of the book, in Chap. 7 Andrea Ferrarin, Josanco Floreani and Maurizio Polato investigate the asset management industry focusing on the Italian market. After the escalation of the global financial crisis and the consequent turmoil of the whole banking system, the asset management industry in EU has undergone a significant growth in the last decade, distinguishing itself as the most vibrant segment within the financial intermediation field. Using a sample of 44 Italian asset management firms from 2006 to 2016, this chapter provides an empirical investigation of the major systematic risk determinants, which have featured Italian asset managers across the financial crisis. Results show that operating efficiency represents a crucial factor for the pricing of the systematic risk exposure of asset managers, having a positive impact on market beta.

Chapters 8 and 9 address another very important element for the firm financing in the fintech era—crowdfunding as financing tool for SMEs. In particular, Chap. 8, authored by Francesca Battaglia, Francesco Busato and Maria Manganiello, focuses on the role of signalling in equity crowdfunding by examining the determinants of funding success in the Italian context. By using a unique dataset of 192 successful and unsuccessful campaigns launched between 2014 and November 2018 on the leading Italian equity crowdfunding platforms, they analyse the signalling role played towards external investors by the disclosure of financial information, by the share of equity retained by founders and by the size of their social network. Results show that the disclosure of financial information, the equity retention retained and the social capital of entrepreneurs have a positive and significant impact on funding success and can be interpreted as effective signals by external investors.

Chapter 9 focuses instead on a different issue—the strategies and business models adopted by lending-based crowdfunding (LBCF) companies, a topic currently neglected by the academic literature. The authors, Stefano Cosma, Francesco Pattarin and Daniela Pennetta, aim at the definition of a more correct classification of LBCF companies, grounded on several dimensions that characterize their business models. In particular, they find that the existing classification can be improved by simultaneously considering strategic choices concerning target customers (borrowers and lenders), the intermediation model and the additional risk management services provided by platforms. This chapter analyses an original worldwide sample of 30 LBCF companies, for which the authors collected several qualitative features. They use a clustering algorithm to group LBCF companies based on the financial and commercial fundamentals of their activity. The chapter identifies four business models denoted by their strategies, financial services, risk positions and customer target. This methodology improves on the existing classifications as it is both more sensitive and more specific, and it provides a clearer picture of LBCF companies' strategic choices and business models.

Chapter 10 concentrates on a different financing tool for SMEs, that is, mini bonds. Mini bonds are a relatively new form of corporate debt financing available to Italian SMEs that may be described as fixed-income securities with a medium-long-term expiration date, issued by listed or non-listed SMEs aimed at supporting growth projects, future developments or refinancing operations. The authors Nicola Carta and Caterina Cruciani focus on a specific, economically relevant area in Italy—the North-East including Veneto, Trentino Alto Adige and Friuli Venezia Giulia—and look at the difference between listed and non-listed issues of mini bonds. In fact, mini bonds may or may not be listed on the ExtraMotPro, the professional segment of the ExtraMot market managed by Borsa Italiana. This chapter explores whether this choice is structurally determined and how recent normative developments may affect it and the overall demand for mini bonds by investors. Moreover, the chapter explores the literature trying to identify criteria for the determination of potential emitters and show that existing criteria likely underestimate the true potential supply and are largely ignored by firms.

Finally, Chap. 11 by Giulia Baschieri, Giorgio S. Bertinetti and Gloria Gardenal analyses the role of the initial capital structure decisions on the success and duration of entrant manufacturing start-up firms. Focusing on all the Italian manufacturing companies incorporated in the database Aida Bureau van Dijk in 2009, this chapter includes financial variables such as leverage (measured as a debt-to-asset ratio) and studies their impact on firm survival through the implementation of duration analysis as an estimation technique on the time span 2009–2016. The analysis confirms that the relationship between leverage and firm hazard is positive and significant, meaning that higher levels of initial bank debt increase the probability of default for Italian manufacturing SMEs. This suggests that start-ups should rely more on alternative financing tools at their initial stages and use debt at a later stage.

The chapters contributed to this book and presented at an internationally recognized conference confirm that the academic debate regarding financial markets and institutions is not at all out of step with the issues that businesses and firms are facing. Financial markets and instruments are continuously evolving in response to the evolution of standards, technologies and goals. This volume aims at providing an overview of this complex and rich debate, providing original solutions and responses to the main research questions in the Banking and Finance field and highlighting the interplay between all of these dimensions ranging from policy and regulation to new financing tools.

PART I

Financial Institutions and the Evolution of European Market and Policy Framework

CHAPTER 2

ECB and FED Governors' Speeches: A Topic Modeling Analysis (2007–2019)

Marika Carboni, Vincenzo Farina, and Daniele A. Previati

2.1 Introduction

Central bank communication has evolved largely in the last decades. Prior to the 1990s, monetary policymakers did not say much to the public (Blinder et al. 2008), with central banks saying little to clarify what they were doing and the reason why (Vayid 2013). That approach changed in the last years of the twentieth century, when central banks reinforced their communication strategy (Blot and Hubert 2018). Starting from those years, central banks have taken significant steps in communication, trying to strengthen transparency and accountability (Vayid 2013).

M. Carboni (✉) • D. A. Previati
Department of Business Studies, University of Rome III, Rome, Italy
e-mail: marika.carboni@uniroma3.it; daniele.previati@uniroma3.it

V. Farina
Department of Management and Law, University of Rome Tor Vergata, Rome, Italy
e-mail: vincenzo.farina@uniroma2.it

C. Cruciani et al. (eds.), *Banking and Beyond*, Palgrave Macmillan Studies in Banking and Financial Institutions,
https://doi.org/10.1007/978-3-030-45752-5_2

Communication can represent a valuable part of the central bank's set of resources, since it is able to make the predictability of monetary policy decisions stronger, move financial markets, and also help reach the macroeconomic goals of central banks (Blinder et al. 2008). That is why central banks communicate their monetary policy framework and objectives nowadays. Additionally, they normally publish both their analysis and projections of economic conditions (Vayid 2013).

Several types of communications have been employed in previous research, such as introductory statements of the European Central Bank (ECB) President at the monthly press conferences (Berger et al. 2006), Financial Stability Reports, and speeches by central banks (Born et al. 2011, 2013). Those papers analyze the content and/or the effects of central bank communication. For example, on the one hand, with respect to the content, Berger et al. (2006) found that, over time, the relative amount of words related to the monetary analysis decreased; on the other hand, with respect to the effects, Born et al. (2011) showed that communication by monetary authorities on financial stability issues are able to affect financial market developments.

Our research is related to the first group of papers, aiming to analyze the content of central bank communication. Specifically, we aim to investigate the content of the ECB and the Federal Reserve (FED) Governors' speeches, with a focus on possible differences and evolution over time of central banks' functions, for the year period spanning 2007–2019.

By employing the topic modeling approach, coding the content of texts into a set of topics containing meaningful words, we find that both ECB and FED Governors' speeches are extensively related to monetary policy, with respect to both the achievement of stable prices and the effects on macroeconomic variables. The topic of financial stability is also relevant, especially in the United States, where, additionally, the issue of consumer protection emerges.

Our chapter contributes to two main strands of literature. The first one broadly relates to central bank communication to the public (see, for example, Born et al. 2011, 2013; Montes and Scarpari 2015; Ehrmann and Talmi 2017; Montes and Nicolay 2017; Blot and Hubert 2018; de Mendonça and de Moraes 2018; Gertler and Horvath 2018). The second one relates to the evolution over time of central banks' functions and role (see, for example, Goodhart 1988, 2011; Nier 2009; Rochon and Rossi 2015; Bordo et al. 2016; Masciandaro and Romelli 2018).

The rest of the chapter is organized as follows: in Sect. 2.2, we review relevant past papers; data and methodology are provided in Sect. 2.3, and we discuss our results in Sect. 2.4. Section 2.5 concludes the chapter.

2.2 Literature Review

Our chapter is closely related to two branches of literature. The first one relates to central bank communication to the public. The second one relates to the evolution of central banks' role and functions.

Central bank communication evolved largely in recent decades (Blinder et al. 2008; Vayid 2013). Previously, central bankers thought that monetary policymakers should provide the public with little information. This belief started to change in the last decade of the twentieth century, when economists finally understood the importance of communication; specifically, they realized that an appropriate communication strategy could make central banks able both to affect the expectations of economic agents and to improve the performance of monetary policy (Janikowski and Rzonca 2018). Policymakers started to think that communication could be employed as a tool to both anchor inflation expectations and orient financial markets. As a consequence, central banks started to disseminate their policies more strongly, as proven by the increasing number of speeches released by representatives of central banks since the end of the 1990s (Lustenberger and Rossi 2017). A large empirical evidence shows that central bank communication has finally strengthened the transmission of the monetary policy, both before and during the financial crisis (Blot and Hubert 2018), supporting the above-mentioned (more recent) belief. Additionally, central bank communications are proven to affect bank risk-taking (Montes and Scarpari 2015), financial markets (Gertler and Horvath 2018), for example, stock market returns (Born et al. 2013), stock prices (Born et al. 2011), and financial stability (de Mendonça and de Moraes 2018), which both the ECB and the FED are committed to promote.

As reported by Janikowski and Rzonca (2018), central banks usually employ the following communication tools: (i) press conferences; (ii) minutes and voting records; (iii) reports (such as annual reports, inflation reports, quarterly and/or monthly bulletins); (iv) official hearings and testimonies (e.g., in parliament); (v) interviews with individual monetary policy committee members. The authors highlight that combining tools is necessary for reaching an effective communication; for example, press conferences are useful to communicate the reasons of a specific monetary policy decision quite rapidly, and at the same time they are able to contain misunderstandings related to central banks' communication, since they allow media to ask clarifying questions. However, press conferences are able to provide only a limited amount of information at once, suggesting that other tools to provide additional information are required.

A crucial point concerning the press releases, announcing and explaining monetary policy decisions, is related to how they are drafted. Central banks usually start from the past statement, and update the previous text at the margin. Interestingly, Ehrmann and Talmi (2017) find that similarity is connected to more stability: specifically, similar press releases are able to generate lower market volatility, whereas more textual changes, after a series of similar statements, generate much larger volatility.

Several types of communications have been employed in past papers, for example, introductory statements of the ECB President at the monthly press conferences (Berger et al. 2006), Financial Stability Reports and speeches by central banks (Born et al. 2011, 2013), ECB press conferences (Ehrmann and Fratzscher 2009). The content of such communications can reveal the evolution over time of central banks' functions and role, which have been studied by different scholars in past papers (see, for example, Goodhart 1988, 2011), especially after the 2007 financial crisis (see, for example, Nier 2009; Rochon and Rossi 2015; Bordo et al. 2016; Masciandaro and Romelli 2018). For example, Bordo et al. (2016) focus on the strengthened central banks' role to guarantee financial stability in the wake of the global financial crisis, while Masciandaro and Romelli (2018) highlight the increased involvement of central banks in supervision following the crisis.

Central banks are involved in processes such as money creation and control, price and financial stability control, and payments system management, having a tremendous impact on society and citizens' welfare (Farina et al. 2019). It is supposed that central banks should align their communication efforts to macroeconomic variables, developments, and trends, but this does not always appear in such a clear way (Farina et al. 2018). The (probably) most influential central bank in the world, the FED, basically shows the same functions of the ECB (conducting monetary policy, maintaining financial stability, supervising financial institutions, fostering payment and settlement system safety and efficiency), even if the former also explicitly communicates to promote consumer protection and community development.[1] Conversely, the ECB and the FED differ with respect to their goals. The main goal of the ECB is to achieve price stability, while the FED's statute states multiple goals, without providing a clear guidance on their relative importance. Specifically, the FED should promote the goals of maximum employment, stable prices, and moderate long-term interest rates. The comparative absence of clarity opens the interpretation of its mandate, posing challenges for the FED (Orphanides 2013), even though, in order to achieve these objectives, the Federal Open Market Committee (FOMC), responsible for open market operations, tries to explain its monetary policy decisions to the public as clearly as possible. As reported on the website of the FED: "Clarity in policy communications facilitates well-informed decision-making by households and businesses, reduces economic and financial uncertainty, increases the effectiveness of monetary policy, and enhances transparency and accountability, which are essential in a democratic society".[2]

On the other side of the Ocean, the ECB makes efforts to strengthen communication; its commitment is proven, for example, by its first conference on communication organized at the end of 2017.[3] From an academic point of view, clarity of central bank communication has been proven to improve the credibility of monetary policy (Montes and Nicolay 2017).

2.3 Data and Methodology

We collected publicly available data, specifically related to ECB and FED Governors' speeches, in the period going from 2007 to 2019.[4] Therefore, we built a unique dataset, characterized by a 13-year coverage.

To conduct our analysis, we applied a topic modeling approach, which enables analysis of large volumes of texts, and groups words according to their co-occurrences (Ferri et al. 2018). Those groups of words form specific topics, which are automatically generated and represent our focus of

[1] The importance given to the consumer protection issue in the United States is also highlighted by the Dodd-Frank Wall Street Reform and Consumer Protection Act, the legislation signed into law by President Barack Obama in 2010 in response to the financial crisis.

[2] See the following webpage: https://www.federalreserve.gov/faqs/money_12848.htm (accessed May 2019).

[3] See the following webpage: https://www.ecb.europa.eu/pub/conferences/html/20171114_communications_challenges_policy_effectiveness.en.html (accessed May 2019).

[4] We are still not able to collect all the speeches related to the year 2019.

analysis. According to Ferri et al. (2018) and DiMaggio et al. (2013), topic modeling shows different advantages if compared to human analysis. In fact, topic modeling is (a) more effective, especially when corpora are very large; (b) more reliable, since it produces objective topics, so that other researchers may easily reproduce the analysis; (c) not requiring the imposition of a priori categories for the analysis of corpora, because topics are automatically generated following a bottom-up approach. Specifically, in this chapter we employ an unsupervised probabilistic model, called Latent Dirichlet Allocation (Blei et al. 2003), which is used to discover latent themes in a document and is the most diffused implementation of topic modeling. This technique makes two different assumptions: (1) documents are produced from a mix of topics, so that each document belongs to each of the topics to a specific degree; (2) each topic is a generative model that generates words of the vocabulary having specific probabilities (words often occurring together will have more probability than others).

As observed by DiMaggio et al. (2013), in order to capture patterns of co-occurrences, which are important in the assignment of words to topics, the LDA trades off two different goals that are at odds: (i) for each document, it allocates its observed words to few topics; (ii) for each topic, it assigns high probability to very few words from the vocabulary. On the one hand, if a document exhibits one topic it is harder to assign few words high probability, since observed words must all have probability with respect to that topic. On the other hand, in the presence of a set of topics, each of which shows very few words with high probability, it is harder to assign documents to a few topics.

To perform the LDA analysis, we used a specifically developed Python script on the basis of the NLTK and Gensim libraries. Three parameters are needed in order to run the LDA model: (1) the number of topics, which should be extracted from the corpus; (2) the number of terms composing a single topic; (3) the maximum number of iterations, which are allowed for an LDA algorithm for convergence. Therefore, even if topics are automatically produced, researchers can still decide the number of topics the model should generate (as reported by DiMaggio et al. 2013, a statistical test for the optimal number of topics is not available), whether they must contain (or not) the same number of words, and the number of iterations for convergence. In our chapter, we started to look at the 5-topic model and 10-topic model, with 10 terms composing each topic and 50 iterations allowed to the LDA algorithm, related to both ECB and FED Governors' speeches. Each co-author looked at the models independently, trying to label the produced topics. Since we agreed that the 5-topic model generated topics that were too aggregated, we chose the 10-topic model.

In order to study the various topics communicated by the ECB and the FED and their representation during the time, we respected the following steps for our LDA analysis. The first step refers to the selection of all the text documents (corpus). The first corpus consists of 313 speeches of Governors Jean-Claude Trichet and Mario Draghi of ECB, during the period January 2007—February 2019. The second corpus consists of 193 speeches of Governors Ben Bernanke, Janet Yellen, and Jerome Powell of the FED, during the same time period.

By using the NLTK library of Python, we then performed the removal of punctuations and stop words from each corpus. Moreover, by using the same library, we normalized the corpora with lemmatized words in order to bring both inflectional forms and derivationally related forms to a common base form.

In order to obtain the conversion into a document-term matrix and to run the LDA model for each corpus, by using the previously defined parameters (10 topics to be extracted, 10 terms composed in a single topic and 50 iterations), we employ the Gensim library of Python. Finally, as an outcome we obtained two models for ECB and FED, where terms are listed based on TF*IDF (term frequency–inverse document frequency) weighting, to adjust the prevalence of each term within a topic for prevalence within the corpus as a whole. In other words, in Tables 2.1 and 2.2, terms are listed in order of decreasing relevance within each topic. The library also allows the inference of topic distribution on text documents for the ECB and FED corpora, reported in Tables 2.3 and 2.4. The relative weights of ECB and FED topics are reported in Figs. 2.1 and 2.2.

The last step consists of the interpretation of the topics, which is devolved to the authors (DiMaggio et al. 2013). That feature obliges the researchers to explain all the adopted decisions and undertaken steps, calling the reader, who basically can agree or disagree with the construction of the categories, to actively participate in the process.

2.4 Results

In this section, we interpret the topic solutions we obtained by employing the topic modeling approach. At this stage we just compare the topics respectively to the tasks and the functions of the ECB and the

Table 2.1 10-topic solution, 10 words, ECB Governors' speeches

Topic 0	*Topic 1*	*Topic 2*	*Topic 3*	*Topic 4*	*Topic 5*	*Topic 6*	*Topic 7*	*Topic 8*	*Topic 9*
Financial	Euro	European	Risk	Euro	Pension	European	Systemic	Euro	Global
Bank	Area	Integration	Price	Area	Insurer	Europe	Risk	Policy	Financial
Market	Economy	Market	Market	Policy	Esas	Union	Esrb	Area	Economy
Risk	Country	Union	Financial	Growth	Ceiops	Euro	Data	Monetary	Market
Crisis	Economic	Europe	Future	Price	Settingup	Single	Macroprudential	Bank	Economic
System	Market	Today	Macroeconomic	Monetary	Eighth	Currency	Tool	Economic	Country
Central	Global	Action	Premia	Market	Rulebook	Ecb	EU	Inflation	Productivity
Policy	Also	People	Asset	Inflation	Disaggregated	Would	Intermediary	Rate	Finance
Liquidity	World	U	Premium	Labour	Addressee	Today	See	Ecb	Growth
Stability	Financial	Gasperi	Oil	Rate	Gathering	Central	Instability	Market	International

This table reports the 10-topic solution, 10 words, related to the sample of ECB Governors' speeches, over the time period 2007–2019. Words are ordered in terms of decreasing relevance within each topic

The presence of the letter "U" in this table is probably due to a set of used acronyms in the text

Table 2.2 10-topic solution, 10 words, FED Governors' speeches

Topic 0	*Topic 1*	*Topic 2*	*Topic 3*	*Topic 4*	*Topic 5*	*Topic 6*	*Topic 7*	*Topic 8*	*Topic 9*
Woman	Financial	Policy	Economic	Inflation	Community	Mortgage	Policy	Mortgage	Rate
Labor	Bank	Monetary	Economy	Expectation	Bank	Fiscal	Reserve	Foreclosure	Inflation
Participation	Market	Financial	Percent	Price	Reserve	Government	Federal	Housing	Policy
Text	Federal	Economic	Growth	Cost	Federal	Federal	Bank	Borrower	Federal
Return	Reserve	Economy	Market	Economic	Business	Market	Monetary	Home	Monetary
Work	Risk	Inflation	Country	Measure	Financial	State	Central	Loan	Price
Force	Firm	Rule	State	Change	Small	Budget	Economic	Economic	Market
Economic	Credit	Pp	U	Board	Board	Housing	Financial	May	Year
Family	Institution	Board	Year	Public	Development	Spending	Return	Rate	Economic
Productivity	System	Bank	Return	Pp	Economic	Credit	Text	Lender	Percent

This table reports the 10-topic solution, 10 words, related to the sample of FED Governors' speeches, over the time period 2007–2019. Words are ordered in terms of decreasing relevance within each topic

Table 2.3 ECB topic distribution

Topic	*2007*	*2008*	*2009*	*2010*	*2011*	*2012*	*2013*	*2014*	*2015*	*2016*	*2017*	*2018*	*2019*	*Total*
0	16	16	13	5	8	1	2	1	2	3	3	1	0	71
1	5	10	2	2	1	1	1	2	2	0	0	2	0	28
2	0	0	0	0	1	0	0	0	0	0	1	0	0	2
3	0	1	0	0	0	0	0	0	0	0	0	0	0	1
4	5	18	2	0	1	1	1	1	2	1	2	0	1	35
5	0	0	0	0	0	0	0	0	0	0	0	0	0	0[a]
6	2	5	5	3	4	2	1	1	2	7	3	2	2	39
7	0	0	0	0	0	0	1	0	0	0	0	0	0	1
8	1	0	11	22	14	12	17	9	12	8	11	7	2	126
9	0	1	4	3	1	0	0	0	0	0	0	1	0	10
Total	29	51	37	35	30	17	23	14	20	19	20	13	5	313

This table reports the number of ECB Governors' speeches, for each year and for each topic. The external row and column report the total number of speeches for each year and topic, respectively. As reported, the total number of speeches considered over the time period 2007–2019 is equal to 313

[a]This result is possible since one document could be related with a certain (very high) probability to a specific topic, and with a certain (very low) probability to another topic

Table 2.4 FED topic distribution

Topic	*2007*	*2008*	*2009*	*2010*	*2011*	*2012*	*2013*	*2014*	*2015*	*2016*	*2017*	*2018*	*2019*	*Total*
0	0	0	0	0	0	0	1	1	0	0	1	0	1	4
1	1	13	14	9	5	3	4	2	2	0	1	1	0	55
2	2	0	1	1	0	0	0	0	1	1	0	1	0	7
3	2	1	1	0	5	2	0	2	1	1	0	0	0	15
4	2	1	1	0	0	0	0	0	0	0	0	0	0	4
5	1	3	3	5	2	3	4	6	2	1	4	4	3	41
6	2	3	1	4	4	0	0	0	0	0	0	0	0	14
7	0	0	0	3	2	2	6	0	1	0	0	1	0	15
8	1	3	1	1	0	3	0	1	0	0	1	0	0	11
9	1	0	0	2	0	3	1	2	4	3	6	4	1	27
Total	12	24	22	25	18	16	16	14	11	6	13	11	5	193

This table reports the number of FED Governors' speeches, for each year and for each topic. The external row and column report the total number of speeches for each year and topic, respectively. As reported, the total number of speeches considered over the time period 2007–2019 is equal to 193

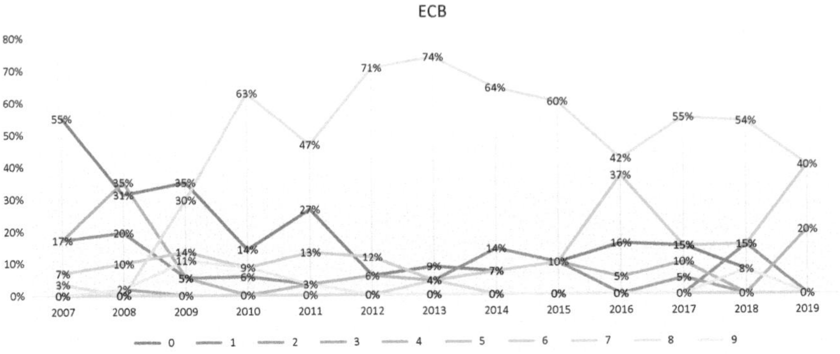

Fig. 2.1 ECB topics (relative weights). This figure reports the relative weights of each topic, for each year of our sample (2007–2019). Specifically, to compute the relative weight and therefore build the graph, we divided the number of speeches, associated to each topic in a specific year, by the total number of speeches collected for that year

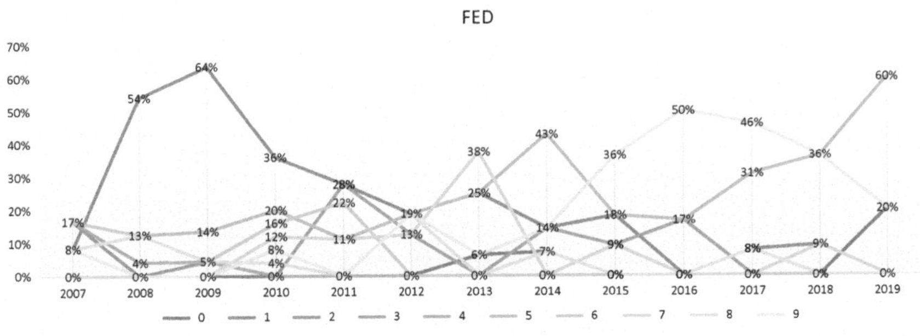

Fig. 2.2 FED's topics (relative weights). This figure reports the relative weights of each topic, for each year of our sample (2007–2019). Specifically, to compute the relative weight and therefore build the graph, we divided the number of speeches, associated to each topic in a specific year, by the total number of speeches collected for that year

FED. Specifically, as reported on the website of the ECB,[5] the Eurosystem is responsible for (i) the definition and the implementation of monetary policy; (ii) the conduction of foreign exchange operations; (iii) the

[5] See the following webpage: https://www.ecb.europa.eu/ecb/tasks/html/index.en.html (accessed May 2019).

holding and the management of the euro area's foreign currency reserves; (iv) the promotion of the smooth operation of payment systems. The ECB carries out specific tasks in the areas of banking supervision, banknotes, statistics, macroprudential policy and financial stability, international and European cooperation. Consequently, starting from the ECB Governors' speeches, we interpret the terms composing the topics 0 and 7 (see Table 2.1) as related to the task of financial stability and macroprudential policy. Specifically, the terms "System" and "Stability", linked to the word "Risk", support our decision to associate topic 0 with the task of financial stability and macroprudential policy; at the same time, the words "Systemic" and "Risk", together with the more explicit terms "Esrb" and "Macroprudential", justify our decision to link topic 7 with the above-mentioned task. It is not surprising that a large number of speeches related to the task of financial stability and macroprudential policy concerns the time period 2007–2011 (see Table 2.3 and Fig. 2.1), consistently with the huge attention given to the topic of financial stability in that specific time period. Additionally, the European Systemic Risk Board (Esrb), which is responsible for the macroprudential supervision of the financial system in the European Union, was established in 2010.

The terms "Global" and "World" suggest that topic 1 is mainly related to international affairs. At the same time, the word "Global", together with the term "International", support our decision to link topic 9 with the same task.

Conversely, the presence of such terms as "European", "Integration", "Union", "Europe", and especially "Gasperi" (Alcide De Gasperi was a great supporter of a united Europe) suggests linking topic 2 with European relations. At the same time, the massive presence of such terms as "European", "Europe", "Union" and "Euro" composing topic 6 motivates our choice to connect it with the same task.

As expected, the majority of the speeches is related to the monetary policy: specifically, we refer to topics 3, 4, 5, and 8. We refer to monetary policy in a wide way, since we consider both groups of such terms as "Inflation", "Rate", "Monetary", which are associated to the goal to achieve stable prices, and such words as "Macroeconomic", "Growth", "Labour", which instead refer to the effects of monetary policy on macroeconomic variables, as related to the same task.

As reported on the website of the FED,[6] it performs five functions. Specifically, it conducts the nation's monetary policy, fosters payment and settlement system safety and efficiency, and promotes consumer protection and community development, the stability of the financial system, and the safety and soundness of individual financial institutions. By taking into account the FED Governors' speeches, we consider the terms composing topic 1 (see Table 2.2) as related to the promotion of financial system stability. Specifically, our choice is motivated by the presence of such terms as "Risk" and "System" composing that topic, which we also found among terms composing topic 0 related to the sample of ECB Governors' speeches (see Table 2.1). Conversely, topics 5, 6, and 8 are related to the promotion of consumer protection and community development, which is a specific function of the FED. Terms such as "Community", "Housing", and "Mortgage" link these three topics to that task, since the FED works to ensure that the financial institutions it supervises comply with the laws protecting consumers, including those laws related to mortgage lending.

The remaining topics (0, 2, 3, 4, 7, and 9) are related to monetary policy. As previously explained, we refer to monetary policy in a wide way, since we consider both the goal of the stable prices and the effects on macroeconomic variables as issues related to it. Specifically, we signal the presence of the terms "Woman", "Labor", and "Participation" composing topic 0, showing the importance of the female employment issue for the FED.

Finally, unlike the European case, the largest number of FED Governors' speeches is related to the promotion of financial stability (topic 1), especially with respect to the time period 2008–2010 (see Table 2.4). That is not surprising, since the financial crisis originated in the United States in 2007 and the financial stability issue had to be a relevant topic to discuss about in the following years.

2.5 Concluding Remarks and Research Perspectives

As far as we are aware, after an in-depth research on the most important economics and management literature databases, this is the first work trying to investigate the content of Governors' speeches over time and space,

[6] See the following webpage: https://www.federalreserve.gov/aboutthefed/pf.htm (accessed May 2019).

by using the topic modeling approach. Consequently, we can sketch some concluding remarks and we can hint some research perspectives, on contents and methodology sides, for further insights.

We obtain a confirmation of the presence, in Governors' speeches, of traditional topics linked to the tasks and functions of central banks (above all monetary policy and financial stability). The financial crisis period, considered in our analysis, supports the relevance of these traditional matters the central banks cope with, while new challenges (i.e., topics referring to social responsibility, with special reference to environmental sustainability) leave small measurable tracks in these speeches (as already emerged, analyzing central banks' annual reports in one previous research effort; see Farina et al. 2019).

The emerging coherence between emerged topics and traditional tasks can suggest a more precise cause-effects analysis, taking into consideration the differences between Europe and United States, at different points in time. Following this perspective, in the near future it can be useful to enlarge the number of countries, especially including Asian ones. It could also be interesting to measure the relationships between topics' evolution and some macroeconomic variables subject to central banks' control, applying topic modeling instead of other text analysis methods (as in Farina et al. 2018).

Viewing the new challenges, we believe that central banks are not institutions impervious to change: for sure, they are under scrutiny by many societal stakeholders, and communication tools, with special regard to Governors' speeches, are going to adopt new themes and new words. Topic modeling offers a useful methodological opportunity for analyzing future developments of Governors' talking.

Besides, and for now concluding, it is interesting to discuss our results with different central banks' stakeholders, trying to label and comment the ten topics from different perception perspectives.

Combining an inductive approach (topic modeling) with a deductive one (discussion) we think we can better our understanding of central banks' Governors' speeches evolution over time and in different countries and regional areas.

References

Berger, H., J. De Haan, and J-E. Sturm. 2006. Does Money Matter in the ECB Strategy? New Evidence Based on ECB Communication. CESifo Working Paper No. 1652.

Blei, D.M., A.Y. Ng, and M.I. Jordan. 2003. Latent Dirichlet Allocation. *Journal of Machine Learning Research 3*: 993–1022.

Blinder, A.S., M. Ehrmann, M. Fratzscher, J. De Haan, and D.-J. Jansen. 2008. Central Bank Communication and Monetary Policy: A Survey of Theory and Evidence. *Journal of Economic Literature 46*: 910–945.

Blot, C., and P. Hubert 2018. Central Bank Communication During Normal and Crisis Times, Monetary Dialogue, September.

Bordo, M.D., Ø. Eitrheim, M. Flandreau, and J.F. Qvigstad, eds. 2016. *Central Bank at a Crossroads*. Cambridge University Press.

Born, B., M. Ehrmann, and M. Fratzscher. 2011. Macroprudential Policy and Central Bank Communication. BIS Papers Chapters. In *Bank for International Settlements*, ed. Macroprudential Regulation and Policy, 60, 107–110. Bank for International Settlements.

———. 2013. Central Bank Communication on Financial Stability. *The Economic Journal 124*: 701–734.

DiMaggio, P., M. Nag, and D. Blei. 2013. Exploiting Affinities Between Topic Modeling and the Sociological Perspective on Culture: Application to Newspaper Coverage of U.S. Government Arts Funding. *Poetics 41*: 570–606.

Ehrmann, M., and M. Fratzscher. 2009. Explaining Monetary Policy in Press Conferences. *International Journal of Central Banking 5*: 41–84.

Ehrmann, M., and J. Talmi. 2017. Starting from a Blank Page? Semantic Similarity in Central Bank Communication and Market Volatility. Working Paper No. 2023.

Farina, V., G. Galloppo, and D.A. Previati. 2018. Central Banks' Communication Strategies: Just Words? In *Contemporary Issues in Banking. Regulation, Governance and Performance*, ed. M. García-Olalla and J. Clifton. Palgrave Macmillan Studies in Banking and Financial Institutions, Palgrave Macmillan.

———. 2019. Central Banks' Commitment to Stakeholders: CSR in the Eurosystem: 2006–2016. In *Frontier Topics in Banking. Investigating New Trends and Recent Developments in the Financial Industry*, ed. E. Gualandri, V. Venturelli, and A. Sclip. Palgrave Macmillan Studies in Banking and Financial Institution, Palgrave Macmillan.

Ferri, P., M. Lusiani, and L. Pareschi. 2018. Accounting for Accounting History: A Topic Modeling Approach (1996–2015). *Accounting History 23*: 173–205.

Gertler, P., and R. Horvath. 2018. Central Bank Communication and Financial Markets: New High-Frequency Evidence. *Journal of Financial Stability 36*: 336–345.

Goodhart, C. 1988. *The Evolution of Central Banks*. 1st ed. MIT Press Books, The MIT Press.

———. 2011. The Changing Role of Central Banks. *Financial History Review 18*: 135–154.

Janikowski, L., and A. Rzonca. 2018. Central Bank Communication at Times of Non-standard Monetary Policies, Monetary Dialogue September.

Lustenberger T., and E. Rossi. 2017. Does Central Bank Transparency and Communication Affect Financial and Macroeconomic Forecasts? SNB Working Papers, 12/2017.

Masciandaro, D., and D. Romelli. 2018. Central Bankers as Supervisors: Do Crises Matter? *European Journal of Political Economy 52*: 120–140.

de Mendonça, H.F., and C.O. de Moraes. 2018. Central Bank Disclosure as a Macroprudential Tool for Financial Stability. *Economic Systems 42*: 625–636.

Montes, G.C., and R.T.F. Nicolay. 2017. Does Clarity of Central Bank Communication Affect Credibility? Evidences Considering Governor-Specific Effects. *Applied Economics 49*: 3163–3180.

Montes, G.C., and A. Scarpari. 2015. Does Central Bank Communication Affect Bank Risk-Taking? *Applied Economics Letters 22*: 751–758.

Nier, E.W. 2009. Financial Stability Frameworks and the Role of Central Banks: Lessons from the Crisis. IMF WP/09/70.

Orphanides, A. 2013. The Federal Reserve and Global Central Banking, Statement Before the Subcommittee on Monetary Policy and Trade of the Committee on Financial Services, United States House of Representatives.

Rochon, L.-P., and S. Rossi, eds. 2015. *The Encyclopedia of Central Banking*. Edward Elgar.

Vayid, I. 2013. Central Bank Communications Before, During and After the Crisis: From Open-Market Operations to Open-Mouth Policy. Bank of Canada Working Paper 2013.

CHAPTER 3

Analyzing Policy Options in the Resolution of Systemically Important Banks: Comparing the "Bailout" and "Bail-In" Tool in Selected Case Studies

Ewa Miklaszewska and Jan Pys

3.1 Introduction

The 2007–2009 financial crisis revealed many weaknesses of the banking industry, which included low capitalization, inadequate risk management practices and a complexity of business models of global banks, and demonstrated how the economy was exposed to the banking crisis due to the systemic risk (Laeven et al. 2014). The governments of many European countries realized that the failure of the country's largest banks would have dramatic consequences and had to bail out, assist with liquidity or even nationalize the failing banks (Gropp and Tonzer 2016). The direct fiscal cost of banks' stabilization measures was on the average 5% of the EU GDP in the 2007–2009 period, but it was accompanied by large indirect assistance,

E. Miklaszewska (✉) • J. Pys
Cracow University of Economics, Cracow, Poland
e-mail: uumiklas@cyf-kr.edu.pl

C. Cruciani et al. (eds.), *Banking and Beyond*, Palgrave Macmillan Studies in Banking and Financial Institutions,
https://doi.org/10.1007/978-3-030-45752-5_3

including a necessity to nationalize 29 Systemically Important Banks (SIBs) (Laeven and Valencia 2010; World Bank 2016b). Consequently, the total stabilization costs could be ultimately assessed only after bank reprivatization (Millaruelo and del Río 2017). Public intervention helped to stabilize the banking sector, but it had its price—in many countries it changed the market structure, incentives to take risks, cost of capital or competitive conditions.

Before the crisis, there was a lack of a consistent bank resolution framework, both in the EU and globally, so the post-crisis reforms recognized the need for the creation of a formalized resolution framework, which would allow for efficient restructuring of troubled banks, with no or limited use of public funds (Vaillant and Cernov 2018). The bank resolution regulations aimed at reducing the restructuring costs and improving its net efficiency, thanks to a compromise between fiscal costs and benefits from financial stability (Čihák and Nier 2012). New resolution tools did not eliminate stabilization costs, but transferred most of them from taxpayers to creditors, including large depositors and bank bond holders. However, the new resolution framework does not completely eliminate public support, including the precautionary recapitalization, but the use of public funds should be only a last resort, not the first choice (Véron 2017).

An in-depth analysis of the costs and effectiveness of the various resolution actions is not yet possible due to few and differently implemented resolution programs and the short time from the full entry into force of the new regulations in 2016. This chapter examines the costs and benefits of various resolution programs applied to large banks during the 2008 crisis and in the post-crisis period, based on the available case studies, and conducts in-depth analysis of three cases: the restructuring of the largest bank in Germany (Deutsche Bank), in the Netherlands (ING Group) and one of the biggest banks in the UK (Royal Bank of Scotland [RBS]). All three banks were heavily affected by the crisis and required government assistance, but their restructuring took a different form. Then, selected resolution cases led by the Single Resolution Board (SRB) and the National Resolution Authorities (NRA) are compared, with an aim to analyze how successful was the restructuring of large banks under the bailout and bail-in regimes. The aim is to demonstrate that the new European resolution framework addressed many issues identified during the crisis and contained a handful of new instruments and options allowing for an efficient resolution of large banks (Allen et al. 2016). However, its application was socially and politically sensitive, and its inflexibility created difficulties in the diverse European banking systems, where the national regulatory organs still have important responsibilities and impacts (Bank of Italy 2018).

3.2 Motivation and the Literature Review

Following the financial crisis, the EU has changed the way banks are supervised and resolved by the creation of the banking union, which is currently built on two pillars: the Single Supervisory Mechanism (SSM) and the Single Resolution Mechanism (SRM) with the third pillar in a form of the European Deposit Insurance Scheme (EDIS) to be implemented. From a legal perspective, SRM is based on the Bank Recovery and Resolution Directive (BRRD) and Single Resolution Mechanism Regulation (SRMR). BRRD explains that "an effective resolution regime should minimize the costs of the resolution of a failing institution borne by the taxpayers" (EP 2014). One of the other key objectives of resolution is to ensure continuation of the critical functions of institutions, defined as "activities, services or operations the discontinuance of which is likely in one or more Member States, to lead to the disruption of services that are essential to the real economy or to disrupt financial stability due to the size, market share, external and internal interconnectedness, complexity or cross-border activities of an institution or group".

The BRRD provided for the creation of a resolution authority—the Single Resolution Board (SRB), responsible for preparation of resolution plans for Eurozone significant and cross-border institutions, which are under the supervision of the ECB. The SRB also decides on the usage of the Single Resolution Fund (SRF), which is financed by the banking industry. The SRB is also responsible for other tasks, such as setting the minimum requirement for own funds and eligible liabilities (MREL), which aims to increase the bail inability of liabilities and therefore increase loss absorption by investors and limit the need for bailouts, funded by the taxpayers. BRRD requires each Member State to designate the National Resolution Authorities (NRA)—usually national central banks or other administrative authorities (The World Bank 2016a)—and describes a set of resolution tools, such as sale of business; bridge institution, a temporary structure, where the critical functions of the failing bank are transferred; asset separation in the form of a "good bank" and "bad bank" and bail-in tool, which allows the resolution authorities to convert the eligible liabilities into loss-absorbing common equity or even completely write them off (Philippon and Salord 2017).

Some liabilities are excluded from the bail-ins, such as deposits protected under the deposit guarantee scheme, secured liabilities, liabilities resulting from the holding of customers' goods, interbank liabilities (except those within the same banking group) with a maturity of less than seven days, liabilities deriving from participation in payment systems with a residual maturity of less than seven days and debts to employees, commercial payables and tax liabilities, if these are privileged under bankruptcy law. Losses that have not been absorbed by the creditors can be transferred to the resolution fund, which can intervene up to a ceiling of 5% of total liabilities, provided that a minimum bail-in of 8% of total liabilities has been applied.

The BBRD assumes that a bank should be "resolvable"—its restructuring should be a safe process, with minimal costs for the taxpayer and efficient maintenance of critical functions (Huertas 2016). However, resolution actions are a result of cost-benefit optimization and must balance the interests of different stakeholders (Dermine 2017; Dewatripont and Freixas 2011). Moreover, the applicability of irresolution tools is affected by the legal and operational structure of the restructured banks and by the diversified structure of the European banking market. Problems may also be created by an unclear definition of critical functions and a need for liquidity during and after the restructuring process (Schoenmaker 2016). Specific problems with the use of restructuring mechanisms are also possible for cooperative banks (Lastra et al. 2016). Hence, there are voices calling for more flexibility in applying the resolution tools, particularly the bail-in mechanism (Micossi et al. 2014).

During the 2008 crisis there were very limited options for bank restructuring: either the application of national bankruptcy regulations, as in the case of Lehman Brothers but then there were problems with critical functions or the recapitalization from public money (bailouts, guarantees, nationalization), which caused large costs for taxpayers and generated moral hazard. The new resolution regulations aimed at widening the restructuring options and minimizing the costs incurred by taxpayers, allowing the banks to be restructured in a predictable and repeatable manner. In terms of the assumed goals, resolution regulations stressed bank stability, with an insufficient emphasis on the creation of incentives for the long-term efficiency improvement of the restructured banks, as illustrated by analyzing the outcome of public aid granted to the EU-28 banks in 2004–2016 period (Table 3.1) in a panel data model (Table 3.2), based on data on total capital ratio (TCR), a comprehensive Multi Level Performance Score (MLPS) and a bank stability indicator (the *Z*-score index).

Table 3.1 Number of banks with public aid (A) and without aid (B) in 2004–2016, EU-28

	AT	*BE*	*BG*	*CY*	*CZ*	*DE*	*DK*	*EE*	*ES*	*FI*	*FR*	*GB*	*GR*	*HR*	
Group A	7	3	–	2	–	7	–	–	11	–	5	6	8	–	
Group B	432	176	40	42	65	2932	177	22	325	79	793	747	36	80	
All	439	179	40	44	65	2939	177	22	336	79	798	753	44	80	
	HU	IE	IT	LT	LU	LV	MT	NL	PL	PT	RO	SE	SI	SK	All
Group A	–	4	3	1	–	–	–	3	–	6	–	2	5	–	73
Group B	78	109	1096	16	214	33	27	166	98	166	48	176	36	39	8248
All	78	113	1099	17	214	33	27	169	98	172	48	178	41	39	8321

Source: Miklaszewska and Kil (2019), based on data on public aid in Iwanicz-Drozdowska (2016)

Table 3.2 The results of public aid for restructured bank (group A) and for other banks (group B) in the EU-28, 2004–2016, period

	TCR	*Z-score*	*MLPS*
Group A[a]	14.90	10.77	−3.30
I	12.53	6.18	−7.28
I + 1	14.96	7.97	−7.75
I + 2	15.57	11.43	−6.38
I + 3	15.88	12.81	−4.52
I + 4	18.66	12.43	−4.70
Group B	19.42	81.56	−0.13
Total (A + B)	19.34	80.76	−0.17

Source: Miklaszewska and Kil (2019)

[a]In group A, the intervention period was denoted as "I", and the four-year period after the intervention was denoted as I + 1, I + 2, I + 3 and I + 4

As a result of receiving public aid, group A recorded a fairly significant increase in the value of its capital adequacy ratio and there was a significant convergence for group A and B in this respect. However, different results were obtained when bank stability (*Z*-score) and performance (MLPS) were analyzed (as explained in Miklaszewska and Kil 2016). For both indicators, in the four years after the intervention both bank stability and performance either were stable or have deteriorated (Table 3.2). Thus, public aid led to an improvement in capitalization, but did not contribute to a long-term improvement of bank performance.

3.3 Lessons from Large Banks' Restructuring Based on the Bailout Tool: The Case of Deutsche Bank, the ING Group and the RBS

Public intervention during the global crisis helped to stabilize the banking sector, but it had its price, changing the market structure, the incentives to take risks, the cost of capital and competitive conditions. Did it also change the strategies and performance of SIBs? To answer this question, the case studies of resolution processes for three large banks—Deutsche Bank in Germany, the ING Group in the Netherlands and the RBS in the UK—were conducted. All three banks were heavily affected by the crisis and required government assistance; however, their restructuring took a different form. Deutsch Bank, the ING Group and the RBS, although having a common European supervisor (SSM), have been working in a different environment and under different regulatory attitudes of their domestic supervisors, which have affected their restructuring outcomes.

The analysis of the three institutions starts with looking at them prior to the crisis; though their performance may appear similar, a number of differences can be noted. In 2006, the ING Group was nearly 8% larger than Deutsche Bank based on the asset size and nearly 5% smaller than the RBS. The RBS was the largest institution based on the number of total employees, followed by the ING Group and DB. There are multiple reasons for these differences, including different scope of operations, for example, in 2006 the ING Group consisted of both banking and insurance sections. Regardless of the differences, all three institutions showed strong financial results in 2006; the RBS reported equivalent of EUR 9.6 billion net profit, the second ING achieved EUR 7.7 billion net profit whilst Deutsche Bank reported nearly EUR 6 billion profit. In case of the ING Group nearly 50% of their 2006 profit before tax was generated from insurance activities. Corrected for the insurance activities, the profitability from banking activities of ING is substantially below the result of Deutsche Bank which achieved nearly 62% more profit before tax on banking operations. All the three institutions had relatively good efficiency in the range of 40–70% cost-to-income ratio, with RBS being a clear cost efficiency leader. Market capitalization was highest for RBS, second with ING and lowest for DB, which can be explained by the size difference, better diversification related to insurance business and higher profitability of both the UK and Dutch institutions (Table 3.3).

Attention should be paid to the possible differences between jurisdictions and applicable accounting standards. For example, the balance sheet of Deutsche Bank showed total assets under US Generally Accepted Accounting Principles (GAAP), to be at EUR 891 billion as of year-end 2009, compared with EUR 1501 billion under International Financial Reporting Standards (IFRS). The main reason for this significant difference was argued to be a disparity in accounting standards for the netting of derivatives (Petitjean 2013). However, ignoring these reporting differences, a conclusion can be made that all the three institutions can be considered as large, profitable and efficient in the pre-crisis year. This was also reflected in the long-term credit rating at the investment grade level assigned by leading rating agencies such as Moody's and S&P.

The 2008 financial crisis had a very negative impact on all the three banks. The ING Group, RBS and Deutsche Bank all had substantial exposure to the US market where the crisis originated, which had a very

Table 3.3 Pre-crisis comparison of Deutsche Bank, the ING Group and RBS

Key metrics (2006)	*Deutsche Bank*	*ING Group*	*RBS*
Size			
Total assets	EUR 1126 billion	EUR 1226 billion	GBP 871 billion
Total capital	EUR 33 billion	EUR 38 billion	GBP 45 billion
# of employees	68,849	119,801	135,000
Solvency			
BIS core capital	8.9%	7.63%	11.7%
Profitability			
Net profit	EUR 5986 million	EUR 7692 million	GBP 6497 million
Basic earnings per share	13.31	3.57	2.00
Dividend per share	4.00	1.32	0.91
Efficiency			
C/I ratio	70.2%	64%	42.1%
Market value			
Share price	EUR 101.34	EUR 33.59	GBP 17.55
Market capitalization	EUR 53.2 billion	EUR 74 billion	GBP 62.8 billion
P/E ratio	7.6	9.4	8.75
Long-term credit rating			
Moody's	Aa3	Aa2	Aa1
S&P	AA-	AA-	AA

Source: Own calculation based on Deutsche Bank (2006), the ING Group (2006) and RBS (2006) (EUR/GBP 0.6743)

negative impact on their risk profile, profitability and solvency and required an intervention of their supervisors and state support from the local governments where these institutions were domiciled. The state had to get involved due to the significant size of these institutions as compared to the gross domestic product (GDP) of the country of origination.

- *The outcome of ING Group bailout*

In October 2008, the Dutch government invested EUR 10 billion in the ING Group in the form of capital injection and on 26 January 2009 the Dutch state took over the majority of risk (c. 80%) on a US high-risk mortgage book. In order for state aid to be granted, an agreement on the number of restructuring measures was made with the European Commission. As a result of this agreement, the ING Group was required to carry out an internal headcount reduction and restructuring program (45% balance sheet reduction). In addition, the ING was obliged to divest several ING insurance brands and complete the separation of banking and insurance business operations by the end of 2013. ING Direct US (considered to be core by the group) and a new company for Dutch retail financial market (composed of mortgage and consumer credit activities) were also in scope of divestments as required by the European Commission (EC). Another measure was a price leadership ban for the EU on certain retail and SME banking products for a three-year maximum period. Finally, ING also received an acquisition ban for a three-year maximum period (Centre For European Policy Studies 2010).

In the years following the crisis, the outcome of the bailout from the Dutch government perspective turned out to be positive. Starting from 12 May 2009, the ING Group started repaying its debt to the Dutch government in a number of tranches scheduled to run between 2009 and 2015. The ING managed to meet the deadlines set by the European Commission and repaid the final tranche to the Dutch government on 7 November 2014. The repayment of the capital injection coupled with the share in proceeds from sale of the high-risk US mortgage book allowed the Dutch state to make a substantial return on the total bailout operation, which amounted to EUR 4.9 billion. The ING indicated that the main sources used to repay the state aid were from the issuance of new capital, proceeds from the sale of businesses and profits from operations in the post-crisis years (Table 3.4).

In summary, it took ING six years to fully repay the debt that arose from the bailout and the Dutch state not only recovered the funds invested in ING but also made a substantial gain on the operation.

- *The outcome of the RBS bailout*

Table 3.4 Return for Dutch state on state aid to the ING Group

Capital flows	*Risk guarantee*
EUR 10 billion (Oct. 2008)	Takeover of risk on 80% of portfolio of EUR 27.7 billion (Jan. 2009)
EUR 13.5 billion repaid (Nov. 2014)	Portfolio sale completed (Feb. 2014)
State return: EUR 3.5 billion	State profit: EUR 1.4 billion

Source: www.ing.com

The Royal Bank of Scotland (RBS) Group PLC was one of the largest financial services groups in Europe and in the world. In 2007, just before the crisis, the RBS had participated in the three-bank consortium acquisition of the Dutch-based ABN AMRO. The crisis resulted in liquidity and capital issues at RBS (EC 2009). The crisis triggered substantial losses at RBS leading to a total of GBP 24 billion loss for financial year 2008 of which GBP 16.2 billion related to the impairment of goodwill that arose on acquisition of ABN AMRO. The reminder of the loss related to the write-downs in the credit portfolio including the Asset-Backed Security (ABS) portfolio and US residential mortgages. The RBS attempted to respond to the crisis with a GBP 12 billion rights issue in 2008 and two disposals of material subsidiaries. However, taking into account the magnitude of the problems, the UK government had to intervene to save the bank from insolvency. In October 2018, the state injected approximately GBP 15 billion into RBS in exchange for the ordinary shares leading to the acquisition of a 58% stake in the company and further GBP 5 billion in the form of preference shares. The following year proved that further assistance was needed, and the UK government announced an additional package consisting of GBP 25.5 billion recapitalization and a contingent GBP 8 billion of capital in case of further deterioration in solvency of RBS. In addition to all the recapitalization measures, the RBS also participated in the impaired assets relief program (APS), which was an unfunded guarantee scheme of the UK government covering up to 90% of losses in excess of an initial amount ("the first-loss position") for selected portfolios. The participation of the RBS in the APS measure amounted to the total of GBP 281 billion, consisting mainly of a Corporate Lending, Commercial Real Estate and Securities portfolio. The RBS also participated in the Credit Guarantee Scheme and Liquidity Assistance (EC 2009) (Table 3.5).

Similar to the case of ING, in order for RBS to participate in the state aid program, EC required a restructuring plan from the institution. The restructuring plan included a strategic review of RBS activities and its division into core and non-core activities with subsequent disposal of the latter. The RBS has committed to exit from the non-core markets outside the UK, Ireland and the US in an effort to limit the operations and reduce the size of the balance sheet. In addition, the restructuring plan assumed a group-wide cost reduction program and return to stable profitability (EC 2009). Compared to the case of the ING Group, the outcome of the bailout to the UK state in case of RBS is not as positive. Between 2015 and

Table 3.5 Aid measures received by RBS

Recapitalization stage	*Funds received*
First recapitalization 13.10–1.12 2008	GBP 20 billion
Second recapitalization announced 3.11.208:	GBP 25.5 billion
– upfront recap in B shares	GBP 8 billion
– contingent capital in B shares	
Total recapitalization	
– nominal	45.5 (53.5 with contingent capital) GBP billion
– as % of RWA	7.8% (9.3% with contingent capital)
Additional recapitalization	Payment of the APS fee in B shares
Participation in the APS (asset covered)	GBP 282 billion with a first-loss position of 60 billion
State guarantees under CGS	
Liquidity assistance granted by the Bank of England (BoE) (Oct.–Dec. 2008)	

Source: Based on EC (2009)

2018, the UK government started exiting its investment in RBS, selling shares at a loss ranging between 169 and 228 pence per share. A decade after the bailout of the RBS, the UK state still owns 62% of the bank with limited prospects to exit their involvement. The state plans laid out in March 2018 were to continue selling around GBP 3 billion worth of shares every year until 2022–2023. This would mean a complete exit could be achieved 17 years after the first bailout, while the estimate of the bailout costs to the state is at GBP 23 billion (Mor 2018).

- *The State assistance to Deutsche Bank*

In case of Deutsche Bank, the bailout took a different route. During the crisis, the German government managed to get an approval from parliament for a EUR 480 billion package of bailout for German banks. Deutsche Bank decided not to participate in this government bailout program. However, the bank did use a number of facilities offered by the US Federal Reserve (Fed) as part of the massive bailout commitment program. The Fed took a very active role during the crisis and fulfilled its obligations as lender of last resort. Deutsche Bank was one of the top beneficiaries of the Fed lending programs, participating in a number of them. In March 2008, the Fed decided to conduct a series of term (28 days) repurchase transactions initially expected to reach a total of USD

100 billion. In the period between July and December 2008, the Fed executed 375 transactions accumulating to the total funds lent of USD 855 billion and monthly amounts reaching the expected USD 100 billion level (Felkerson 2011).

According to Fed data, Deutsche Bank was the second biggest participant in this program with participation equal to USD 101 billion, which translates to nearly a 12% share in the program. At the same time, in addition to the repo program, the Fed decided to extend its Treasury lending program called the Term Securities Lending Facility (TSLF) which was aimed to "promote liquidity in the financing markets for Treasury and other collateral and thus to foster the functioning of financial markets more generally" (Federal Reserve 2008). Deutsche Bank was among the top participants in this program with total participation amounting to USD 277 billion and becoming the third highest beneficiary of TSLF. The last phase of the Fed's bailout program was aimed at the purchase of long-term securities in order to support the functioning of credit markets (Bernanke 2009). In total, 16 institutions participated in this program with Deutsche Bank being the largest beneficiary with sales amounting to USD 293 billion (Felkerson 2011).

- *Post-crisis recovery: comparison of ING, RBS and DB*

Following the crisis and the bailout, each bank needed to find its own way to recovery. This included a number of issues, including agreements with the European Commission, required as a condition for accepting the bailout applicable to both the ING Group and RBS. In the case of the ING Group, this meant a number of divestments of the insurance activities such as NN which pre-crisis constituted a substantial part of the group. In 2006, the profit before tax attributable to the insurance activities of the ING Group amounted to 49.6%. Divestment of these activities, required by the European Commission and the De Nederlandsche Bank (DNB), was a time-consuming and difficult task both from the financial and from the operational perspective. Similar to ING, the RBS also needed to follow a restructuring plan aimed at shrinking down its operation to key activities and markets and reducing costs to ensure return to profitability. In contrast, Deutsche Bank did not have to make such significant divestments; however, it did have some own issues to face. The research on the performance of banks after the bailout showed evidence that any post-bailout performance improvement in the rescued banks is slow at best (Gerhardt and Vennet 2017).

Table 3.6 Post-crisis comparison of Deutsche Bank, the ING Group and RBS

Key metrics (2018)	*Deutsche Bank*	*ING Group*	*RBS*
Size			
Total assets	EUR 1348 billion	EUR 887 billion	GBP 694 billion
Total capital	EUR 62 billion	EUR 51 billion	GBP 46 billion
# of employees	91,737	52,233	67,000
Solvency			
Common equity Tier 1 ratio	13.6%	14.50%	16.2%
Profitability			
Net profit	EUR 341 million	EUR 4703 million	GBP 2084 million
Earnings per share	0.00	1.21	0.13
Dividend per share	0.11	0.68	0.02
Efficiency			
C/I ratio	92.7%	54.8%	43.0%
Market value			
Share price	EUR 6.97	EUR 9.41	GBP 2.17
Market capitalization	EUR 14.4 billion	EUR 37.1 billion	GBP 26.2 billion
P/E ratio	–	7.8	16.05
Long-term credit rating			
Moody's	Baa3	Baa1	Baa2
S&P	BBB-	A-	BBB-

Source: Own calculation based on Deutsche Bank (2018), ING Group (2018) and RBS (2018) (EUR/GBP 0.89148)

Comparing the three banks based on the data of 2018 shows significant differences in number of aspects such as profitability, efficiency and other market indicators. Even though Deutsche Bank has the substantially biggest balance sheet, with assets more than 50% higher than the ING Group and 70% higher than RBS, other indicators show significantly lower profitability, efficiency and market perception of the value of DB. In 2018, the ING Group was leading in most financial metrics. For example, the ING Group managed to generate almost 14 times more net profit than Deutsche Bank and twice as much net profit as RBS, where RBS was leading at 43% cost-to-income (C/I) ratio with second ING showing nearly 55% C/I ratio. In case of Deutsche Bank, the cost inefficiency was a clear problem as for each euro of income DB generates nearly 93 cents of costs. The significant differences in the financial performance were also reflected in the market valuation of the three banks, where again the Dutch institution was a leader (Table 3.6).

Table 3.7 Deutsche Bank, the ING Group and RBS: relative transformation between 2006 and 2018

Key metrics: 2018 versus 2006	*Deutsche Bank*	*ING Group*	*RBS*
Size			
Total assets	222	−339	−177
Total capital	29	13	1
# of employees	22,888	−67,568	−68
Solvency			
Common equity Tier 1 ratio	4.7%	6.9%	4.5%
Profitability			
Net profit	−5645	−2989	−4.413
Earnings per share	−13	−2	−1.87
Dividend per share	−4	−1	−.89
Efficiency			
C/I ratio	22.5%	−9.2%	0.9%
Market value			
Share price %	−93%	−72%	−88%
Market capitalization	−38.8 billion	−36.9 billion	−36.6 billion
Long-term credit rating			
Moody's	−6 notches	−5 notches	−7 notches
S&P	−6 notches	−3 notches	−7 notches

Source: Own calculation

Before the crisis Deutsche Bank, RBS and the ING Group had similar asset size and similar level of profitability, but the post-crisis picture looks significantly different for the benefit of the ING Group. In 2006, the ING Group consisted of both banking and insurance activities with the latter contributing a substantial portion of results. At that time, the profit before tax (PBT) related to the banking activities of ING was nearly 38% lower than that of Deutsche Bank. Ten years later, that proportion was reversed and the PBT related to the banking activities of ING was 466% higher than that of Deutsche Bank (Table 3.7).

The European Commission indicated that the banking restructuring plans under state aid rules have helped to save many European banks. Their data showed significant improvements in operational and risk indicators, and funding and solvency positions. In general, banks that received aid during the financial crisis are today as healthy as other banks (European Commission 2015). The findings of the EC can be supported by the ING case. The bank was forced to focus on efficiency optimization and organic growth, which resulted in the development of the Think Forward Strategy in 2014, described as: Our Purpose, Our Customer Promise, Our Strategic Priorities and Our Enabler"). In the years 2008–2013, the RBS focused on remaining a full-service universal bank, with a significant global network, including a large lending portfolio in the US, and a substantial investment bank; however, that strategy became problematic as capital requirements were increasing and remaining losses were higher than expected. From 2013, a new approach was agreed with the UK Treasury refocusing the bank on its core UK and Irish business while exiting or limiting the number of businesses and activities amongst others in the US (RBS News and Opinion 2018). The change of the strategic view and delayed execution resulted in slower recovery of RBS as compared to the ING Group. This could also be one of the reasons of the high bailout costs to the UK state and failure to exit from the involvement in the bank without substantial losses. In 2015, Deutsche Bank also announced their new Strategy 2020, with the following strategic goals:

> First, to become simpler and more efficient by focusing on the markets, products, and clients where we are better positioned to succeed, which should lead to greater client satisfaction and lower costs. Second, to become less risky by modernizing our technology and withdrawing from higher-risk client relationships. Third, to become better capitalized. Fourth, to run Deutsche Bank with more disciplined execution.

3.4 Lessons from First Resolution Cases Led by SRB After 2016

The post-crisis resolution regulation brought the possibility of using a wider catalog of restructuring tools than nationalization, guarantees and recapitalization. However, the implementation of the resolution processes so far has presented a mixed picture. Since resolution laws were fully in force in 2016, the Single Resolution Board (SRB) was involved in decisions for five banks: Monte dei Paschi di Siena (MPS) in Italy, Banco Popular in Spain, Veneto Banca and Banca Popolare di Vicenza in Italy (the Veneto banks), and ABLV Luxembourg in Luxembourg. According to the World Bank Report, the most effective restructuring tool was the sale of assets combined with the bail-in mechanism, although in some cases it was also the most socially and politically sensitive (World Bank 2016b).

The first resolution case based on the new regulation—the Spanish BPE Bank (the sixth banking group in Spain)—was carried out according to rules and achieved its objectives. The SRB applied bail-in of shareholders and subordinated creditors; and the sale of assets to Banco Santander for EUR 1 took place, which in turn recapitalized BPE with EUR 7 billion (SRB, Banco Popular 2017). However, further examples, especially in Italy, were more problematic. NRA (Bank of Italy) decided to conduct the domestic resolution process for banks in the Venetian region (Veneto Banca and Banca Popolare di Vicenza), although the SRB did not consider them to be systemically important and indicated that they should undergo liquidation according to domestic regulations (Asimakopoulos 2018). The Italian government spent a total of EUR 17 billion on restructuring of both banks (including EUR 5 billion for Intesa Sanpaolo to support the acquisition of "good bank" assets and a EUR 12 billion guarantee for dealing with the bad assets of the restructured banks). The EU Commission approved state aid provided by the Italian government in order to mitigate contagion risks.

The case of a larger Italian bank—MPS (Monte dei Paschi di Siena—fourth banking group)—showed yet another way of implementing state assistance under SRMR: precautionary recapitalization by the state at the time when the bank was still solvent, but had to raise capital, instead of applying full bail-in to creditors. The Italian government had recapitalized MPS for more than 5 billion EUR and provided government guarantees for the sale of a large pool of bad loans worth 26 billion EUR. In return, the bank committed to a business reorientation—closing 600 branches by 2021, and cutting down 20% of employees (KPMG 2017). The most recent case of resolution process was the forced liquidation of ABLV Luxembourg, following allegations by the US authorities for money-laundering practices by the subsidiary and its Latvian parent institution. This is also a controversial case, since the national commercial court in Luxembourg decided against the EU authorities and ordered the reorganization of the bank instead of its liquidation (Asimakopoulos 2018).

Thus, the idea to rigorously limit public spending in the resolution processes has not been fully implemented in the first resolution cases (Bowman 2017). Moreover, in Italy, to safeguard economic and social stability, privately owned funds, owned mostly by banks, were created to compensate the bailed-in stakeholders and to protect some small Italian banks from full application of resolution procedures, with a possible consequence of transmitting risk to the whole sector.

3.5 Preliminary Lessons from the Resolution Led by the NRA: Resolution of the Polish Cooperative Bank PBS by the Bank Guarantee Fund in 2020

In Poland, the Bank Guarantee Fund (BFG) is the NRA, based on the 2016 Act on the Deposit Guarantee Scheme and Resolution. According to the Act, BFG can sell failing institutions in whole or in part, establish a bridge institution, transfer doubtful assets to a specialized entity and write down certain obligations of the restructured institution in order to cover its losses or convert them into shares (the bail-in tool).

Polish commercial banks are in a stable condition and do not pose a systemic risk (IMF 2019). However, the cooperative sector, although small (7% of the banking sector assets), presents a constant regulatory challenge. In 2015, the largest cooperative bank—SK Bank—went bankrupt, based on the national bankruptcy law, followed in 2016 by another small cooperative bank. On the 4 December 2019, Polish bank regulator PFSA (KNF) informed the Bank Guarantee Fund that the second large cooperative bank—Podkarpacki Bank Spółdzielczy (PBS)—is failing or likely to fail, with losses estimated at 182.8 million PLN. As of June 2019, PBS assets were of 2.8 billion PLN and CET1 capital ratio declined to 0.32%; the bank was also outside the Institutional Protection Scheme (IPS). In 2019 there were 541 Polish cooperative banks, 515 affiliated with 2 IPSs and 26 outside, out of which 15 were large banks, with capital of over EUR 5 million. When SK Bank went bankrupt in 2015, guaranteed deposits exceeded 2.2 billion PLN. For PBS, in 2018 all deposits were estimated at 2.6 billion, so the scale of the deposit insurance operation would have been similar.

Although Polish cooperative banks are small and not of systemic importance, they have a large, even a critical share in servicing local administrative bodies, whose deposits are uninsured. Hence, the BFG decided that the PBS bank is "too local to fail", having a critical function in financing local authorities (mostly 34 small cities) whose deposits in the case of bankruptcy would be irreversibly lost and the bank went into resolution. BFG created a bridge bank—Bank Nowy BFG SA—owned by the BFG, with capital of 100 million PLN. The clients and employees were transferred to the new bank. Insured and large deposits (above EUR 100,000) of individual clients and SMEs were also transferred to the new bank, while large deposits of local administrative bodies and big firms were only partially transferred (57.4%), deducting the part which was proportional to bank losses. As a result, local authorities lost around 80 billion PLN. Also, subordinated bonds of 100 million PLN were cancelled and there was a redemption of all capital of bank owners.

From a technical point of view, the resolution program went very smoothly—there was only a four-day-long disruption of bank activity and individual clients were not affected. Also, the resolution operation was largely self-financing. However, social and economic problems will follow, as was the case of the Italian cooperative banks. First, there is an estimated large jump in deposit insurance and resolution fund contributions. In 2018, the total deposit insurance contribution was 2.2 billion; in 2019 it increased by 27% to 2.79 billion, out of which 2 billion went to the bank resolution fund. For 2020, the preliminary BFG announcement suggests an increase of 15% to 3.1 billion PLN, in addition to bank corporate tax and bank asset tax introduced in 2016 and amounting to 3–4 billion PLN annually. The result is that listed banks' cost of equity capital was estimated by the IMF (2019) at 11%, while ROE for Polish banks remained between 6% and 7% on average in 2017–2019 (ZBP 2019). This tendency is very dangerous for sustainable growth and for technological investment. Secondly, it will be increasingly difficult to place a large volume of bank bonds on the market, as required by MREL requirements. Finally, the local authorities which lost 50% of their deposits are unable to provide their social contribution and the Ministry of Finance has already announced some funds transfer, followed by a special loan program, so eventually the cost of the resolution program will be much higher. Finally, although the failure of the largest cooperative bank, the SK Bank, in 2015 was efficiently managed without serious political and social consequences, after the resolution of PBS in 2020 all other troubled banks will expect an individually negotiated resolution package, with an active participation of various groups of interests. The rescue programs are financed to a large degree by the commercial banking sector via its contributions to the Bank Guarantee Fund, passing the problems of small banks to the entire banking system.

3.6 Conclusions

The post-crisis bank restructuring and resolution experience have indicated that the resolution of SIBs have to combine several solutions and to resolve many different concerns, so in all cases they must be individually negotiated and flexibly managed (Landier and Ueda 2014). Moreover, large banks have remained Too Big to Fail (TBTF) and are involved in risky market-based activities and thus the question of the efficiency of different restructuring programs is still of vital importance. On the one hand, the chapter analyzes the outcome of Deutsch Bank's, the RBS's and the ING Group's restructuring based on state aid and nationally led restructuring programs, negotiated with the EU. The three banks before the crisis were performing relatively well, while post the crisis there is a significant difference in their performance. The Dutch institution managed to come out of the crisis in a good shape, which can be attributed to a number of factors, but the important issue has been that the restructuring agreement related to the state aid that was made with the European Commission, while Deutsche Bank did not have such an obligation toward the EC or domestic regulator. The scope of the strategic reorientation can be one of the reasons why ING and RBS are today more cost efficient and profitable, particularly the fundamental reorientation away from the insurance sector and toward digital channels on the part of the ING Group. At the same time, the performance of DB shows its inability to curb size and costs and to reorient its business model. The comparison of those banks' current performance illustrates that the bailout restructuring offers flexibility and generates opportunity for fundamental reorientation; and if efficiently executed, might be successful. On the other hand, the first examples of resolution programs, led by both the SRB and the NRA, pose a mixed picture. Judging from the first resolution cases, the common challenge for the resolution process is the conflict between the European and the National Resolution Authorities and the importance of environmental factors, particularly the relative importance of bank stakeholders for domestic and local economies. These all raise a significant concern as to the effectiveness of the post-crisis resolution framework (Asimakopoulos 2018).

References

Allen, F., E. Carletti, J. Gray, and G.M. Gulatui, eds. 2016. *Filling the Gaps in Governance: The Case of Europe*. Florence: European University Institute.

Asimakopoulos, I.G. 2018. The *Veneto Banks Resolution: It Shall Be Called 'Liquidation. European Company Law Journal 15* (5): 156–162.

Bank of Italy. 2018. Financial Stability Report 2, November.

Bernanke, B.S. 2009. *The Crisis and the Policy Response*. Speech at the Stamp Lecture, London School of Economics, London, England, January 13.

Bowman, L. 2017. *The Italian Job*. Euromoney. www.euromoney.com.

Centre For European Policy Studies. 2010. *Bank State Aid in the Financial Crisis—Fragmentation or Level Playing Field?*, A CEPS Task Force Report, October.

Čihák, M., and E. Nier. 2012. The Need for Special Resolution Regimes for Financial Institutions—The Case of the European Union. *Harvard Business Law Review* 395: 396–434.

Dermine, J. 2017. *Europe's Single Resolution Mechanism Is Creating Instability.* INSEAD Knowledge, October 10. https://knowledge.insead.edu.

Deutsche Bank. 2006. Financial Report.

———. 2018. Annual Report.

Dewatripont, M., and X. Freixas. 2011. Bank Resolution: A Framework for the Assessment of Regulatory Intervention. *Oxford Review of Economic Policy 27* (3): 411–436.

European Commission. 2009. State Aid No N 422/2009 and N 621/2009—United Kingdom Restructuring of Royal Bank of Scotland Following Its Recapitalisation by the State and Its Participation in the Asset Protection Scheme, Brussels, 14.12.2009, C(2009)10112 Final.

———. 2015. State Aid to European Banks: Returning to Viability, Competition State Aid Brief, Issue 2015–01, February.

European Parliament and of the Council. 2014. Directive 2014/59/EU of the of 15 May 2014 Establishing a Framework for the Recovery and Resolution of Credit Institutions and Investment Firms.

Federal Reserve. 2008. Federal Reserve Actions. Federal Reserve Monetary Policy Release, March 11.

Felkerson, J. 2011. $29,000,000,000,000: A Detailed Look at the Fed's Bailout by Funding Facility and Recipient, Levy Economics Institute of Bard College, Working Paper No. 698.

Gerhardt, M., and R.V. Vennet. 2017. Bank Bailouts in Europe and Bank Performance. *Finance Research Letters* 22: 74–80.

Gropp, R., and L. Tonzer. 2016. *State Aid and Guarantees in Europe.* In *The Palgrave Handbook of European Banking*, ed. T. Beck and B. Casu. Palgrave Macmillan.

Huertas, T. 2016. European Bank Resolution: Making it Work! CEPS Task Force Report.

IMF. 2019. *Republic of Poland Financial Sector Assessment Program, Technical Note—Stress Testing and Systemic Risk Analysis.* Country Report No. 19/120, May.

ING Group. 2006. *Annual Report.*

———. 2018. *Annual Report.*

Iwanicz-Drozdowska, M., ed. 2016. *European Bank Restructuring During the Global Financial Crisis.* Houndmills and New York: Palgrave Macmillan.

KPMG. 2017. *SRB: Contrasting Outcomes for Banks*, July.

Laeven, L., and F. Valencia. 2010. Resolution of Banking Crises: The Good, the Bad, and the Ugly. IMF Working Paper, WP/10/146.

Laeven, L., L. Ratnovski, and H. Tong. 2014. Bank Size and Systemic Risk. IMF Staff Discussion Note, May.

Landier, A., and K. Ueda. 2014. The Economics of Bank Restructuring: Understanding the Options. In *Financial Crises: Causes, Consequences, and Policy Response*, ed. S. Claessens, M.A. Kose, L. Laeven, and F. Valencia. Washington, DC: IMF.

Lastra, R.M., R. Ayadi, R. Olivares-Caminal, and C. Russo. 2016. *The Different Legal and Operational Structures of Banking Groups in the Euro Area and Their Impact on Banks' Resolvability*. European Parliament IPOL EGOV.

Micossi, S., G. Bruzzone, and M. Cassella. 2014. Bail-in Provisions in State Aid and Resolution Procedures: Are They Consistent with Systemic Stability? CEPS Policy Paper, No. 318.

Miklaszewska, E., and K. Kil. 2016. The Impact of 2007–2009 Crisis on the Assessment of Bank Performance: The Evidence from CEE-11 Countries. *Transformations in Business & Economics* 15 (2A): 459–479.

———. 2019. *Skutecznośc rozwiązań i mechanizmów stabilizujących banki systemowo waěne*, Bank i Kredyt, No. 2.

Millaruelo, A., and A. del Río. 2017. *The Cost of Interventions in the Financial Sector since 2008 in the EU Countries*. Banco de Espana.

Mor, F. 2018. Royal Bank of Scotland Bailout: 10 Years and Counting House of Commons Library. https://commonslibrary.parliament.uk/parliament-and-elections/government/royal-bank-of-scotland-bailout-10-years-and-counting.

Petitjean, M. 2013. Bank Failures and Regulation: A Critical Review. *Journal of Financial Regulation and Compliance* 21 (1): 16–38.

Philippon, T., and A. Salord. 2017. *Bail-ins and Bank Resolution in Europe—A Progress Report*. International Center for Monetary and Banking Studies, Geneva Reports on the World Economy Special Report 4, March.

RBS. 2006. *Annual Report and Accounts*.

———. 2018. *Annual Report and Accounts*.

RBS News and Opinion. 2018. Chairman Howard Davies Looks Back at the Financial Crisis. https://www.rbs.com/rbs/news/2018/09/chairman_howard_davies_looks_back_at_the_financial_crisis.html.

Schoenmaker, D. 2016. *The Different Legal and Operational Structures of Banking Groups in the Euro Area, and their Impact on Banks' Resolvability*. http://bruegel.org/wp-content/uploads.

SRB. 2016. *Introduction to Resolution Planning*. Luxembourg: Publications Office of the European Union.

———. 2017. *Banco Popular*. https://srb.europa.eu/en/content/banco-popular.

Vaillant, I., and M. Cernov. 2018. Business Models in Prudential Policies. SUERF Policy Note 50, www.suerf.org/policynotes.

Véron, N. 2017. *Precautionary Recapitalisation: Time for a Review*. European Parliament, IPOL EGOV, July.

World Bank Group. 2016a. *Bank Resolution and Bail-in in the EU: Selected Case Studies Pre and Post BRRD*. FinSAC, November.

———. 2016b. *Understanding Bank Recovery and Resolution in the EU: A Guidebook to the BRRD*. FinSAC, November.

ZBP. 2019. *Polska i Europa*, September.

CHAPTER 4

Recent Innovation in the Regulation of Covered Bonds in Europe: Who Will Benefit from the New Legislative Framework?

Giusy Chesini and Elisa Giaretta

4.1 Introduction

Covered bonds are debt instruments with a long history, given that they were first issued in Prussia in 1769 (Larsson 2013). They can be considered a sub-category of corporate bonds, but differently from other corporate bonds, they are collateralised by high-quality loans that are ring-fenced to provide covered bond investors a preferential claim in case of issuer default. In addition to this specific collateralisation, covered bonds present a number of further characteristics, making them a very safe debt instrument that is closely competitive with government bonds.

G. Chesini (✉)
Department of Business Administration, University of Verona, Verona, Italy
e-mail: giusy.chesini@univr.it

E. Giaretta
Department of Management, Economics and Quantitative Methods, University of Verona, Verona, Italy
e-mail: elisa.giaretta@unibg.it

C. Cruciani et al. (eds.), *Banking and Beyond*, Palgrave Macmillan Studies in Banking and Financial Institutions,
https://doi.org/10.1007/978-3-030-45752-5_4

Covered bonds are issued by financial institutions because they are the only institutions that possess very high volumes of loans and that need financial tools that allow the refinancing of their lending activities.

In addition to their long existence, covered bonds have constituted a growing sector of the fixed-income market in Europe over the past two decades, continuing to expand with new jurisdictions and borrowers coming on stream.

Originally issued in domestic markets and placed with local investors, covered bonds became increasingly popular in Europe in the 1990s with the launch of a new benchmark format designed to attract large institutional investors. This format was important because it led to the internationalisation of formerly domestic markets (Avesani et al. 2007). Initially, in 1995, Germany started with large-size issues under the name of "jumbo" covered bonds (ECB 2007).[1] France and Spain followed in 1999. Since then, the covered bond market has greatly expanded within Europe (Mastroeni 2001). Almost all European countries in the first decade of the new millennium implemented new covered bond legislation or updated existing rules to incorporate this development while also responding to the considerable growth in mortgage lending in the European Union in those years (Cross 2008).

In 2003, the first "structured" covered bond was issued in the UK with the help of securitisation techniques based on contractual agreements in the absence of a dedicated legal framework. This innovative product was widely accepted by the market and rapidly imitated by other lenders, not only in the UK but also all across Europe, paving the way for a variety of new products to enter the arena (Chesini and Tamisari 2009).[2]

Covered bonds were traditionally characterised by a high degree of standardisation and homogeneity, requiring limited analytical effort from domestic investors. However, the impressive market growth has increased

[1] German mortgage banks introduced the so-called "Jumbo Pfandbrief" with the purpose of internationalising their funding base. In contrast to traditional Pfandbriefe, Jumbo Pfandbriefe were provided with a rating and, even more importantly, with a high degree of liquidity. The two main components used to bolster liquidity were a minimum issue size and a market-making obligation by the underwriting banks.

[2] Proposal for a Directive of the European Parliament and of the Council on the issue of covered bonds and covered bond public supervision and amending Directive 2009/65/EC and Directive 2014/59/EU. The proposal for a directive is complemented by a proposal for a regulation amending EU Regulation No. 575/2013 (the Capital Requirements Regulation).

the diversity in the covered bond universe. New demand from investors and more stringent requirements from rating agencies have led to an increased combination of traditional features with structured finance elements providing credit enhancement. The ever-broader range of products has offered investors an enhanced degree of asset diversification while requiring additional credit analysis.

Since November 2004, the industry, through the European Covered Bond Council (ECBC), which represents covered bond issuers, analysts, bankers, investors, rating agencies and other stakeholders, has been very attentive to all the developments in the markets and has worked to protect the robustness of the covered bond product (Hardt 2004). For example, in 2012, the ECBC introduced the covered bond label (ECB 2017).[3] Since its launch, the label has significantly developed, showing the industry's ability to "keep up" and to even proactively lead in regard to market needs.

To better integrate the regulation and usage of this instrument in Europe, in recent years, an increasing number of reports by European institutions and financial authorities on harmonising the European covered bond legal frameworks have been issued. In particular, at the end of 2019, in the context of the ambitious Capital Markets Union project, the European Commission issued a new regulatory framework aiming to further foster the development of covered bonds across the European Union.

This chapter analyses the reasons behind the growing success of covered bonds and the novelties and impacts of the new regulations on issuers and investors. After a general description of the market and its evolution, attention is paid to the recent regulatory developments that aim to solve the problems arising when different legal frameworks coexist in a global financial market. In fact, very diverse rules across the EU (European Union) member states have affected the market strength of these instruments: while these instruments are very important in some member states, they are less developed in others. Currently, the same financial instruments have different names in different countries and present some slight differences that require attentive analyses by investors. On the other hand, the judgement on the instrument per se is very positive; thus, the new

[3] EU Parliament legislative resolution of 18 April 2019 on the proposal for a directive of the European Parliament and of the EU Council on the issue of covered bonds and covered bond public supervision and amending Directive 2009/65/EC and Directive 2014/59/EU.

regulations have had to consider the good results achieved to date and avoid undermining the growth of the market by imposing useless regulatory burdens.

4.2 The Covered Bond Concept and the Expansion in Europe

Covered bonds are bank obligations collateralised by a dynamic pool of financial assets, to which bondholders have a priority claim over unsecured creditors. Typical features include restrictions on the business activities of the issuer, eligibility criteria for the cover pool, specific asset valuation rules, asset-liability matching requirements and specific post-bankruptcy procedures.

As long as the credit institution is not insolvent or bankrupt, covered bonds behave like normal unsecured debt. Interest and principal on outstanding bonds are paid by the credit institution out of their own funds, regardless of the performance of the assets in the cover pool. Once the credit institution becomes insolvent or goes bankrupt, covered bondholders benefit from a direct claim against the cover pool similar to securitisations (Packer et al. 2007). The proceeds generated by the assets in the cover pool are used to satisfy the covered bondholders who have priority over the unsecured creditors of the credit institution. In addition, should the cover pool prove insufficient to fully satisfy the claims of covered bondholders, the latter will rank *pari passu* with the unsecured creditors of the insolvent financial institution (Schwarcz 2010).

Covered bonds issued by a single issuer are collateralised by the same cover pool, which is actively and conservatively managed by the issuer, with new assets entering the pool as others mature or become ineligible. In the event of the credit institution becoming insolvent, the cover pool will turn static and will be separated from the insolvent estate. The cover pool and pertaining bonds will be managed as a separate entity, usually by a specifically appointed administrator, ensuring that investors will continue to receive the payments due according to contractual dates.

Due to their low-risk profile, covered bonds offer credit institutions a cost-efficient instrument to raise long-term funding, mainly for mortgage or public sector loans.

Following the overwhelming success of this product in Germany, since the end of the 1990s, a number of countries across Europe have enacted their own covered bond legislation in recent decades (Golin 2006). In other countries, such as the UK, in the absence of a specific legal framework, issuers started "replicating" covered bonds via contractual agreements on the basis of existing legislation.

The issuance of covered bonds is generally subject to the banking supervision of a specific country, with a legal framework specifying the key safety features such as the type and quality of eligible assets. In many frameworks, the composition and value of the cover pool are observed by an independent cover pool monitor, who usually reports to the banking supervisory authority. In the case of "structured" covered bonds, the monitoring of the cover pool is mainly conducted by the rating agencies.

The particularity of covered bonds lies in the fact that many countries have adopted their own covered bond legislation (European Parliament 2019). The local investors of a country that adopts covered bond legislation participate in the project, first by investing in the local brand of covered bonds and then by investing in its foreign varieties. With many countries—including non-European countries—allowing national credit institutions to issue covered bonds, the number of previously locally focused investors interested in all types of covered bonds has risen significantly (European Mortgage Federation 2018; Stocker 2011).[4]

At present, the market for covered bonds is far more diversified in terms of the geographical distribution of issuers than it was some years ago. In 2001, German Pfandbriefe accounted for nearly 87% of the outstanding covered bonds in the market. In 2003, the market share of German issuers was 59% (ECBC 2007)[5]; at the end of 2006, it was 34%; and at the end of 2018, it was less than 15.5% (ECBC 2019), as shown in Fig. 4.1.

The global market for covered bonds is substantial, with more than €2500 billion in covered bonds outstanding in 2018 (see Fig. 4.2), and these bonds having been issued by more than 320 issuers from 25 countries. Europe is the oldest and largest covered bond market, with Germany being home to the largest investor base. Covered bonds represent the second largest bond market in Europe, with only sovereign debt representing a larger market. As one of the most dynamic segments of the

[4] EU Directive 2019/2162 amending Directives 2009/65/EC and 2014/59/EU on the issue of covered bonds and covered bond public supervision and EU Regulation 2019/2160 amending Regulation (EU) No. 575/2013 regarding exposures in the form of covered bonds were published on December 18th, 2019, in the Official Journal of the European Union (OJ).

[5] See ECBC, The European Covered Bond Fact Book, August 2007.

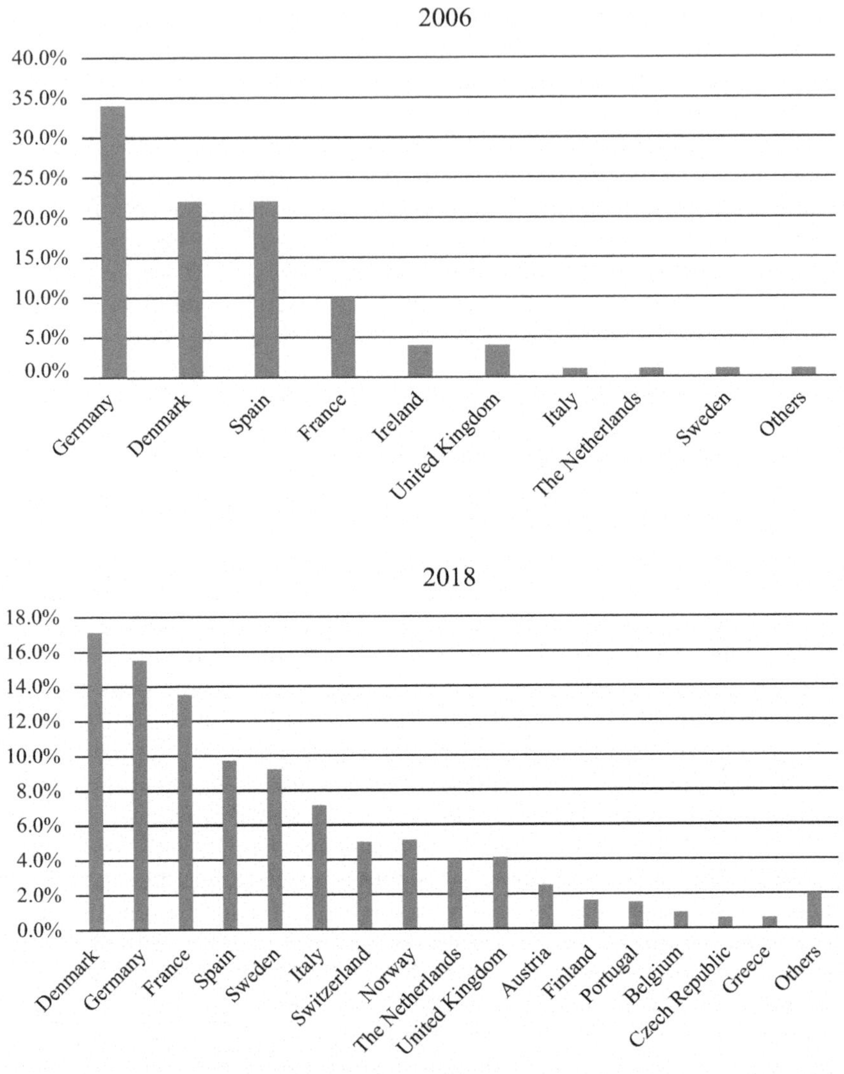

Fig. 4.1 Percentage of outstanding covered bonds by country in Europe (Source: Own elaboration from ECBC statistics)

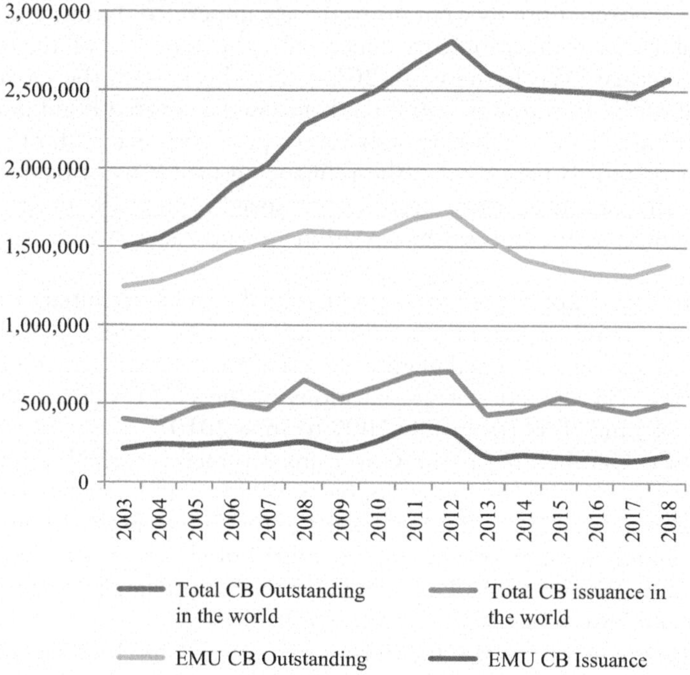

Fig. 4.2 Trend of outstanding and issuance of covered bonds in the world and in EMU (European and Monetary Union) countries, 2018 (in million euros). (Source: Own elaboration from ECBC statistics)

European capital market, covered bonds are a main driver of the integration of European financial markets.

Taking a retrospective view, we observe that the covered bond market showed no signs of a slowdown in growth until the 2008 financial crisis and the subsequent sovereign debt crisis. Demand for covered bonds continued to accelerate globally as new types of investors started diversifying into asset classes for various reasons. After 2012, we see a stronger decline in the covered bonds outstanding following the decline in the issuance of covered bonds (Standard and Poor 2019). This trend must be specifically tied to the sovereign debt crisis, which involved many countries in Europe. However, if we separate the issuers considering their respective countries, we also observe a similar trend for the countries outside the Eurozone (see Fig. 4.2).

Even if covered bonds were not seriously imperilled during the global financial crisis, some problems concerning the liquidity of the issuing banks emerged (Van Rixtel et al. 2015). For this reason, the Governing Council of the European Central Bank adopted a covered bond purchase programme (CBPP) in 2009 to stabilise the post-crisis market for this kind of security and to help resolve the refinancing problems of banks (ECB 2011). In particular, there were three specific purchase programmes implemented by the Eurosystem (Markmann and Zietz 2017):

- On 7 May 2009, the Governing Council decided to initiate the covered bond purchase programme (CBPP), under which the Eurosystem purchased eligible covered bonds (a volume of €60 billion). The operational specifications of the CBPP were announced on 4 June 2009 (from July 2009 to June 2010).
- On 6 October 2011, the Governing Council launched a new covered bond purchase programme (CBPP2): the purchases of euro-denominated covered bonds issued in the Eurozone, for an intended nominal amount of €40 billion, distributed across the Eurozone. Ultimately, it involved a lower volume of approximately €16 billion (from November 2011 to October 2012).
- On 4 September 2014, the European Central Bank (ECB) announced its plan to buy covered bonds. This covered bond purchase programme (CBPP3) came as a surprise to the markets. The CBPP3 was originally scheduled until October 2016 (from October 2015 to October 2016). In January 2015, however, it was embedded in a broader asset purchase programme including sovereign debt as well as international and supranational institutions and agencies (ECB 2017). This programme was extended until year-end 2018.

With all these purchases, the ECB will remain an important player within the covered bond market for quite some time, unless at some point the Central Bank sees the economic rationale to actively reduce its covered bond holdings by unwinding its portfolio.

Finally, it must be stressed that covered bonds also play an important role in the financial system by contributing to the integration of European mortgage markets (Issing 2005). In fact, there is a close link between the origination and funding of mortgages. Indeed, financial innovation on the funding side heavily influences the supply and price of mortgage credit products (Rossignoli and Chesini 2009). In this respect, covered bonds may lead to increased efficiency, improved product diversity and a higher degree of competition in EU mortgage markets. The consequent reduction in the cost of credit for end-customers may contribute to the efficient allocation of capital and, ultimately, to economic growth (London Economics 2005).

4.3 The Relevance of Regulation and the Recent Regulatory Steps Taken to Arrive at the European Directive

The growing pressure to set up common standards was clearly driven by the ever-increasing internationalisation of the market. The huge variety of covered bonds presents a great challenge to investors—especially those from outside Europe—in determining which structures are the best for achieving geographical diversification. This in turn raises the issue of whether a certain degree of standardisation and homogeneity in the market would help further develop this market, resulting in limited analytical effort for investors.

One main question that has arisen from the debate on a definition of covered bonds at the industry level is whether or not minimum standards should be enshrined in law (Moore 2007).[6] The benefit of such a move would be to protect the instrument's "brand name", thereby preventing the risk of free riders entering the market and negative headlines spreading, unfiltered, across the entire sector. By contrast, a legal definition would be a disadvantage in terms of flexibility since the market might be unable to react quickly enough to rapid market developments. In fact, the market drives financial innovation in the industry. The competition between different products enhances the quality of the covered bond instrument, stimulating continuous improvements and the development of new solutions that better respond to the needs of issuers and investors. Even if legislation helps benefits spread throughout the entire system, market changes are much faster than legislative changes.

In brief, both regulation and the market itself help the industry grow. The interplay between regulatory and market developments in the covered bond universe is well represented by the dynamic between "structure" and "law".

[6] For a more detailed analysis of the relevance of the current debate, see Moore, P., Covered bonds debate: Covered bond issuers take on the global market, in Euromoney, June 2007.

In this respect, an interesting case study is that offered by the UK experience in the field. In the early 2000s, in the absence of specific legislation at the national level, UK issuers started issuing covered bonds via contractual agreements. The first covered bond in the UK was issued in July 2003 by HBOS. The deal was structured with the help of securitisation techniques on the basis of existing legislation and succeeded in being accepted by the market as a covered bond even though the UK at that time had no national covered bond legislation. Following the success of the new "structured" covered bond, other UK lenders entered the market with similar products. Then, the covered bond market in the UK reached a certain level of saturation without being regulated. At that point, the national banking regulatory body decided to acknowledge and recognise the existing covered bond structures and implemented a general regulation based on market practice, which incorporated the structured covered bonds that had already been issued (Treasury and FSA 2011). A similar pattern at the national level can be observed in the Netherlands.

Both the UK and the Netherlands have underlined the fact that there was a clear trend in the market of moving from a structure-backed system to a legislated system. In fact, it could be argued that there was a tendency towards transforming the self-regulatory standards established by the industry itself into general rules, namely, law-based prescriptions, with the purpose of achieving the objectives of systemic stability and investor protection.

However, rules easily become outdated due to market developments. In 2006, the cases of two new market entrants, BNP Paribas and HSBC, clearly illustrate this point. Both banks entered the market with new innovative products.

The French bank designed a tailor-made structured covered bond on the basis of the contractual methodology—even though there was specific covered bond legislation in France—to better combine high investor protection with specific internal needs. HSBC set up an innovative programme that provides a unified platform to issue both covered bonds and RMBS notes backed by a single portfolio of residential mortgage-backed loans, thus helping to save fixed costs and to promptly respond to the final implementation of Basel II and shifts in demand for both types of debt (Credit Suisse 2006). In both cases, the search for efficiency and flexibility, in relation to market changes, was the main driver of innovation and led the two banks to break with established rules.

These examples support the fact that as the covered bond market grew and developed, there were more variations in and interpretations of what was actually the basic concept of covered bonds. Although there was a clearly recognisable move from structured covered bonds back to a legal framework, this did not signal the end of the structured covered bond market, and both markets continued to grow in tandem.

In summary, once a financial innovation is successfully introduced into the market and starts spreading throughout the system as increasingly more players adopt it, a certain degree of regulation is required to achieve the objectives of systemic stability and investor protection.

In the financial industry, market standards and law-based prescriptions have represented two equally valuable forms of governance. Market standards emerged endogenously from prevailing industry practices, while law-based provisions stemmed from exogenous public intervention.

Sometimes, market standards emerge as a primary means of governance when no formal legal structures exist, and they are subsequently replaced by public regulation. In principle, market standards represent a tool that is more flexible than public regulation, as they are able to adjust more quickly and flexibly to financial innovation. In contrast, the implementation of a set of formal rules might hinder further innovation in rapidly changing financial markets.

Interestingly, the developments in the covered bond market have confirmed these dynamics. A clear desire to set up common standards has emerged at the international level as a result of the internationalisation of formerly domestic markets (Gottlieb 2005). This has led to various initiatives at the industry level that aim to reach an agreement on common rules among market participants.

The establishment of new rules has had an impact on the legislative process of EU institutions. In fact, in recent years, an increasing number of reports on harmonising European covered bond frameworks have been published. In March 2018, all these efforts culminated in the EC (European Commission) proposal for a European regulatory framework for covered bonds.

Analysing the recent evolution of regulations, we observe that it is possible to say that the process of regulatory harmonisation started very effectively in July 2014 when the European Banking Authority (EBA) published its view on the preferential risk weight treatment of covered bonds (EBA 2014).[7] The EBA concluded that preferential risk weight treatment was warranted, but it also noted that more convergence was necessary to increase the safety and robustness of the covered bond instrument, which

[7] EBA, Report on EU covered bond frameworks and capital treatment, July 2014.

would enhance financial stability and safeguard the preferential risk weight treatment. Overall, the EBA identified some areas where convergence of legal frameworks was necessary in the medium to longer term. The key areas were as follows: (1) the dual recourse mechanism; (2) the segregation of cover assets; (3) the bankruptcy remoteness of covered bonds; (4) cover pool features; (5) the valuation of cover assets and loan-to-value (LTV) limits as well as other requirements for cover assets; (6) the coverage principle and legal over-collateralisation; (7) stress testing, the use of derivatives for hedging and liquidity risk mitigation; (8) covered bond monitoring; (9) the role of the supervisor; and (10) investor reporting.

Subsequently, the European Commission (EC) took the discussion on covered bond harmonisation to another level in 2015, when it published a consultation paper on covered bonds in the European Union (EU) that was part of the EC's action plan to build a Capital Markets Union (EC 2015).[8] Overall, the aim of the EC was to "evaluate signs of weaknesses and vulnerabilities in national covered bond markets as a result of the crisis, with a view to assessing the convenience of a possible future integrated European covered bond framework that could help improve funding conditions throughout the Union and facilitate cross-border investment and issuance in Member States currently facing practical or legal challenges in the development of their covered bond markets". Ultimately, the EC proposed three options for convergence:

1. voluntary convergence of the member states' covered bond laws
2. an EU covered bond legislative framework seeking to harmonise existing national laws
3. a new EU legal framework for covered bonds (29th Regime)

The industry's response by means of the European Covered Bond Council (ECBC) was that a cautious approach to harmonisation would be welcomed. The ECBC also noted that the national differences were a "consequence of historical national differences in terms of mortgage markets, housing policies, consumer behaviour, insolvency law, credit an evaluation regulation, etc." and that full harmonisation of EU covered bond laws was a "utopia". However, the ECBC further noted that it saw room for convergence in specific areas. In general, the industry's message to the EC was that a pan-EU framework should be flexible and principle based.

[8] EC, Covered bonds in the European Union, Consultation document, 2015.

In September 2016, the EC decided to request a cost-benefit analysis on introducing an EU legislative framework for covered bonds (ECB 2017).[9] Interestingly, this report examined the proposals of the EBA report published in July 2014 (EBA 2014).

In the meantime, however, the EBA was still working on this topic and published a follow-up report in December 2016 that included recommendations on harmonising covered bond frameworks in the EU (EBA 2016). Now, it seems that these proposals were the blueprint for an EU directive.

Moreover, the EU Parliament—with which the EC (and the EU Council) had to agree with regard to the final text of legislation—ultimately published its own initiative on the harmonisation of covered bond frameworks. It supported the EBA proposals (EBA 2018) and mentioned that it would also have supported the inclusion of European secured notes (ESNs) in a new directive as a separate asset class next to covered bonds. The EU Parliament text[10] was voted on and approved in early July 2017. The key points of the EU Parliament are that this body favoured a cautious approach, stressing that the covered bond market had functioned well while also saying that diversity among covered bonds needed to be maintained (European Parliament 2017). Therefore, it noted that an integrated framework needs to be principle based, built on high-quality standards and aligned with best practices.

Interestingly, the EU Parliament preferred that the new European directive should distinguish between "premium covered bonds", which adhere to Art. 129 of the Capital Requirements Regulation (CRR), and "ordinary covered bonds", which comply with only Art. 52(4) of the UCITS Directive. Thus, premium covered bonds should receive better regulatory treatment than ordinary covered bonds, which should be treated more favourably than other forms of collateralised debt.

Like the European Commission, the EU Parliament also wants covered bonds to be backed by mortgages or public sector loans, while ESNs could finance riskier assets, such as SME loans, consumer credit, or infrastructure loans without a government guarantee. The EU Parliament closely followed the EC and EBA in regard to defining covered bonds while calling for a reassessment of the eligibility of ship loans as cover assets. It also noted that covered bonds issued by credit institutions from developing

[9] EC, Covered Bonds in the European Union: Harmonisation of legal frameworks and market behaviours' May 2017.

[10] EU Parliament, 'Own-initiative report on Covered Bonds', June 2017.

countries should receive similar regulatory treatment if the legal, institutional and supervisory environment is equivalent to that in the EU. As such, EU legislation could act as a benchmark for the global covered bond market.

Following the publication of these different reports, the EC did indeed decide to go ahead with a legislative proposal for an EU framework for covered bonds. The aim had become clear: to create a more integrated covered bond market in the EU without undermining the quality of existing covered bonds. This again suggests that the legislation should be of high quality and principle based.

The EC published the detailed proposal of the EU framework on covered bonds in March 2018.[11] The proposal considered all the previous studies and, in particular, closely followed the recommendations set out by the EBA.

4.4 The New European Covered Bond Framework

On 18 April 2019, the EU Parliament and the EU Council provisionally approved the proposal for a new regulatory framework composed of a directive on the issue of covered bonds and covered bond public supervision[12] and a regulation amending Regulation (EU) No. 575/2013 regarding exposures in the form of covered bonds.

Finally, on 27 November 2019, EU Directive 2019/2162 of the EU Parliament and of the EU Council was issued together with EU Regulation 2019/2160.[13] This framework represents an important part of the Capital Markets Union action plan, and, in general, it is an important step forward in strengthening capital markets and investment in the EU.

[11] Proposal for a Directive of the European Parliament and of the Council on the issue of covered bonds and covered bond public supervision and amending Directive 2009/65/EC and Directive 2014/59/EU. The proposal for a directive is complemented by a proposal for a regulation amending EU Regulation No. 575/2013 (the Capital Requirements Regulation).

[12] EU Parliament legislative resolution of 18 April 2019 on the proposal for a directive of the European Parliament and of the EU Council on the issue of covered bonds and covered bond public supervision and amending Directive 2009/65/EC and Directive 2014/59/EU.

[13] EU Directive 2019/2162 amending Directives 2009/65/EC and 2014/59/EU on the issue of covered bonds and covered bond public supervision and EU Regulation 2019/2160 amending Regulation (EU) No. 575/2013 regarding exposures in the form of covered bonds were published on 18 December 2019, in the *Official Journal of the European Union* (*OJ*).

In particular, the new European covered bond framework sets the conditions that these bonds must meet to be recognised under EU law. It also strengthens investor protection by imposing specific supervisory duties on the issuers. The directive is complemented by a regulation amending the Capital Requirements Regulation (CRR), which adds further requirements to the cover pool with the aim of strengthening the conditions for granting preferential capital treatment to investors.

Pursuant to European law, a regulation is usually directly binding on member states, whereas a directive will require member states to adopt its provisions into national law within a specified timeframe. In this specific case, the new framework was published in the *Official Journal of the European Union* on 18 December, and the new covered bond directive and the related regulation entered into force on 6 January 2020. Member states will need to adopt both texts in their national legislations by 8 July 2021, and they will need to implement those measures no later than 8 July 2022.

In particular, starting from the analysis of the directive, this is articulated in six titles that do the following:

1. provide common *definitions* of covered bonds and their specific characteristics that will represent a consistent reference for purposes of prudential regulation;
2. define the *structural features* of the instrument (dual recourse, quality of the assets backing the covered bond, liquidity and transparency requirements, etc.);
3. define the tasks and responsibilities for the *supervision* of covered bonds;
4. set out the rules allowing the use of the *"European covered bond" label*;
5. list the amendments to other directives; and
6. provide final provisions.

The first title of the directive defines the financial instrument in a very simple way, specifying the terminology used in the following chapters of the regulatory text.

More importantly, the second title (Art. 4–17) describes the structural features of covered bonds (Fig. 4.3)*. Art. 16 is particularly relevant; it states that member states will ensure investor protection by imposing that the cover pool will include at all times a liquidity buffer composed of liquid assets available to cover the net liquidity outflow of the covered bond

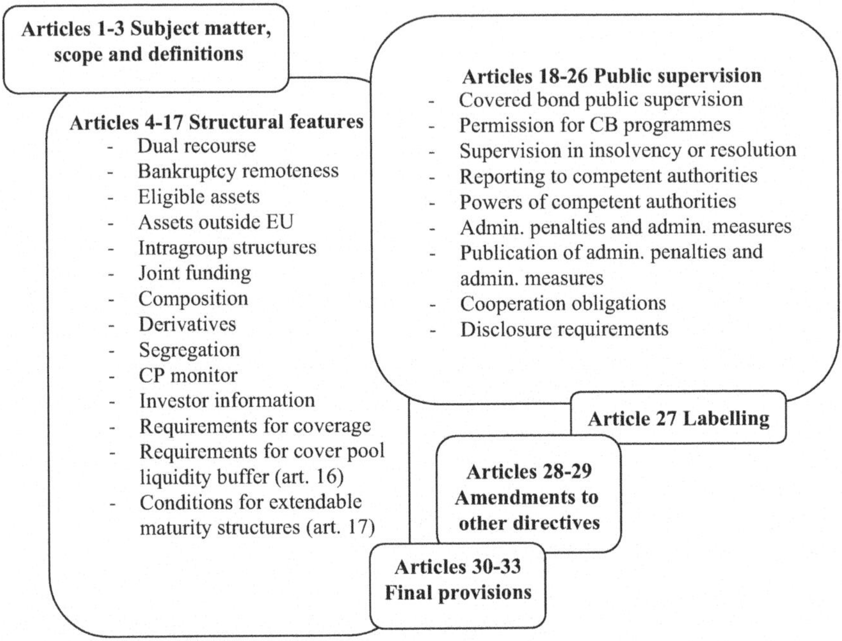

Fig. 4.3 Overview of the covered bond directive

programme. The cover pool liquidity buffer has to cover the maximum cumulative net liquidity outflow for 180 calendar days. Member states will ensure that the cover pool liquidity buffer consists of determined kinds of assets, segregated in accordance with Art. 12 of the same directive.

In this regard, it is worth emphasising the content of Art. 17, which presents the introduction of the German-inspired 180-day liquidity buffer required for hard bullet structures. To understand this, it is useful to note that covered bonds can be issued with a hard or a soft bullet structure. At present, most covered bond programmes are issued as soft bullet structures because they include provisions that enable the maturity of the covered bond to be extended. The standard extension period is one year, with the interest rate being tied to a floating rate index, but there are differences. There is no uniform wording as to when and under what circumstances covered bonds can be extended—rather, extendibility is at the discretion of the issuer.

Considering the new directive, covered bonds, which are extendible, are not subject to a 180-day liquidity buffer; however, compared with the current situation, the criteria for extensions are tightened. Considering this rule, it is possible to forecast that hard bullets will become a rarity outside Germany. It is also likely that some German issuers will move away from hard bullets over time and start issuing soft bullets.

As opposed to hard bullets, where the indirect cost of maintaining a liquidity buffer is incurred by the issuer, the cost of extendibility on soft bullet structures is incurred by the investor.

Under the new framework, investor protection on future soft bullet structures will be ensured to a much higher degree. In this regard, Art. 17 specifies what is needed to fulfil the new criteria for extendibility:

- the maturity can be extended only subject to objective triggers in national law and not at the discretion of the credit institution issuing covered bonds; and
- the maturity extension triggers are specified in the contractual terms and conditions of the bond.

Consequently, most covered bond programmes will be changed. Most likely, national laws will specify objective triggers, which could differ between countries, or individual contractual terms will be included in the covered bond programmes, and they will differ between issuers.

As a result, a harmonised common set of objective triggers will be achieved, either through national law or through contractual terms and conditions. Investor protection will also be enhanced under the new legal framework, as extension triggered at the discretion of the issuer will no longer be possible (Table 4.1).

Table 4.1 Bond type definitions before and after the new directive

Time	*Hard bullet*	*Soft bullet*
Before the new directive	The final maturity cannot be extended	The final maturity can be extended often at the discretion of the issuer
After the new directive	The final maturity cannot be extended (but liquidity buffer has to maintained)	Extension subject to objective/ specified triggers

The third title of the directive (Art. 18–26) disciplines the specific domestic public supervision of covered bonds. In fact, to ensure investor protection, the issue of covered bonds in each member state is subject to competent domestic supervision. For this purpose, every member state has to designate one or more competent authorities and communicate their names to the European Commission and to the EBA.

The competent authorities must have the expertise, operational capacity, powers, resources and independence necessary to carry out their functions. Furthermore, they must cooperate closely with other authorities performing the general supervision of credit institutions and with the resolution authority in the event of the resolution of a credit institution issuing covered bonds.

In addition, the covered bond competent authorities must cooperate closely with each other. This cooperation must include providing one another with any information relevant to the exercise of the other authorities' supervisory tasks under the national provisions transposing this directive. They must also cooperate with the EBA or, where relevant, the ESMA.

In particular, member states must ensure that the following information is published by the covered bond competent authorities once they are designated:

(a) the texts of their national laws, regulations, administrative rules and general guidance adopted in relation to the issue of covered bonds;
(b) the list of credit institutions permitted to issue covered bonds; and
(c) the list of covered bonds that can use the "European covered bond" label and list of covered bonds that can use the "European covered bond (premium)" label.

The competent authorities have to provide the lists of credit institutions and covered bonds to the EBA on an annual basis. Moreover, the published information must be sufficient to enable a meaningful comparison of the approaches adopted by the competent authorities of the different member states.

To ensure investor protection, every member state must require permission for a covered bond programme to be obtained by the financial intermediary before issuing covered bonds under that programme. Clearly, the power to grant such permission belongs exclusively to the competent authorities. Member states will set requirements for permission, at minimum including the following:

(a) an adequate operational programme that sets out the issue of covered bonds;
(b) adequate policies, processes and methodologies aimed at investor protection for the approval, amendment, renewal and refinancing of loans included in the cover pool;
(c) management and staff who are dedicated to the covered bond programme and who have adequate qualifications and knowledge regarding the issue of covered bonds and the administration of the covered bond programme; and
(d) an administrative set-up of the cover pool and the monitoring thereof that meets the applicable requirements set in the national provisions transposing this directive.

Member states must ensure investor protection by giving the competent authorities all supervisory, investigatory and sanctioning powers necessary to perform their task. These powers will at minimum include the following:

1. the power to grant or refuse permission;
2. the power to regularly review the covered bond programme to assess compliance with the directive;
3. the power to carry out on-site and off-site inspections;
4. the power to impose administrative penalties and other administrative measures in accordance with the national provisions; and
5. the power to adopt and implement supervisory guidelines related to the issue of covered bonds.

In the event of the resolution of a credit institution that was previously the issuer of covered bonds, to ensure that the rights and interests of the covered bondholders are preserved, the competent authorities must cooperate with the resolution authority, at minimum including control of the continuous and sound management of the covered bond programme during the period of the resolution process.

Member states may appoint a special administrator to ensure that the rights and interests of investors are preserved, at minimum by verifying the continuous and sound management of the covered bond programme during the necessary period. Where member states use this option, they may require their competent authorities to approve the appointment and dismissal of the special administrator, and, at minimum, they will require that the competent authorities be consulted regarding the appointment and dismissal of the special administrator.

Member states must ensure investor protection by requiring the credit institutions issuing covered bonds to report the information on covered bond programmes to the competent authorities. This reporting must be carried out on a regular basis and upon request by those competent authorities.

Member states must also provide rules on reporting by the issuer to the competent authorities in the event of insolvency or resolution of the credit institution.

Without infringing the right of member states to impose criminal penalties, member states must set rules establishing appropriate administrative penalties and other administrative measures.

Finally, the EBA maintains a central database of administrative penalties and other administrative measures communicated by the competent authorities. This database is accessible only to the competent authorities and must be updated on the basis of the information that they provide.

The fourth title of the directive includes only Art. 27. It differentiates between "European covered bonds" and "European covered bonds (premium)". The distinction is the following:

- a European covered bond has to meet the requirements of the directive; and
- a European covered bond (premium) has to meet the requirements of both the directive and the regulation.

Under the new framework, only premium covered bonds will receive preferential treatment (e.g., lower risk weight) from investors.

Finally, the fifth title specifies the amendments to other directives, while the sixth title introduces the tap issuance exemptions. In particular, the directive opens a two-year exemption period for covered bonds that are tap issued, that is, issued before 8 July 2022. Tap-issue bonds are still subject to certain limits:

- an absolute limit on size: they must not exceed €6 billion or the domestic currency equivalent;
- a relative limit on size: twice the total size of the covered bonds outstanding on that date; and
- a maturity limit on tap-issue bonds: the maturity date is before 8 July 2027.

As previously stated, the new regulatory framework also includes a regulation and the consequent changes to Art. 129 of the Capital Requirements Regulation (CRR). Notably, this regulation introduces an over-collateralisation (OC) rule and clarifies the dimension of the loan-to-value (LTV) ratio.

Most importantly, a new minimum level of 5% over-collateralisation (OC) is introduced. This level can be lowered to a minimum of 2% but only if the bank uses a formal approach that takes into account the underlying risk of the assets or if it is based on mortgage lending value (ECBC 2019).

Furthermore, the LTV wording is clarified in the regulation. Limits of 80% for residential loans and 60–70% for commercial loans and ships do not determine whether a loan can be included in a cover pool but only what share can be included. The regulation also stresses that the LTV ratio has to be maintained throughout the maturity of the loan.

The new European covered bond framework should certainly be able to harmonise minimum technical and product standards based on existing national regulations, establish a common regulatory treatment for covered bonds in member states, improve investor confidence and create the conditions for the further development of this instrument.

4.5 Conclusion

Covered bonds have been increasingly used in the marketplace as a funding instrument, in addition to savings deposits and mortgage-backed securities (MBS). Among the two capital market funding tools, the covered bond market is the most developed and the largest capital market.

Covered bonds offer many relevant advantages to both issuers and investors. This accounts for their success and the ultimate development of the market during recent decades. The replication of issuances in different jurisdictions has favoured the introduction of products with some characteristics that differ from the original model, although a certain degree of standardisation has tended to be preserved within the global market.

Since the changes introduced by the Capital Requirements Directive (CRD) adopting Basel II, issuers have started to rethink and reshape their securitisation and funding strategies. The CRD defines covered bonds in more detail and maintains a favourable treatment with regard to covered bond exposures if they fulfil certain eligibility criteria, which are specifically defined. Therefore, covered bonds traditionally benefit from a lower risk weighting than MBS, even though uncertainty remains in certain areas of application due to numerous national discretions. Nevertheless, covered bonds and asset-backed securities (ABS) continue to be complementary funding instruments, mainly because they target different investor bases.

Since 2014, the opportunity to harmonise the different domestic rules disciplining covered bonds in Europe has become evident. The new regulatory framework at the end of 2019 is built on principle-based rules and provides minimum harmonisation inspired by well-functioning and mature national markets. At the same time, the rules offer sufficient room for national specificities. The text covers all necessary elements for a sound covered bond product, thus achieving the objective of justifying preferential treatment in terms of capital requirements for investors. In particular, the amendments of Art. 129 of the Capital Requirements Regulation (CRR), which aim to reinforce and complement the requirements for the preferential capital treatment of covered bonds, make the regulatory framework more consistent and up-to-date.

In particular, the new framework aims to protect investors, and this objective should undoubtedly be achieved. It is also widely considered positive for the overall product, with Moody's recently saying that it would maintain and enhance the credit strength of European covered bonds. In particular, the directive sets a minimum level of over-collateralisation, defines the sorts of assets that can secure the issuance and calls for a cash buffer with enough liquidity to cover the next 180 days of payments.

On the issuer side, in some member states, credit institutions will benefit from the new regulatory framework, while in others, they will be disadvantaged. In this regard, the Spanish covered bond statutory framework is one of the frameworks most affected by the new European framework because the regulation in Spain is so different from the regulation in the rest of Europe. Spanish authorities have approximately two years to bring the Cédulas framework into line with the new covered bond directive. The greatest single problem is that under the current regime, investors have a claim on the entire mortgage portfolio of the issuing bank. Amending the law will probably require a more definitive separation of the cover pool assets from the issuer's balance sheet, which will dilute investors' claim and, according to the Moody's rating agency, be a negative for the Cédulas credit rating. Under the new law, issuers will have to transfer a substantial portion of the best mortgages to their new programmes. Moody's believes that this will lead to a material reduction in both the size and the quality of existing cover pools.

Furthermore, the new harmonised framework for European covered bonds will surely impact the Nordic countries, some more than others. In these countries, the Swedish domestic covered bond market is a hard bullet market. Although most market participants would prefer the current market structure to remain, there exists a high probability of a "forced" conversion to soft bullet issues.

The new regulatory framework offers a certain level of certainty with regard to what a covered bond actually is as well as provides a strong guidepost for CEE countries to develop new covered bond laws.

However, real work has yet to be done. It is now up to the respective national supervisors to make improvements to existing covered bond legislations.

Since the directive gives national supervisors discretion with regard to many topics, there is room for interpretation as the directive is incorporated into national law, and there will still be variations between national regimes. The flexibility and the principle-based characteristics of the new regulatory framework not only bring many advantages but also continue to permit a certain degree of discretion among member states.

References

Avesani, R.G., M.E. Ribakova, and A.G. Pascual. 2007. *The Use of Mortgage Covered Bonds*. IMF working paper, 07/20.

Chesini, G. and M. Tamisari. 2009. The Regulatory and Market Developments of Covered Bonds in Europe. *Financial Innovation in Retail and Corporate Banking*, Edward Elgar Publishing.

Credit Suisse. 2006. Covered Bonds and Basel II, 16 March.

Cross, G.H. 2008. The German Pfandbrief and European Covered Bonds Market. In 2004, *The Handbook of European Fixed Income Securities*, ed. F.J. Fabozzi and M. Choudhry. United States: Wiley.

European Banking Authority (EBA). 2014. Report on EU covered bond frameworks and capital treatment, July.
———. 2016. Report on Covered Bonds. Recommendations on Harmonisation of Covered Bond Frameworks in the EU, 20 December.
———. 2018. EBA report on the European Secured Notes (ESNSs). 24 July.
European Commission (EC). (2015). Covered bonds in the European Union. Consultation document.
European Central Bank (ECB). 2007. The Dynamics of Bank Spreads and Financial Structure, Working Paper Series, No. 714, January.
———. 2011. The Impact of the Eurosystem's Covered Bond Purchase Programme on the Primary and Secondary Markets. Occasional Paper Series, No. 122, January.
———. 2017. The Macroeconomic Impact of the ECB's Expanded Asset Purchase Programme (APP). Working Paper 2075, June.
European Commission. 2006. Report of the Mortgage Funding Experts Group, Bruxelles, 22 December.
European Covered Bond Council (ECBC). 2007. European Covered Bond Fact Book, August 2007, Second Edition.
———. 2019. European Covered Bond Fact Book, August 2019, Fourteenth Edition.
European Mortgage Federation. 2018. Hypostat 2018, September.
European Parliament (2017). Own initiative report on Covered Bonds. June.
———. (2019). Covered bonds – Issue and supervision, exposures. Briefing. Eu legislation in progress. Febrary 25.
Golin, J.L., (Ed). 2006. *Covered Bonds: Beyond Pfandbriefe: Innovations, Investment and Structured Alternatives*. Euromoney Books, Euromoney Institutional Investor. London.
Gottlieb, C. 2005. The European Covered Bond Market: Too Big to Ignore. ECMI Commentary No. 2, 23 December.
Hardt, J. 2004. Covered Bonds Wake Up to a New World, in The Banker, 4 November.
HM Treasury and FSA. 2011. Review of the UK's Regulatory Framework for Covered Bonds, April.
Issing, O. 2005. Mortgage Markets and Monetary Policy: A Central Banker's View. In *Speech Delivered at the European Mortgage Federation Annual Conference*, Brussels.
Larsson, C.F. 2013. What did Frederick the great know about financial engineering? A survey of recent covered bond market developments and research. *North American Journal of Economics and Finance* 25: 22–39.
London Economics. 2005. The Costs and Benefits of Integration of EU Mortgage Markets, Report for the Commission, DG-Internal Market and Services, August.

Markmann, H. and J. Zietz. 2017. Determining the Effectiveness of the Eurosystem's Covered Bond Purchase Programs on Secondary Markets. *The Quarterly Review of Economics and Finance* 66: 314–327.

Mastroeni, O. 2001. Pfandbrief-style Products in Europe, BIS Paper No. 5. October.

Moore, P. 2007. Covered Bonds Debate: Covered Bond Issuers Take on the Global Market, Euromoney, June.

Packer, F., R. Stever, and C. Upper. 2007. The Covered Bond Market. *BIS Quarterly Review*, September.

Rossignoli B. and G. Chesini. 2009. Il finanziamento dei crediti ipotecati e le obbligazioni bancarie garantite. In (a cura di) Comana, M., Brogi, M., *Saggi in onore di Tancredi Bianchi*, Bancaria Editrice.

Schwarcz, S.L. 2010. The Conundrum of Covered Bonds. *Business Law* 66: 561.

Standard & Poor's (2019). S&P Global Ratings' Covered Bonds Primer. June, 20.

Stocker, O. 2011. Covered Bond Models in Europe: Fundamentals on Legal Structures. *Housing Finance International* Winter: 32–40.

Van Rixtel, A., L.R. González, and J. Yang. 2015. *The Determinants of Long-term Debt Issuance by European Banks: Evidence of Two Crises.* BIS Working Paper No. 513, September.

CHAPTER 5

Subordinated Debt and Banking Regulation: An Overview

Giulio Velliscig, Josanco Floreani, and Maurizio Polato

5.1 Introduction

Subordinated debt is a liability that ranks junior with respect to senior debt in case of default, which means that subordinated creditors are not paid out until senior creditors are paid in full. There exist different levels of subordination—for instance, a liability L2 may be senior to L3 but subordinated to L1. Common equity can be seen as the most subordinated claim whereas secured bonds can be regarded as the most senior.

Subordination can be obtained in three ways: it may be statutory when following from legal provisions that identify certain liabilities as subordinated; structural when the liability is issued by a non-operative holding or sub-holding; contractual when it follows from clauses indicated on the bond's term sheet.

G. Velliscig (✉) • J. Floreani • M. Polato
Department of Economics and Statistics, University of Udine, Udine, Italy
e-mail: velliscig.giulio@spes.uniud.it; josanco.floreani@uniud.it; maurizio.polato@uniud.it

C. Cruciani et al. (eds.), *Banking and Beyond*, Palgrave Macmillan Studies in Banking and Financial Institutions,
https://doi.org/10.1007/978-3-030-45752-5_5

Subordinated debt is part of the bank's regulatory capital since 1988 when Basel Accords included it into their own funds with the specific purpose of absorbing losses in case of default. As a result, subordinated debt is often referred to as *gone concern* capital. Although its status remained unaltered throughout all the Basel Accords issued by the Basel Committee on Banking Supervision (BCBS), a recent debate in literature has started questioning the risk profile and functions of subordinated bondholders under the European Bank Recovery and Resolution Directive (BRRD).

In order to cope with the expensive bank bail-outs that occurred during the Great Financial Crisis (GFC), the BRRD introduces the bail-in tool that transfers the risk of a bank's default from taxpayers to bailinable creditors. The bail-in tool requires bailinable instruments to be written off and/or converted into common equity in the event of resolution. As a result, the BRRD requires banks to meet a minimum amount of own funds and eligible liabilities (MREL) in order to grant the effectiveness of the bail-in tool. Moreover, the subordination feature of the MREL requires banks to pile up the buffer of bailinable liabilities partly using subordinated liabilities.

Bailinable liabilities include all liabilities but deposits protected by the Deposit Guarantee Scheme (DGS), secured liabilities and those explicitly excluded from bail-in. The MREL, instead, represents a sub-sample of bailinable liabilities that mostly consist of unsecured debt. Furthermore, the MREL subordination requirement requires banks to pile up part of the MREL buffer using subordinated liabilities. The Directive 2017/2399, amending the BRRD, introduces the new "Tier 3" asset class, which consists of non-preferred senior debt that is eligible to meet the MREL subordination requirement.

According to bail-in rules, therefore, even senior debt may be subjected to a write-down thereby causing hefty reputational damage for banks. To prevent such a scenario, banks are going to issue larger amounts of subordinated bonds, including "Tier 3" bonds, to pile up the bail-in buffer. As a result, an MREL which is adequately met with equity and subordinated debt may be able to reassure investors who want to buy relatively safer senior bonds without facing the impending threat of a bail-in. Subordinated debt plays, therefore, a crucial role in complying with the MREL and needs more research on the evolving risk profile and functions of its investors under recovery and resolution rules.

An attractive feature of subordinated debt consists of the incentives it provides to market participants to monitor the bank's risks as it bears a substantial amount of losses in case of default. However, the expensive bail-outs granted by governments during the GFC deterred unsecured investors from properly incorporating the bank's risk into securities' prices. This phenomenon is acknowledged by literature as creditor inertia. The BRRD addresses this issue turning unsecured debt into bailinable aiming to resume the market monitoring function of unsecured investors thereby restoring market discipline (Goodhart and Avgouleas 2014). Thus, research on the interplay between BRRD and subordinated debt should focus on the ability of subordinated investors to correctly understand changes in the bank's risk profile and incorporate this assessment into securities' prices.

However, for the BRRD to lead investors out of creditor inertia successfully, the market requires a solid resolution framework and a prompt and resolute application of the bail-in tool in case of bank distress. In this regard, recent literature has pointed out the severe credibility issue suffered by the bail-in tool detecting its weaknesses in the political (Hadjiemmanuil 2015) and regulator's discretion (Walther and White 2014) that might hamper its application. As a result, the credibility of the bail-in tool needs to be taken into account when assessing the risk profile and functions of subordinated investors. This further complicates the assessment of the new role of subordinated bondholders under the BRRD but strengthens the need for shedding light on it.

This chapter aims to deepen the role of subordinated bondholders within the evolving resolution framework starting to frame the question in literature and providing the theoretical and empirical grounds for future research. We first review the ongoing literature about subordinated debt and explore its evolving role under banking regulation. We then provide our contribution by reviewing three branches of literature, in accordance with a theoretical framework we developed, in order to ground in literature the study of subordinated bondholders under the BRRD.

As the ongoing literature lacks studies on the linkage between subordinated bondholders and BRRD, we borrow from unsecured debt literature when providing our contribution in order to draw conclusions regarding how subordinated bondholders may be affected by rules on recovery and resolution.

Our theoretical framework hinges on a credible bail-in tool and claims that a prompt and resolute application of bail-in rules might turn unsecured creditors out of creditor inertia that hampered their risk sensitivity following the too-big-too-fail (TBTF) subsidies provided by governments during the GFC to save ailing banks. As a result, the BRRD would be able to resume the active monitoring function of unsecured investors, thereby restoring market discipline.

Grounding on the interplay between resolution regulation and the cost of funding, we identify the three branches of literature useful to the purpose of this study in the stream investigating the credibility of the bail-in, in the stream assessing the impact of the TBTF bias on debt spreads, and finally in the stream of market discipline testing BRRD progresses in restoring the monitoring function of unsecured investors. We deem that these three branches of literature are crucial to providing future research with the coordinates able to shed a light on the interplay between subordinated bondholders and BRRD.

The chapter is organized as follows: Sect. 5.2 provides a review of recent theoretical and empirical developments in subordinated debt literature; Sect. 5.3 links subordinated debt to regulation in a review of European implementations of Basel Accords; Sect. 5.4 grounds the question of the role of subordinated bondholders within the EU resolution framework in literature and lays the bases for future research; Sect. 5.5 concludes and calls for future research.

5.2 Literature Review

This section provides a literature review on subordinated debt from the earlier debate over its design to the latest development of its theoretical and empirical stand.

5.2.1 Subordinated Debt Proposals

The debate on the evolution of bank regulatory design saw scholars questioning the traditional rule-based regulatory supervision in favor of an incentive-compatible approach focused on market discipline and subordinated debt. This question gave birth to the stream of literature known as mandatory subordinated debt market discipline, which led both scholars and regulators questioning the suitability of a mandatory subordinated debt policy. The purpose of such policy consists of creating a sufficiently large class of unsecured investors that, due to their low ranking in the creditor insolvency hierarchy, are enticed to actively monitor and discipline banks' risk thereby providing the relevant market signal and a valid disciplinary option to the regulatory authorities. Table 5.1 provides a

Table 5.1 A summary of mandatory subordinated debt proposals

References	*Recognition phase criteria*		*Control phase criteria*	
	Debt maturity	*Frequency of issue*	*Debt size*	*Additional control features*
Horvitz (1984, 1987)	×	×	✓ Discussed, but no specific details proposed	✓ Discusses the control characteristics of debt holder covenants, but no specific details proposed
Benston et al. (1986)	✓ Discussed, but no specific details proposed	✓ Discussed, but no specific details proposed	✓ 3–5% of deposits	✓ Covenants to restrict risky banks' activities ✓ Some debt is puttable
Keehn (1989)	✓ Subordinated bonds would have maturities of greater than 5 years	✓ Staggered to ensure debt maturity in any 1 year is greater than 10% but less than 20% of issued subordinated debt	✓ Minimum of 4% of subordinated debt to risk assets	✓ Progressively increased sanctions as a bank's performance deteriorates (similar to the prompt corrective action provisions of FDICIA)
Cooper and Fraser (1988)	✓ Should not be long term	✓ Rolled over at frequent intervals	✓ 3% of deposits	✓ Bonds would be puttable at 95% of par ✓ Failure by the bank to repurchase within a prescribed period would trigger revocation of its charter

(*continued*)

Table 5.1 (continued)

References	*Recognition phase criteria*		*Control phase criteria*	
	Debt maturity	*Frequency of issue*	*Debt size*	*Additional control features*
Wall (1989)	✓ Minimum maturity of 90 days	✓ Discussed, but no specific time period proposed	✓ Minimum of 4–5% of RWA	✓ Bonds would be puttable ✓ Exercise of put would force a bank to raise new debt or sell assets to meet debt size criteria within 90 days; otherwise, it would be deemed insolvent ✓ Restrictions on % of debt owned by insiders
Evanoff (1993)	✓ Long enough to tie debt holders to the bank (e.g. 5 years)	✓ Semi-annual calls on the market	✓ A significant proportion of total regulatory capital (e.g. 50%)	✓ Progressively increased sanctions as a bank's performance deteriorates (similar to the prompt corrective action provisions of FDICIA) ✓ Possible issue of puttable debt, the exercise of which would force a bank to raise new debt within 90 days; otherwise, it would be taken over by regulators

(*continued*)

Table 5.1 (continued)

References	*Recognition phase criteria*		*Control phase criteria*	
	Debt maturity	*Frequency of issue*	*Debt size*	*Additional control features*
Calomiris (1997)	×	✓ Discusses the rollover of overlapping generations of debt, but no specific time period proposed	✓ 2% of nonreserve assets or 2% of RWA	✓ Debt yield would be restricted to 50 basis points above a riskless rate ✓ "Insiders" excluded from holding sub-debt
Litan and Rauch (1997)	✓ At least 1 year	✓ A fraction due in each quarter	✓ Minimum of 1–2% of RWA	×
Bankers Round Table (1998)	×	×	✓ Minimum of 2% of liabilities	×
Calomiris (1999)	✓ 2 years	✓ 1/24th of the issue would mature each month	✓ Minimum of 2% of risky assets	✓ Debt rates would be capped at a spread above treasury rates
US Shadow Financial Regulatory Committee (2000)	✓ At least 1 year	✓ At least 10% of debt would have to mature in each quarter	✓ Minimum of 2% of risky assets	✓ Progressively increased sanctions as a bank's performance deteriorates (similar to the prompt corrective action provisions of FDICIA) ✓ Debt must be sold at arm's length

(*continued*)

Table 5.1 (continued)

References	*Recognition phase criteria*		*Control phase criteria*	
	Debt maturity	*Frequency of issue*	*Debt size*	*Additional control features*
Evanoff and Wall (2001)	✓ 5 years	✓ Minimum two issues per year, with each issue at least 2 months apart	✓ Minimum of 3% of RWA	✓ Tie debt yields to the "trip wires" under prompt corrective action such that progressively increased sanctions are imposed as a bank's performance deteriorates

Note: Key, ✓, issue considered; ×, issue not considered; FDICIA, Federal Deposit Insurance Corporation Insurance Act

Source: Hamalainen (2004)

summary of mandatory subordinated debt proposals developed between 1984 and 2001. Based on the distinction of the recognition and control phases of the bank's risk that characterizes the market discipline activity of subordinated investors, Table 5.1 summarizes the different proposals according to maturity, frequency of issue, debt outstanding and control features. The maturity date ranges from a minimum of one year to a maximum of five years. The authors suggest a frequency of subordinated debt issuances that ranges from two to four times per year. Other proposals just recommend the percentage of subordinated debt that has to mature within a specified period. The size of the outstanding subordinated debt is based on different accounting measures: it ranges from 1% to 5% of risk-weighted assets, from 3% to 5% of deposits; other authors set a minimum of 2% of liabilities; others require subordinated debt to account for at least 50% of the total regulatory capital. Additional control features require bonds to be puttable, impose restrictions on percentages of subordinated debt held by insiders and sanctions tied to bank's performance deterioration.

5.2.2 *Theoretical Literature*

Recent theoretical literature has been focused mostly on testing the effectiveness of subordinated debt in enhancing market discipline. Early studies are still influenced by the debate on the suitability of a mandatory subordinated debt policy.

Hamalainen et al. (2010) draw from the debate outlined in the previous section to test the feasibility of a mandatory subordinated debt policy (MSNDP) for the largest global institutions. The authors employ a descriptive approach to analyze the characteristics of the subordinated debt issuances in the UK, deepening the study on a bank level. They then compare the results with EU and US subordinated debt markets, along with mandatory subordinated debt policy (MSNDP) characteristics set out in the literature. As a result, they conclude raising some concerns about the feasibility of an MSNDP for the largest global credit institutions since it would alter their funding structures from the unconstrained optimum, thereby distorting the international level playing field.

Scholars then focus their interest on the market monitoring and market influence streams of the market discipline literature. To correctly place both streams into the general framework of the market discipline literature it is crucial to recall the difference between the two. Market monitoring is the process through which investors assess the bank's risk profile and embed it into securities' prices whereas market influence is the process through which a change in securities' prices causes bank managers to address the deterioration in the bank's resilience condition.

Regarding the former, Chauhan and Sundaram (2016) develop a model of a bank with endogenous risk choices where the monitoring activity played by an active market of subordinated debt helps in containing excessive risk-taking in the presence of deposit insurance. The model helps to derive the optimal level of subordinated debt able to reach the equilibrium where banks choose risk levels consistent with the first best as envisaged by a social planner, which could be compared to a regulator or a government agent who aims to maximize social welfare. Furthermore, the optimal quantity of subordinated debt helps to eliminate any risk-shifting associated even with risk-insensitive premiums.

Regarding market influence, Chen and Hasan (2011) develop a model to test the effectiveness of subordinated debt in disciplining banks. They conclude that subordinated debt regulation is effective as it reduces incentives for managers of distressed banks to benefit from taking value-destroying actions. Moreover, they claim that subordinated debt regulation and bank capital requirements are complementary in tackling the moral hazard issues. The authors conceive five crucial features for their subordinated debt regulation proposal. First, regulators assess the ability of banks to place subordinated debt into the market; on this basis, they decide whether to take corrective actions or not. Second, regulators scrutinize banks which do not fulfill subordinated debt requirements. Third, the government can impose ceilings on interest rates of subordinated debt. Fourth, subordinated debt converts into equity as the government takes over or provides assistance to the bank. Fifth, market discipline is indirect. As a result, the authors suggest that regulators impose ceilings on the interest rate of subordinated debt, forbid collusion between banks and investors in subordinated debt and require the conversion of subordinated debt into equity as the government assists the bank.

Among these studies, some scholars have started questioning the informative content of subordinated debt quotes. The study conducted by González-Rivera and Nickerson (2006) argues the informative content of the secondary market price of a single subordinated bond. The authors find the support of their thesis in the decentralization of secondary markets and the ambivalent responsiveness of subordinated debt yields to default risk. To address these difficulties, they conceive a multivariate dynamic signal that combines fluctuations in equity prices, subordinated debt, and senior debt yields. The signal appears able to have practical value since it captures joint movements in equity prices, subordinated debt yields and senior debt yields. As a result, the authors suggest that regulators and investors consider all market information jointly since the only subordinated debt yield spreads are noisy measures of a bank's risk of default and might embed several other information (i.e. liquidity issues, state of the business cycle, etc.).

The accuracy of subordinated debt market quotes to reflect the bank's risk of default is crucial for the BRRD to achieve its primary objective of an enhanced market discipline. However, the recent theoretical literature on the interplay between subordinated debt and the new rules on bank recovery and resolution has instead focused on the risk profile and functions of subordinated debt investors as well as the compatibility of subordinated debt market with the bail-in regime.

Resti (2016) investigates the role played by subordinated bonds within the new recovery and resolution framework focusing on the possible concerns in terms of consumer protection for retail investors. This study first raised the question of whether the BRRD, by easing resolution proceedings and minimizing public support, has increased the risk faced by subordinated bondholders. After discussing how subordinated bonds may be affected by new rules on recovery and resolution, the author provides some suggestions on how to enhance European regulations in order to prevent aggressive selling techniques and unsuitable advice that might mislead the investment decisions of retail clients.

Martino (2017) further explores the role of subordinated bonds under the BRRD. Employing a Law and Economics methodology, the author analyzes the economic consequences of the new legal framework pointing out the incompatibility between the current regulatory framework and the necessity of a well-functioning and dynamic market for subordinated debt. The author claims the inefficiency of a pure-mandatory bail-in mechanism for subordinated debt because of the spillover effects on the market of these instruments on a dynamic perspective. As a result, he suggests the adoption of a contractual bail-in regime, tailored on the contingent capital model, to enhance certainty amongst the contractual parties.

These results raise the question of whether more clarity is required by the BRRD in order to build up a credible framework that subordinated debt investors might discount into market quotes, eventually disentangling the uncertainty regarding their role under recovery and resolution rules.

5.2.3 *Empirical Literature*

Like theoretical literature, empirical studies are also influenced by the debate on the most suitable mandatory subordinated debt proposal.

Evanoff et al. (2011) analyze the relationship between the bank's risk and the subordinated bonds' yield spreads accounting for an environment characterized by a fully implemented mandatory subordinated debt program. They exploit a sample that consists of subordinated bond issues for 19 banks and 39 bank holding companies for the period 1990–1999. The results show that the risk-spread relationship is stronger during the period around new debt issuance, pointing out liquidity and transparency as main drivers. Overall, the authors claim that the degree of market discipline would be enhanced by a fully implemented subordinated debt program, suggesting a crucial role for subordinated debt in capital requirement regulation and requiring banks to issue regularly on the market to maintain it deeper, more transparent and informative.

Among those studies that ground on market discipline, an exception is provided by Kato and Hagendorff (2010) who, instead of testing for subordinated bond yields' risk sensitivity, study subordinated debt as a driver for bank fundamentals to better predict default. In detail, their study analyzes the role of subordinated debt in driving the ability of accounting-based indicators of risk to predict the distance to default, measured using market data, for a sample of US bank holding companies (BHCs) over the period 1998–2007. Their results show that for banks that have issued subordinated debt, a larger number of bank fundamentals help to predict default. Moreover, for banks that issued subordinated debt, the authors find that higher charter values and lower capitalizations further enhance the predictive ability of bank fundamentals.

Literature then empirically addresses the question of whether a higher proportion of subordinated debt within the capital structure can enhance market influence. The study by Belkhir (2013) contributes to the market discipline literature by analyzing whether the presence of subordinated debt among liabilities affects risk management decisions. The author employs a two-stage regression approach exploiting a dataset of 500,000 quarterly observations on the population of US insured commercial banks over the 1995–2009 period. In detail, the study compares the use of derivatives between banks that hold high and low levels of subordinated debt. The results point out that the impact of subordinated debt on risk management decisions depends mostly upon whether this debt is held by investors who hold the bank's equity claims or not. In the first case, holding subordinated debt should enhance risk-monitoring. In the second case, more subordinated debt should induce moral hazard incentives in management decisions. The solution suggested by the author consists of a regulation that forces the parent holding company to hold at least a share of the subordinated debt issued by its affiliated banks.

Another study by Nguyen (2013) investigates the disciplinary role of subordinated debt in mitigating bank risk-taking. The sample consists of publicly listed commercial banks and bank holding companies with an available date over the period 2002–2008. Using regression analysis, the author provides evidence supporting the role played by subordinated debt in mitigating bank risk-taking. Moreover, the author finds that national bank regulations and both legal and institutional conditions are crucial drivers of such relation.

A substantial contribution to literature is then provided by two studies that focus on the interplay between subordinated debt and the measures developed by rating agencies. In particular, the former contributes to market discipline literature by exploring the subordinated bond yields' sensitivity to risk measures developed by rating agencies whereas the latter contributes to the literature about the informational content of debt ratings focusing on the rating process of subordinated bond issuances.

The first study is conducted by Zhang et al. (2014) who empirically test the sensitivity of subordinated bonds' yield spreads to bank risk in the UK. They use a sample of 631 issues of subordinated notes and debentures between 1997 and 2009. The results point out that subordinated debt yield spreads are sensitive to risk measures developed by rating agencies, in particular, Moody's and Standard & Poor's. As a result, a downgrade causes an increase in spread yields and vice versa. Authors prove that subordinated debt yields reflect bank risk-taking in the UK sustaining the role of subordinated debt as a market discipline tool.

The second study by John et al. (2010) investigates the information content of debt ratings. The authors exploit a sample of 9457 bonds issued by 2109 companies. They employ multivariate analysis to investigate the impact of the notching policy on bond yields. They conclude that the notching policy that rating agencies adopt to capture differences in recovery rates of bonds with similar probabilities of default creates a systematic bias in bond ratings. Specifically, subordinated bonds with a high probability of default are rated conservatively. Moreover, subordinated bonds with a low probability of default are rated too optimistically. The authors conclude that the rating process of subordinated bonds reflects a trade-off between pleasing the issuer and suffering the costs of lawsuits in case of too optimistic judgments.

Empirical research also provides interesting insights into the relationship between subordinated debt and public guarantees and subsidies. In particular, two studies shed light on the role played by government guarantees in driving subordinated debt issuances and hampering the risk sensitivity of subordinated bonds' yields respectively.

The former conducted by Wang et al. (2010) employs a probit model, exploiting half-yearly cross-sectional time-series data from the first half of 2002 to the second half of 2007, to analyze the relationship between commercial banks' decisions to issue subordinated bonds and the banks' risk levels in Taiwan. Their results do not support the market discipline view, highlighting, instead, public guarantees from the government and the poor bond market conditions in Taiwan as the two main drivers of the bank's issuance decisions.

The latter by Millera et al. (2015) empirically assess the ability of market signals relative to accounting-based signals in predicting bank holding companies' distress. They use expected default frequency (EDF) and yield spreads on bank subordinated notes and debentures (SNDs) as proxy variables for market signals. Book signals include a failure probability model, capital ratios, commercial real estate concentration and a *Z*-score. The sample period goes from Q1 2006 to Q4 2012. The results show that in 2008 EDF's signals were more accurate than the other measures but do not lead to economically significant reductions in missed distressing events. As a result, the authors suggest that regulators would have been better off monitoring CRE concentrations in BHCs. As the crisis kicked in, the failure probability model was a more accurate signal. The SND's spreads over treasuries were poor predictors due to the TBTF subsidies bias. For the largest BHCs, the Tier 1 ratio was the most accurate signal. Overall, the results do not provide evidence to support the inclusion of EDFs or SND yield spreads as systematic inputs within bank supervision early warning systems.

The issue raised by this chapter about the low risk sensitivity of subordinated bonds' yields caused by the TBTF bias might turn out useful to shed light on the question posed by theoretical literature in the previous section about the risk profile and functions of subordinated bondholders under the BRRD. The BRRD indeed addresses the TBTF bias disciplining rules on burden-sharing and bail-in, and further constraining the government's ability to support weak banks via state-aid rules. As a result, the recovery and resolution framework may have increased the risk faced by subordinated bondholders and may have further restored the risk sensitivity of subordinated bonds' yields, thereby reshaping the risk profile and functions of subordinated debt investors. However, as suggested by theoretical literature, credibility might be crucial for the BRRD to address the TBTF bias, thereby resuming the market monitoring function of subordinated investors and restoring market discipline.

Section 5.4 grounds such suggestions in literature in order to provide a solid basis for future research on how rules on recovery and resolution are affecting the subordinated debt and investors' status.

5.3 Regulation

This section provides an overview of the European implementation of Basel Accords, drawn up by the Basel Committee on Banking Supervision (BCBS), focusing on the capital adequacy regulation and its contribution in shaping the banks' capital structure. This regulation dictates the minimum capital requirement and the instruments eligible for this purpose.

The Capital Requirements Directive (CRD: [EC 2006]) implements the Basel I (BCBS 1988) and Basel II (BCBS 2006), structuring the own funds on three layers. The first one is called Tier 1, which is required to be 4% of the risk-weighted assets. It consists of Core Tier 1, namely, the highest-quality capital, which is required to contribute at least 2% of the risk-weighted assets. Therefore, hybrid capital instruments are allowed to contribute up to 50% of Total Tier 1. The second layer is called Tier 2 and consists of subordinated debt and hybrid capital. Tier 2 capital can contribute up to 50% of the overall capital requirement. The third layer is Tier 3, which consists of subordinated debt. Following these constraints, a bank could comply with the overall 8% requirement with only 2% of equity.

The Capital Requirements Regulation (CRR: [EC 2013]) implements Basel III (BCBS 2010), which aims to enhance the quality and quantity of the bank's capital. Regarding own funds, Tier 3 is deleted. Tier 1 consists of Common Equity Tier 1 (CET1), which is the highest-quality capital, and Additional Tier 1 (AT1), which consists of subordinated and hybrid instruments. Tier 1 is required to be 6% of the risk-weighted assets, of which 4.5% must be covered with CET1 and the remaining 1.5% could be satisfied with AT1 instruments. Given that the overall capital requirement remains at 8% of the risk-weighted assets, the Tier 2 instruments, which consist of subordinated and hybrid instruments, are allowed up to 2%.

Moreover, Basel III requires three additional buffers of CET1. The capital conservation buffer accounts for 2.5% of risk-weighted assets; the same requirement is applied for the countercyclical buffer which addresses the procyclicality issue, whereas an additional 1% to 5% of CET1 is required for the systemic buffers. Given these constraints, the total CET1 requirement could reach 14.5% of the risk-weighted assets. Compared to Basel II, Basel III significantly reduces the weight of instruments different from CET1.

In 2014, the European Union adopts the Bank Recovery and Resolution Directive (BRRD: [EC 2014]), introducing the bail-in tool. To grant the effectiveness of bail-in, the BRRD requires banks to hold a minimum requirement for own funds and eligible liabilities (MREL). In case of resolution, these securities are available for write-down or conversion into equity.

In 2015, the Financial Stability Board (FSB) established international principles and a term sheet (FSB 2015) regarding the total loss-absorbing capacity (TLAC). It requires Global Systemically Important Banks (G-SIBs) to hold not only equity but also liabilities able to be bailed in.

In 2016, the European Commission proposed in the Banking Package a series of amendments to the banking directives and regulations (CRD IV/CRR, BRRD) to harmonize the MREL framework with the TLAC principles and TLAC Term Sheet. The amendment to the CRR (EC 2016a) introduces the minimum requirement of TLAC for EU G-SIBs, whereas the amendment to the BRRD (EC 2016b) introduces a firm-specific TLAC add-on for G-SIBs and a firm-specific MREL for non-G-SIBs.

Moreover, another amendment to the BRRD (EC 2016c) introduces a new asset class called non-preferred senior debt (i.e. contractually subordinated debt), which aims to tackle the confounding BRRD's provisions that put a heterogeneous stock of debt under the threat of the bail-in, and further let banks efficiently cope with the TLAC/MREL requirement. Indeed, these liabilities rank in insolvency above own funds and subordinated liabilities but below other senior liabilities and further meet the eligibility criteria for the TLAC/MREL subordination requirement, which requires banks to pile up part of the TLAC/MREL buffer with subordinated liabilities.

Although Basel III has shrunk the share of instruments different from CET1, the new resolution framework widens the buffer of other liabilities (MREL-eligible) required to absorb losses again. As a result, the bank's capital structure will require a mix of securities able to comply with different requirements which complicate its structure and composition.

The BRRD's provisions consider all liabilities but guaranteed deposit, secured or covered bonds and other instruments explicitly excluded as bailinable. The TLAC/MREL buffer is a sub-sample of bailinable liabilities mostly consisting of unsecured liabilities. Furthermore, the TLAC/MREL subordination requirement requires banks to pile up part of the TLAC/MREL buffer using subordinated liabilities among which there is also the new type of unsecured senior debt called non-preferred senior debt.

Bail-in rules, therefore, jeopardize even senior bonds. Such a scenario would cause heavy reputational damage for banks which plan to issue larger amounts of subordinated debt, including so-called "Tier 3" bonds, in order to reassure investors who want to buy relatively safer senior bonds without facing the impending threat of a bail-in.

Subordinated debt needs, therefore, to be further investigated by scholars given its crucial role within the capital structure as defined by BRRD provisions. In the next section, we identify three streams of literature that we deem able to better frame the role of subordinated bondholders under recovery and resolution rules.

5.4 Subordinated Bondholders and Bail-In

5.4.1 Theoretical Framework and Streams Identification

The study conducted by Resti (2016) points out the complexity brought by the BRRD within the capital structure. The author further explains the crucial role played by subordinated debt in piling up the MREL buffer, thereby reassuring investors who wish to buy relatively safer senior bonds without facing the impending threat of bail-in. The study then calls for future research on the risk profile and functions of subordinated bondholders under recovery and resolution rules.

We address the question posed by Resti and proceed in the following way. We provide our contribution by reviewing three branches of literature in accordance with a theoretical framework we developed in order to ground in literature the study of subordinated bondholders under the BRRD. Given the lack of research on the interplay between subordinated bondholders and the BRRD, the studies analyzed by this review, as well as the theoretical framework, build upon unsecured debt and its investors in order to draw conclusions on the role of subordinated bondholders under recovery and resolution rules. The three streams of literature we investigate focus on the impact of the absence, the introduction and the objectives of resolution regulation on the bank's cost of funding.

The first branch investigates the role of the TBTF issue in driving the dynamics of the bank's cost of funding. Before the introduction of a resolution regulation, governments used to save ailing banks using public funds. The promise of a government bail-out in case of insolvency discouraged unsecured investors from correctly incorporating the bank risk profile into securities' prices. The resulting scarce monitoring activity conducted by unsecured creditors is recognized by literature as creditor inertia. Such condition resulted in a funding cost advantage for TBTF institutions.

The second branch explores the credibility of bail-in rules in driving changes in the bank's cost of funding. The introduction of a resolution framework by the BRRD has seen scholars initially focusing on the credibility of the bail-in tool, looking for the causes that might hamper and limit its application. Although the BRRD has transferred risks from taxpayers to unsecured bondholders, scholars have brought its application into question calling for empirical research on investors' expectations over bail-in representing a plausible threat. As a result, the empirical literature on this topic has been focusing on the impact of bail-in events that refer to either its legislative process or its application on debt spreads.

Finally, we look at the BRRD's objectives and explore the market monitoring branch of market discipline literature that investigates the progress that the resolution regulation is making in restoring an active market monitoring function of unsecured investors. Indeed, bail-in rules, lowering the expectations of government support, are expected to entice unsecured investors to a more careful assessment of the bank's risk profile, thereby tackling the creditor inertia.

We decide to focus on these three streams of literature according to the following theoretical framework that we deem useful to disentangle the role of subordinated bondholders under recovery and resolution rules. We look at the BRRD as a means for regulators to interrupt the creditor inertia that deters unsecured investors from performing an active monitoring function. However, we consider the credibility of the bail-in tool as crucial in order to make the transfer of risk from taxpayers to unsecured bondholders effective, thereby enticing them to correctly incorporate the bank's risk into securities prices. As a result, we deem that a credible resolution framework would be able to lead unsecured investors out of creditor inertia and restore their market monitoring activity, thereby reshaping their risk profile and functions.

Given that the TBTF issue and the bail-in are pillars of our theoretical framework and crucial branches for our literature review, someone might argue that the conclusions we draw from the study of subordinated bondholders under the BRRD are valid only for large banks and limited to the bail-in tool. We argue, instead, that our study also applies to medium-size banks and further accounts for burden-sharing rules and soft bail-in (equity + subordinated debt). As recognized by literature, bail-in is an option only for large banks because they have access to the market of non-preferred senior debt that can grant them the sufficient loss-absorbency capacity required by bail-in rules. Medium banks, instead, depending on their similarity to small or large banks, can be wound up under normal insolvency proceedings or either resolved via burden-sharing, whose rules provide an intermediate solution between bail-in and bail-out by requiring the write-off or conversion of equity and subordinated debt before the injection of public funds to save an ailing bank, or resolved via soft bail-in. Some medium banks, indeed, that are both too large for liquidation and too small to issue a large amount of bailinable liabilities may lack sufficient loss-absorbing capacity required for the application of the bail-in tool. However, burden-sharing and soft bail-in threaten subordinated bondholders of such banks just like bail-in does for large banks. Indeed, the investors in subordinated debt issued by such banks might see their expectations over bail-out in case of distress, caused by the proximity of their banks' size to that of large banks, threatened by rules on burden-sharing or by soft bail-in. As long as the burden-sharing and the soft bail-in are deemed credible by market participants, subordinated bondholders would, therefore, resume their monitoring function, thereby helping the BRRD in achieving its primary objective of an enhanced market discipline. As a result, the theoretical framework and the conclusions we draw from the literature review also hold for medium banks and further account for burden-sharing rules and soft bail-in.

5.4.2 *Subordinated Debt Literature: What Is Missing*

Given the scarce contribution provided by literature on the linkage between resolution regulation and subordinated bondholders we deem it essential to dig deeper into the streams investigating the TBTF issue, the credibility of the bail-in tool and the market monitoring function from the perspective of the unsecured debt market, to ground both theoretically and empirically the study on the evolving role played by subordinated bondholders within the resolution framework and further pave the way for future research. The literature examined in Sect. 5.2 barely addresses the interplay between subordinated bondholders and resolution regulation.

From a theoretical standpoint, the studies conducted by Resti (2016) and Martino (2017) posed the question of subordinated bondholders concerned about the new recovery and resolution framework. Both studies recognize the new role of subordinated debt designed by the BRRD as a cushion that protects senior creditors from conversion into equity or write-off. As a result, they call for future research on the evolving risk profile and functions of subordinated investors under recovery and resolution rules.

Empirical literature lacks studies conducted on the impact of the BRRD on subordinated debt and its investors. To the best of our knowledge, the only empirical researches conducted on the reaction of the debt market to the introduction of the BRRD are those by Giuliana (2019) and Crespi et al. (2019). These studies hinge on the literature about the credibility of the bail-in. Indeed, Crespi et al. (2019) claim that the question as to whether investors will require higher returns on bank bonds due to bail-in rules is empirical and depends on whether they consider the bail-in as a plausible threat.

In the following paragraph, we dig deeper into the branch of literature exploring the credibility of the bail-in tool to start framing our study on the evolving role of subordinated bondholders under recovery and resolution rules.

5.4.3 The Credibility of Bail-In

The literature on the credibility of the bail-in tool is the first stream we investigate to ground the study of subordinated bondholders within the resolution framework. Borrowing from the theoretical framework developed from unsecured debt literature, we claim that the expectations of subordinated investors over the bail-in are crucial for the BRRD to pose an end to the creditor inertia and restore market discipline. A more credible bail-in, indeed, will entice subordinated investors to better monitor the bank's risk profile, therefore resuming their active market monitoring function.

Although the literature on the credibility of bail-in does not strictly focus on subordinated investors, it provides results on the unsecured debt market that can be extended to subordinated investors as well. Unsecured debt market reactions to bail-in events, being related to their application or their legislative process, are therefore crucial to understand the expectations of subordinated investors over bail-in.

In this regard, Giuliana (2019) studies bail-in events employing a difference-in-differences analysis to assess whether the authorities' commitment toward the bail-in tool causes a repricing of securities in the bond market. His results show an increase in the spread between bailinable and non-bailinable bonds following bail-in events.

Crespi et al. (2019) show similar results by studying the impact of the introduction of the bail-in tool on Italian bank bonds. They find that Italian banks experienced a higher bond funding cost following the introduction of the bail-in. Specifically, their analysis shows an increase of the spread at issuance of bailinable bonds compared to non-bailinable ones. They further point out that the drivers of such an increase lie in the inherent characteristics of each bank. Finally, their results suggest that the introduction of the BRRD has improved market discipline for the bank bonds' primary market.

Both studies show that the regulator and political commitment toward the bail-in tool contribute to debunking its credibility issue among investors. Moreover, Crespi et al. (2019) further suggest a link between the credibility of bail-in and an improved market discipline among bailinable investors, which is crucial in our framework to explain the evolving function of subordinated investors from creditor inertia to an active market monitoring.

Besides the empirical studies of Giuliana (2019) and Crespi et al. (2019), literature has provided interesting insights on the credibility issue also from a theoretical perspective. The focus of these studies is the regulator and political discretion that may hamper the application of the bail-in tool in case of resolution. The loosening eligibility criteria outlined by the BRRD for an instrument to qualify as bailinable also jeopardize senior creditors' investment in case of bail-in. This scenario would entail hefty reputational as well as political repercussions. This possibility led several scholars to question the efficacy of the resolution framework in preventing taxpayers' money from bearing the costs of bank bail-outs.

Hadjiemmanuil (2015) addresses such concerns pointing out the political discretion that lies in the application of the bail-in tool and identifying it as the main driver of the credibility issue. Walther and White (2014) contribute to this literature analyzing the regulator's discretion within the bail-in regime. They develop a model in which regulators decide upon resolution actions with discretion after analyzing private information regarding the bank's viability. Their results show that regulators with bad news and discretion have incentives to conduct excessively weak bail-in policies due to the costly consequences that the signal of a bail-in may trigger, such as bank runs.

Instead of looking at the causes that may hamper the application of the bail-in tool, the study conducted by Philippon and Salord (2017) points out the positive outcome that a credible bail-in may generate. They claim that credibility is crucial to enhance the BRRD as it contributes to form market expectations over bail-in. Their opinion is that if the resolution is effective both theoretically and empirically then there will be no need of applying it any time since bondholders would be more likely to accept a voluntary restructuring due to its more efficient outcome.

5.4.4 *The Link Between Market Discipline and BRRD*

The second layer on which the grounding of our study is based is the market discipline literature. Borrowing from the theoretical framework developed from unsecured debt literature, we claim that before the introduction of the BRRD subordinated bondholders have been bailed out alongside senior creditors by taxpayers and that led to the phenomenon known as "creditor inertia". Instead, the BRRD aims to restart the market monitoring function of subordinated bondholders by ceasing their inertia.

As literature misses the direct link between market discipline and subordinated bondholders under recovery and resolution rules, we review the studies investigating the monitoring function of unsecured investors in a framework evolving from the creditor inertia to a restored market discipline pursued by the BRRD. Insights from the unsecured debt market are crucial to get a grasp of the evolving risk sensitivity of subordinated investors under recovery and resolution rules.

In a speech held at the Conference "Financing the recovery after the crisis—the roles of bank profitability, stability, and regulation" in Milan on 30 September 2013, Benoît Cœuré, member of the executive board of the European Central Bank, highlights the crucial role played by market discipline in contributing to create an efficient resolution mechanism. He specifies further that a good resolution framework cannot be substitutive but only complementary to market discipline and supervisory vigilance.

Although the role of market discipline within the resolution framework is deemed essential, the literature investigating the linkage between investor's risk sensitivity and BRRD is scarce. However, the contribution of a few scholars has provided a solid basis supporting our theoretical framework.

Gleeson (2012), indeed, identifies the bail-outs granted by governments during the Great Financial Crisis to save ailing banks as the event that triggered the creditor inertia. Such condition is then defined as the decrease of unsecured creditors' risk sensitivity due to public backstop in case of bank distress. The author then suggests the credibility of the bail-in tool as a solution that has to be pursued by authorities in order to interrupt creditor inertia and restore market discipline.

Goodhart and Avgouleas (2014) come to a similar conclusion pointing out that turning unsecured liabilities into bailinable should provide creditors with incentives to restore an active market monitoring function, thereby helping to achieve the primary objective of BRRD, namely, an enhanced market discipline.

Overall, these studies suggest that the BRRD is crucial to restore the risk sensitivity of subordinated investors. The review further links the credibility of the bail-in tool to the success of the BRRD in restoring market discipline, thereby supporting our theoretical framework.

5.4.5 *The TBTF Bias*

The third layer on which the rooting of this study is based on is the literature that explores the relationship between the TBTF issue and the bank's cost of funding. Borrowing from the theoretical framework developed from unsecured debt literature, we argue that the implicit subsidies provided by EU governments during the Great Financial Crisis deterred subordinated bondholders from actively monitoring banks' risks, ultimately resulting in a funding advantage for TBTF institutions.

Given that literature overlooks the relation between subordinated bondholders and the TBTF issue, we analyze the dynamics behind the pricing of the TBTF guarantee by unsecured investors. Borrowing from these studies, we draw conclusions on the magnitude of the creditor inertia as well as the potential impact that the BRRD may have on security prices of subordinated investors if resolution regulation manages to restore market discipline.

Acharya et al. (2016) find that credit spreads of unsecured bonds issued by the largest US financial institutions between 1990 and 2012 are not risk-sensitive due to the implicit subsidy provided by the government in case of failure. That finding corroborates the creditor inertia condition that characterizes investors of TBTF institutions. Moreover, they find that the introduction of the Dodd-Frank Act has not mitigated the TBTF expectations of large institutions' bondholders. As the BRRD and the Dodd-Frank Act share the same purposes of addressing the issues related to the TBTF institutions, this result might suggest that the BRRD is not able to reduce investor's expectations of government support. According to our theoretical framework, then, the BRRD would not interrupt creditor inertia, thereby not even restoring market discipline.

The study by Demirgüç-Kunt and Huizinga (2010) shows that the TBTF issue not only has implications for investor's risk sensitivity but further affects the bank's size. Considering an international sample of banks between 1991 and 2008, they document that the number of systemically important banks has declined after 2008 with respect to the two previous years, implying private incentives to downsize in order to further exploit the government subsidy, especially in fiscally constrained countries.

We then review the literature evaluating the TBTF subsidy as the magnitude of such impact on securities prices is crucial to predict the success of the BRRD in resuming the active monitoring activity of subordinated investors. In this regard, literature has provided different evaluation methods as well as different sources and estimates.

Araten and Turner (2012) disentangle the sources of funding for bank holding companies in the US over the business cycle between 2002 and 2011. They find G-SIBs to benefit from the TBTF guarantee only partially for what concerns domestic interest-bearing deposits and credit spreads on senior and unsecured debt. Overall, accounting for all sources of funding, their results point out a funding cost benefit of 9 bps for G-SIBs.

A similar result is also provided by the study conducted by Baker and McArthur (2009) who quantify the value of the government subsidy following the adoption of the Troubled Asset Relief Program (TARP), which formalizes the establishment of a TBTF policy in the US. Using data from the Federal Deposit Insurance Corporation (FDIC) on the funding costs of the TBTF banks and smaller banks, they point out the increase in spread following the TBTF policy results of 0.09 percentage points that are equivalent to an annual subsidy of $6.3 billion.

Employing a market value-based approach, Li et al. (2011) quantify the value of the implicit government guarantee for large EU and US financial institutions, pointing out a potential gap of 50 bps between Credit Default Swap (CDS) spreads and Fair-Value Spreads (FVS). They show that credit spreads are much more affected by implicit subsidy than are equity prices. This result further supports our focus on unsecured debt, in particular, subordinated debt, as being the most affected by the TBTF subsidy and its response to the BRRD could potentially be of much interest. This study further confirms the above-mentioned results regarding the value of the TBTF premium by estimating a value of $293 billion for the top 20 EU banks and a value of $170 billion for the top 20 US banks.

The following study, instead, provides evidence of a higher valuation of the TBTF subsidy. Ueda and di Mauro (2012) quantify the value of structural state guarantees on a large worldwide sample of banks using the expectations of government support embedded in credit ratings as of end-2007 and end-2009. They point out a credit rating bonus of 1.8–3.4 notches at the end of 2007 and 2.5–4.2 at the end of 2009. These values correspond to a funding cost spread of 60 bp and 80 bp, respectively.

Most of the studies agree on a partial advantage taken by large financial institutions from TBTF subsidies and quantify it at around 10 bps. The results from the unsecured debt market suggest, therefore, the likely success of the BRRD in resuming the monitoring activity of subordinated investors since a firm and resolute application of bail-in rules would easily tackle such little bias.

5.5 Conclusion

The recent developments in the EU resolution framework raise the academic debate on the evolving role of subordinated debt. First, it plays a crucial role under the new resolution framework by building the buffer of bailinable liabilities required to grant the application of the bail-in, and, further, it is a direct objective of the BRRD aim to restore market discipline as it is designed to provide incentives to investors to monitor changes in the bank's risk profile.

This chapter provides an overview of subordinated debt literature and its evolution within banking regulation and further contributes to the debate by reviewing three branches of literature, in accordance with the theoretical framework we developed, in order to provide both the theoretical and the empirical bases to ground future research on the role of subordinated bondholders within the EU resolution framework.

Given the lack of studies on the interplay between subordinated bondholders and the BRRD, our review and theoretical framework borrow from unsecured debt literature in order to draw conclusions on the role of subordinated bondholders under recovery and resolution rules.

The theoretical framework is articulated as follows. The BRRD, transferring risk from taxpayers to unsecured bondholders, aims to resume the market monitoring function of the latter thereby restoring market discipline. Indeed, the TBTF subsidies provided by EU governments during the GFC did not entice unsecured investors to correctly price the bank's risk profile leading to the phenomenon acknowledged by literature as creditor inertia. However, for the risk transfer to become effective, the resolution framework must be deemed credible by unsecured investors. The credibility of the bail-in tool, therefore, plays a crucial role in helping the BRRD in achieving its objectives. In short, we build a thread linking the creditor inertia caused by the TBTF bias to the potential turning point that the BRRD might represent resuming the monitoring function of unsecured investors for restored market discipline. We further point out the credibility of the bail-in tool as crucial in making this thread holding.

According to this theoretical framework, we explore the literature that investigates the impact of the absence, the introduction and the objectives of the resolution regulation on the bank's cost of funding. Regarding the absence of a proper resolution regulation, we deepen the literature on the impact of the TBTF issue on debt spreads. Moreover, on the introduction of the resolution framework, we investigate the credibility of the bail-in tool looking at the debt market reactions to bail-in events, which are related to its legislative process or application. Finally, regarding the objectives of resolution regulation, we review those studies that address the changing risk sensitivity of unsecured investors from creditor inertia to the restored market discipline pursued by the BRRD. We claim that the branches of literature highlighted in this study are crucial to pave the way for future research on the role of subordinated bondholders within the EU resolution framework.

We therefore suggest that future research focus on the interplay between both the BRRD's legislative process or applications and subordinated bondholders according to the theoretical framework developed by this study. Borrowing from the literature on the credibility of the bail-in tool, we first call for an empirical investigation of subordinated debt market quotes reaction to bail-in events to study the subordinated investor's expectations over the bail-in. If such events are effective in enhancing the bail-in tool, then researchers will find a positive repricing which would indicate that investors are discounting higher expectation of being bailed in in case of resolution. On the contrary, creditor inertia persists, thereby jeopardizing the monitoring function of subordinated investors. As we highlighted in this study, the expectations of subordinated investors over the bail-in tool are crucial in resuming the market monitoring function that has been mitigated by bank bail-outs. As a result, we call for further research on the risk sensitivity of subordinated debt quotes. Indeed, positive expectations over the bail-in tool are likely to entice subordinated investors to better monitor the bank's risk, thereby resuming an active monitoring function and helping the BRRD in achieving its primary goal of an enhanced market discipline. Finally, to complete the research, we call for a focus on the implications that the impact of bail-in events has for the funding advantage enjoyed by TBTF institutes to better understand the progress made by the BRRD legislative process in freeing subordinated investors from creditor inertia.

References

Acharya, V.V., D. Anginer, and A.J. Warbuton. 2016. The End of Market Discipline? Investor Expectations of Implicit Government Guarantees. *MPRA Paper 79700*, Germany: University Library of Munich.

Araten, M., and C. Turner. 2012. Understanding the Funding Cost Differences between Global Systemically Important Banks (G-SIBs) and Non-G-SIBs in the United States. *JPMorgan Chase*.

Baker, D., and T. McArthur. 2009. The Value of the "Too Big to Fail" Big Bank Subsidy, CEPR Reports and Issue Briefs 2009-36, Center for Economic and Policy Research (CEPR).

Bankers Round-table. 1998. Market-Based Incentive Regulation and Supervision: A Paradigm for the Future, Washington, DC.

BCBS. 1988. International Convergence of Capital Measurement and Capital Standards. Bank for International Settlements, Basel. www.bis.org/publ/bcbs04a.pdf.

———. 2006. International Convergence of Capital Measurement and Capital Standards: A Revised Framework, Comprehensive Version. Bank for International Settlements, Basel. www.bis.org/publ/bcbs128.pdf.

———. 2010. Basel III: A Global Regulatory Framework for More Resilient Banks and Banking Systems. Bank for International Settlements, Basel. www.bis.org/publ/bcbs189.htm.

Belkhir, M. 2013. Do Subordinated Debt Holders Discipline Bank Risk-taking? Evidence from Risk Management Decisions. *Journal of Financial Stability* 9: 705–719.

Benston, G., R. Eisenbeis, P. Horvitz, E. Kane, and G. Kaufman. 1986. *Perspectives on Safe and Sound Banking: Past, Present and Future*. Cambridge, MA: MIT Press.

Calomiris, C.W. 1997. *The Postmodern Safety Net: Lessons from Developed and Developing Economies*. Washington: American Enterprise Institute.

———. 1999. Building an Incentive Compatible Safety Net. *Journal of Banking and Finance* 23: 1499–1519.

Chauhan, G.S., and S.S. Sundaram. 2016. Subordinate Debt, Deposit Insurance and Market Oriented Monitoring of Banks. *IIMB Management Review* 28: 136–146.

Chen, Y., and I. Hasan. 2011. Subordinated Debt, Market Discipline, and Bank Risk. *Journal of Money, Credit and Banking* 43 (6): 1043–1072.

Cœuré, B. 2013. The Implications of Bail-in Rules for Bank Activity and Stability. In *Opening Speech at Conference on "Financing the Recovery after the Crisis—The Roles of Bank Profitability, Stability and Regulation"*, Bocconi University, Milan. https://www.ecb.europa.eu/press/key/date/2013/html/sp130930.en.html.

Cooper, K., and D.R. Fraser. 1988. The Rising Cost of Bank Failures: A Proposed Solution. *Journal of Retail Banking* 10: 5–12.

Crespi, F., E. Giacomini, and D.V. Mascia. 2019. Bail-In Rules and the Pricing of Italian Bank Bonds. *European Financial Management* 25 (5): 1321–1347.

Demirgüç-Kunt, A., and H. Huizinga. 2010. Are Banks Too Big to Fail or Too Big to Save? International Evidence from Equity Prices and CDS Spreads. CentER Discussion Paper Series No. 2010-59.

EC. 2006. Directive 2006/48/EC of the European Parliament and of the Council of 14 June 2006 relating to the taking up and pursuit of the business of credit institutions (recast). *Official Journal of the European Union*, L177, 1–200.

———. 2013. Regulation (EU) No 575/2013 of the European Parliament and of the Council of 26 June 2013 on Prudential Requirements for Credit Institutions and Investment Firms and Amending Regulation (EU) No 648/2012. *Official Journal of the European Union*, L176, 1–337.

———. 2014. Directive 2014/59/EU of the European Parliament and of the Council of 15 may 2014 Establishing a Framework for the Recovery and Resolution of Credit Institutions and Investment Firms and Amending Council Directive 82/891/EEC, and Directives 2001/24/EC, 2002/47/EC, 2004/25/EC, 2005/56/EC, 2007/36/EC, 2011/35/EU, 2012/30/EU and 2013/36/EU, and Regulations (EU) No 1093/2010 and (EU) No 648/2012, of the European Parliament and of the Council. *Official Journal of the European Union*, L173, 190–348.

———. 2016a. Proposal for a REGULATION OF THE EUROPEAN PARLIAMENT AND OF THE COUNCIL Amending Regulation (EU) No 575/2013 as Regards the Leverage Ratio, the Net Stable Funding Ratio, Requirements for Own Funds and Eligible Liabilities, Counterparty Credit Risk, Market Risk, Exposures to Central Counterparties, Exposures to Collective Investment Undertakings, Large Exposures, Reporting and Disclosure Requirements and Amending Regulation (EU) No 648/2012. European Commission, Brussels, 23/11/2016, COM/2016/0850 final—2016/0360 (COD).

———. 2016b. Proposal for a DIRECTIVE OF THE EUROPEAN PARLIAMENT AND OF THE COUNCIL Amending Directive 2014/59/EU on Loss-absorbing and Recapitalization Capacity of Credit Institutions and Investment Firms and Amending Directive 98/26/EC, Directive 2002/47/EC, Directive 2012/30/EU, Directive 2011/35/EU, Directive 2005/56/EC, Directive 2004/25/EC and Directive 2007/36/EC. European Commission, Brussels, 23/11/2016, COM/2016/0852 final—2016/0362 (COD).

———. 2016c. Proposal for a DIRECTIVE OF THE EUROPEAN PARLIAMENT AND OF THE COUNCIL on Amending Directive 2014/59/EU of the European Parliament and of the Council as Regards the Ranking of Unsecured Debt Instruments in Insolvency Hierarchy. European Commission, Brussels, 23/11/2016, COM/2016/0853 final—2016/0363 (COD).

Evanoff, D.D. 1993. Preferred Sources of Market Discipline. *The Yale Journal of Regulation* 10: 344–367.

Evanoff, D.D., and L.D. Wall. 2001. Reforming Bank Capital Regulation: Using Subordinated Debt to Enhance Market and Supervisory Discipline. *Contemporary Economic Policy* 19: 444–453.

Evanoff, Douglas D., Julapa A. Jagtiani, and T. Nakata. 2011. Enhancing Market Discipline in Banking: The Role of Subordinated Debt in Financial Regulatory Reform. *Journal of Economics and Business* 63: 1–22.

FSB, 2015. Principles on Loss-absorbing and Recapitalisation Capacity of G-SIBs in Resolution: Total Loss-absorbing Capacity (TLAC) Term Sheet. Financial Stability Board, 9 November 2015.

Giuliana, R. 2019. Impact of Bail-in on Banks' Bond Yields and Market Discipline, Working Paper.

Gleeson, S. 2012. Legal Aspects of Bank Bail-Ins. LSE Financial Markets Group Paper Series, Special Paper No 205.

González-Rivera, G., and D. Nickerson. 2006. Dynamic Monitoring of Financial Intermediaries with Subordinated Debt. *The Journal of Risk Finance* 7 (5): 463–487.

Goodhart, C., and E. Avgouleas. 2014. A Critical Evaluation of Bail-Ins as Bank Recapitalisation Mechanisms, CEPR Discussion Paper No 10065.

Hadjiemmanuil, C. 2015. Bank Resolution Financing in the Banking Union, LSE Law, Society and Economy, Working Paper No 6.

Hamalainen, P. 2004. Mandatory Subordinated Debt and the Corporate Governance of Banks. *Corporate Governance: An International Review* 12 (1): 93–106.

Hamalainen, P., B. Howcroft, and M. Hall. 2010. Should a Mandatory Subordinated Debt Policy be Introduced in the United Kingdom? Evidence from the Issuance Activity of Banks and Building Societies. *Contemporary Economic Policy* 28 (2): 240–263.

Horvitz, P.M. 1984. Subordinated Debt is Key to New Bank Capital Requirement. *American Banker*, December 31, 5–6.

———. 1987. A Free Market Approach to Saving Troubled Banks. *American Banker*, December 10, 4–5.

John, K., S.A. Ravid, and N. Reisel. 2010. The Notching Rule for Subordinated Debt and the Information Content of Debt Rating. *Financial Management* 39 (2): 489–513.

Kato, P., and J. Hagendorff. 2010. Distance to Default, Subordinated Debt, and Distress Indicators in the Banking Industry. *Accounting and Finance* 50: 853–870.

Keehn, S. 1989. Banking on the Balance: Powers and the Safety Net: A Proposal. Working paper, Federal Reserve Bank of Chicago.

Li, Z., Q. Shisheng, and Z. Jing. 2011. Quantifying the Value of Implicit Government Guarantees for Large Financial Institutions. White Paper, Moody's Analytics Quantitative Research Group.

Litan, R., and J. Rauch. 1997. *American Finance for the 21st Century*. Washington: US Treasury.

Martino, E. 2017. Subordinated Debt Under Bail-in Threat. *University of Bologna Law Review,* [S.l.], 2(2).

Millera, S., E. Olsonb, and T.J. Yeagerc. 2015. The Relative Contributions of Equity and Subordinated Debt Signals as Predictors of Bank Distress During the Financial Crisis. *Journal of Financial Stability* 16: 118–137.

Nguyen, T. 2013. The Disciplinary Effect of Subordinated Debt on Bank Risk Taking. *Journal of Empirical Finance* 23: 117–141.

Philippon, T., and A. Salord. 2017. Bail-ins and Bank Resolution in Europe: A Progress Report. Geneva Reports on the World Economy Special Report No 4.

Resti, A. 2016. Bank Subordinated Debt: A Source of Capital for Lenders or a Source of Concern for Retail Investors? *Banca Impresa Società* 1: 21–37.

Ueda, K., and B.W. di Mauro. 2012. Quantifying Structural Subsidy Values for. Systemically Important Financial Institutions, IMF Working Paper No 12/128.

US Shadow Financial Regulatory Committee. 2000. Reforming Bank Capital Regulation. Policy statement No. 160. Washington: The AEI Press.

Wall, L.D. 1989. A Plan for Reducing Future Deposit Insurance Losses: Puttable Subordinated Debt. *Economic Review*, Federal Reserve Bank of Atlanta (July/ Aug), 2–17.

Wang, C.-Y., Y.-F., Chen, and G.-S. Tung. 2010. Does Subordinated Debt Play a Role for Market Discipline? Evidence from Commercial Banks in Taiwan. *Emerging Markets Finance & Trade* 46 (1): 27–33.

Walther, A., and L. White. 2014. Rules Versus Discretion in Bank Resolution. *The Review of Financial Studies*, ISSN: 0893-9454.

Zhang, Z., W. Song, X. Sun, and N. Shi. 2014. Subordinated Debt as Instrument of Market Discipline: Risk Sensitivity of Sub-debt yield Spreads in UK Banking. *Journal of Economics and Business* 73: 1–21.

CHAPTER 6

The Impact of Monetary Policy on Bank Profitability

Paula Cruz-García

6.1 Introduction

The accommodative monetary policy, carried out by the main central banks in order to combat the effects of the financial crisis that erupted in 2008, has led to an extended period of low—or even negative—interest rates. In late 2008 and early 2009 policy rates fell sharply, reaching values very close to the lower limit of 0% thereafter, as can be seen in Fig. 6.1. The potential side effects of this situation of low interest rates on bank profitability has been a topic of concern in recent years. This issue is especially relevant considering that, in some cases such as the European banking sector, bank profitability is below the cost of raising capital, affecting negatively the prices of banks in the stock markets. This low profitability is due to several reasons (such as the high volume of non-performing assets, regulatory requirements, competition from *fintech* and *bigtech*, etc.), outstanding the pressure of low interest rates to the net interest margin. In

P. Cruz-García (✉)
Department of Economic Analysis, University of Valencia,
Valencia, Spain
e-mail: paula.cruz@uv.es

C. Cruciani et al. (eds.), *Banking and Beyond*, Palgrave Macmillan Studies in Banking and Financial Institutions,
https://doi.org/10.1007/978-3-030-45752-5_6

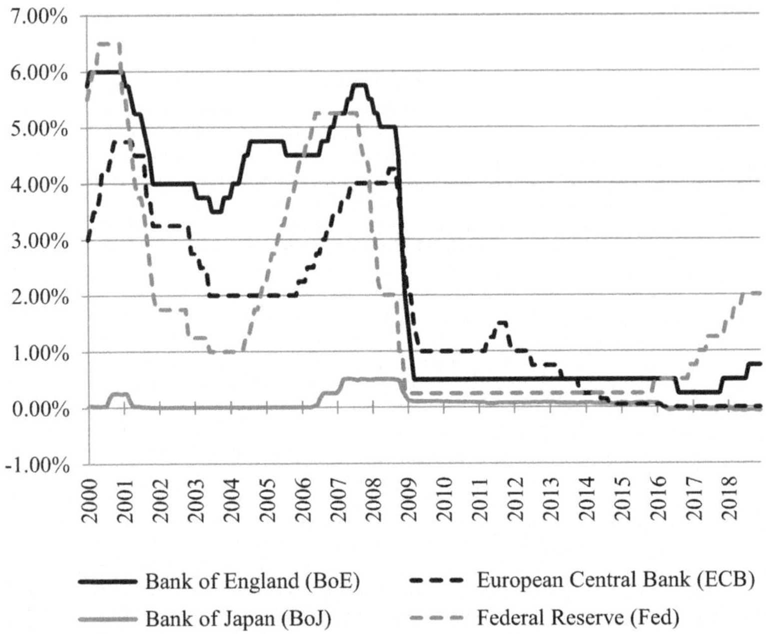

Fig. 6.1 Intervention interest rates by the main central banks (2000–2018). (Source: Bank of England, Bank of Japan, European Central Bank and U.S. Federal Reserve)

addition, in the case of European banks, the negative interest rate on the deposit facility is penalizing banks for excess liquidity, directly affecting their income statement and therefore profitability.

Low interest rates maintained for an extended period may reduce banks' margins and, therefore, their profitability. With negative interest rates, the existence of an effective lower limit on the remuneration of deposits (as customers are not expected to accept a negative deposit interest rate) makes it difficult to transfer the decline in interest rates to the interest on deposits and thus the financial margins narrow.

Monetary policy operates mainly affecting the short-term interest rate and the slope of the yield curve. The central banks directly control the short-term rate through the policy rate, and indirectly the yield curve through both the impact on the expectations about the future policy rate and the large-scale operations in government securities, which have an impact on their price. Very low short-term interest rates typically come hand in hand with a lower and flatter yield curve, which reduces the profit from maturity transformation activities, reducing banks' margins and therefore their profitability.

A large part of the literature that analyzes the effect of monetary policy on bank profitability confirms a positive relationship between the level of interest rates and the profitability of banks (Weistroffer 2013; Alessandri and Nelson 2015—in the long-run—; Genay and Podjasek 2014—only in the short-term—; Busch and Memmel 2015—over the medium- to long-term horizon—; Aydemir and Ovenc 2016—in the long-run—; Sääskilahti 2018; Borio et al. 2017; Claessens et al. 2018; Cruz-García et al. 2019; Angori et al. 2019; among others). Nevertheless, there are some actions that banks can take to mitigate the negative impact of falling interest rates on profitability; for instance, they can reduce interest expenses (Scheiber et al. 2016), increase loan spreads (Sääskilahti 2018), set higher fees and commissions (Turk Ariss 2016) or decrease the importance of deposits as source of funding (International Monetary Fund [IMF] 2016). Due to the boost of the real economy as a result of low interest rates, banks would benefit from the lower provisions thanks to the improved solvency of the borrowers (Albertazzi and Gambacorta 2009; Weistroffer 2013; Genay and Podjasek 2014; Borio et al. 2017; Altavilla et al. 2018; Bikker and Vervliet 2018). However, in this context, banks can also carry out riskier lending strategies to increase their profits, which might deteriorate the quality of the bank's loan portfolio as a result of the increase in credit risk (Albertazzi et al. 2018; Heider et al. 2018; Demiralp et al. 2019). Finally, low interest rates could also positively affect the volume of loans (Demiralp et al. 2019; Rostagno et al. 2016), although the literature on this subject is inconclusive.[1] Thus, the net impact of decreased interest rates on bank profitability depends on how banks manage the aforementioned factors.

In this context, this chapter provides an in-depth analysis on the link between monetary policy and bank profitability. Particularly, it focuses on the effect of both the interest rate levels and the yield curve on both profitability and the banks' main source of earnings, namely net interest

[1] Some papers find that monetary policy is less effective in stimulating credit growth when interest rates are very low (Borio and Gambacorta 2017), and other studies even find that negative interest rates have a contracting effect on the credit supply (Heider et al. 2018; Brunnermeier and Koby 2018). The paper of Arce et al. (2018) suggests that there is no significant difference between the volume of credit offered by banks affected or not by negative interest rates.

margin. Following Sääskilahti (2018), Borio et al. (2017), Bikker and Vervliet (2018), Cruz-García et al. (2019) and Angori et al. (2019), among others, the possible non-linear effect of a scenario of low interest rates on banks' profitability is also analyzed. This allows us to verify that the lower the interest rates and the flatter the yield curve, the greater the negative effect on bank profitability. A possible non-linear relationship between interest rates and net interest margin is also analyzed, as well as between the slope of the yield curve and the interest margin.

This chapter offers new empirical evidence on the impact of the current expansionary monetary policy on bank profitability, also analyzing the main channel through which it is transmitted. This analysis is carried out for 31 OECD countries over the period 2000–2017, which includes the years of economic expansion, the years of financial crisis in which aggressive monetary policy measures were applied and the subsequent economic recovery (characterized by the negative rates policy). The combination of years and country coverage allows us to examine countries or economic areas with different monetary policies. This guarantees enough in-sample variability so that the effects of monetary policy can be properly measured. In addition to monetary policy instruments (level of interest rates and the yield curve slope), this study considers several banks' characteristics, as well as macroeconomic variables.

The main results show that the expansionary monetary policy measures adopted in numerous economies to combat the negative effects of the crisis—with the consequent reduction in interest rates and the flattening of the yield curve—had a negative impact on net interest margins and, therefore, on the bank profitability. In both cases—interest margin and profitability—the impact of interest rates is non-linear (inverted U-shaped). The same relationship is found for the slope of the yield curve. This suggests that the impact is greater the lower the interest rate and the flatter the yield curve are. Therefore, the negative effect of low interest rates on net interest margin is not offset by other factors, being negative the net effect on bank profitability. Therefore, the problem of low profitability suffered by certain banking sectors will persist as long as the current scenario of low interest rates continues, which may also affect financial stability.

After this introduction, this chapter is structured as follows: Sect. 6.2 provides an overview of the related literature. Section 6.3 describes the sample used and the construction of the variables for the empirical analysis. Section 6.4 summarizes the empirical findings. Finally, Sect. 6.5 provides some conclusions and economic policy implications.

6.2 Literature Review

In recent years, the link between monetary policy and bank profitability has gained interest as a research topic. Central banks adopted an expansionary monetary policy to cope with the financial crisis, being one of the causes of the current scenario of low bank profitability. The transmission mechanisms of the monetary policy (both interest rates and the slope of the yield curve) are as follows. On the one hand, as interest rates fell to zero and enter negative territory, financial margins narrow, and it becomes difficult to transfer the decreased interest rates to the interest on deposits. Moreover, the potential for capital gains on asset values becomes very small when there is little room for additional cuts. In addition, the bigger the proportion of loans at a floating rate, the bigger the negative impact on profitability, as the benchmark interest rate has failed more than the banks' cost of funding. Similarly, a large share of funding from deposits has a negative impact on margins when rates are very low, as it is difficult to transfer the decline in interest rates to these deposits.

A large number of works in the previous literature show a positive relationship between bank profitability and the scenario of low interest rates. Weistroffer (2013) studies for the case of Japan the effect of the ultra-low interest rates on banks' profitability. This author finds that Japanese banks have been able to survive ultra-low interest rates for a long period, but they faced a severe decline in the net interest income and pressures to reduce costs. The loss of profitability was compensated by lending to domestic sovereign and expanding credit abroad, without assuming an excessive credit risk. Genay and Podjasek (2014) studied the effect of the interest rate level and the slope of the yield curve on profitability for the United States, finding that a low interest rates scenario is associated with decreases in bank profitability in the short-term, although in the long-term a boosted economic activity could compensate for this effect. Alessandri and Nelson (2015) find that the long-run relationship between profitability and both interest rates and the slope of the yield curve is positive for the case of the United Kingdom. However, in the short-run, increases in market rates compress interest margins due to the presence of loan pricing frictions. For the German banking system, Busch and Memmel (2015) demonstrate that banks' net interest income benefits in the long-term horizon from interest rate increases. Aydemir and Ovenc (2016) found, for the Turkish banking system during 2002–2014, that the relationship between both the short-term interest rate and the slope of the yield curve with profits is negative in the short-run, but it turns positive in the long-run. Sääskilahti (2018) analyzes the relationship between low interest rates and retail bank interest margins in the Finnish retail banking market, allowing for non-linearities and finding that the market interest rates are positively related with the net interest margins of both new operations and stock of operations.

Borio et al. (2017) find a positive effect of both the level of short-term interest rates and the slope of the yield curve on bank profitability for a sample of 14 advanced economies. These authors also analyze the possible non-linear relationship between the banks' profitability and both interest rates and the yield curve slope, finding that the effects on net interest margins are much stronger at lower levels of interest rates and where there is a flatter yield term structure. The effect of monetary policy on the different main components of bank profitability is also analyzed, showing that the effect on net interest income offsets the effect on non-interest income and provisions. Claessens et al. (2018) obtain strong evidence on the negative impact of low interest rates and the flattening of the yield curve on net interest margin and profitability for a sample of 47 countries. Pérez and Ferrer (2018) study the effects of these two variables on bank profits and balance sheet structure in Spain during the 2000–2016 period, finding a positive non-linear relationship between interest rates and profit measures, especially the net interest income.

Arce et al. (2018) find, for the case of the euro area, that those banks whose net interest income is adversely affected by negative rates are lowly capitalized and take less risk. However, no differences in banks' credit supply are found. In the case of Bikker and Vervliet (2018), the authors found that low short-term interest rates compress net interest margins and reduce the levels of credit loss provisions for the United States banking sector, being the effect non-linear. The effect on net interest income offsets the effect on provisions. These results are in line with those obtained by Borio et al. (2017). Cruz-García et al. (2019) analyze, for a sample of 32 OECD countries, the impact of interest rates and the slope of the yield curve on net interest margins, finding a positive and non-linear relationship, although the effect of the flattering of the yield curve is less economically significant than that of interest rates. The same results are obtained by Angori et al. (2019) analyzing, for the case of the euro area, the impact of interest rates and the slope of the yield curve on net interest margins, finding a positive and non-linear relationship between them. Molyneux et al. (2019) investigate the influence of negative interest rate policy

(NIRP) on bank net interest margins and profitability for a dataset of banks from 33 OECD countries. These authors find that bank margins and profits fell in NIRP adopter countries compared to countries that did not adopt the policy.

Other studies find no evidence of a significant effect of the low interest rate scenario on bank profitability. English (2002) finds no evidence of the existence of an effect of interest rates or the slope of the yield curve on net interest margin for many countries (Australia, Canada, Germany, Italy, Japan, Norway, Sweden, Switzerland and the United Kingdom). The exception in this chapter is the United States, where the slope of the yield curve affects the margin significantly and with the positive sign suggested by the conventional vision. Scheiber et al. (2016) analyze, for the case of Denmark, Sweden and Switzerland, the risks of side effects of the negative interest rates on bank profitability and particularly on net interest income. These authors conclude that negative interest rates have not resulted in a significant reduction of net interest income so far, since the decline in interest income has been compensated for by declines in interest expenses. A similar result is found by Turk Ariss (2016) in the case of Denmark and Sweden. Altavilla et al. (2018) study a panel of European banks, not finding evidence of a significant effect of interest rates on profitability when controlling for current and expected macroeconomic conditions. However, they find a positive effect of interest rates on the non-interest income and provisions. Some (few) studies have found a negative relationship between interest rates and bank profitability, such as Kohlscheen et al. (2018), who find that higher short-term interest rates reduce profitability by raising funding costs in 19 emerging market economies.

Some works of the related previous literature, most of them mentioned above, deal with the effects of a low interest rate environment on bank profitability just for a specific country: Weistroffer (2013) for the Japanese case, Genay and Podjasek (2014) and Bikker and Vervliet (2018) for the United States, Alessandri and Nelson (2015) for the United Kingdom, Busch and Memmel (2015) and Entrop et al. (2015) for Germany, Ahtik et al. (2016) for the case of Slovenia, Sääskilahti (2018) for Finland, Aydemir and Ovenc (2016) for Turkey, Pérez and Ferrer (2018) for Spain.

Therefore, the results of the previous literature can be mainly divided into those finding a positive relationship between the current expansionary monetary policy and bank profitability, and those finding an inconclusive effect. This confirms that the net impact of decreasing interest rates on bank profitability depends on how banks manage the rest of the factors that affect profitability such as provisions, fees and commissions, the importance of deposits such as source of funding, etc.

6.3 Data, Variables and Methodology

6.3.1 Sample and Sources of Information

The sample used in the empirical analysis includes banks from 31 OECD countries all over the world[2] over the period 2000–2017, which includes the pre-crisis sub-period, the crisis sub-period and the years of the subsequent economic recovery. Therefore, the analyzed time span covers the period in which many countries implemented expansionary policy measures to cope with the financial crisis.

All banks included in BankScope and Orbis (Bureau van Dijk) databases for the aforementioned countries are considered. The financial statements used are unconsolidated (domestic business in each country), since the dependent variables depend on interest rates (short-term level and slope of the yield curve) and a proper correspondence between them becomes necessary. Consolidated statements will include both domestic and cross-border activities carried out by bank subsidiaries, which will depend on the interest rate of the country of the subsidiary and not on that of the parent bank. The GDP growth is obtained from the World Bank database. Money market and government debt interest rates were from the OECD database. Banks for which there was no information on any of the explanatory variables were excluded from the sample. After filtering, the panel of data used comprised 68,004 observations.

6.3.2 Variables

To perform the empirical analysis, two alternative dependent variables are used: net interest margin (difference between revenue and financial costs) and Return On Assets (ROA), both of them expressed as a percentage of total assets. As determinants of the alternative dependent variables the

[2] Austria, Australia, Belgium, Canada, Switzerland, Colombia, Czech Republic, Germany, Denmark, Spain, Finland, France, United Kingdom, Greece, Ireland, Iceland, Italy, Japan, Luxembourg, Latvia, Netherlands, Norway, New Zealand, Poland, Portugal, Russian Federation, Sweden, Slovenia, Slovak Republic, United States and South Africa.

short-term interest rate and the slope of the yield curve are included as monetary policy indicators, and the growth rate of real GDP as macroeconomic indicator. Bank-specific characteristics habitually included in the literature are also taken into account. These include market power, credit risk, bank size, banks' degree of risk aversion, operating costs, implicit payments, liquidity reserves and an efficiency indicator. Finally, an indicator of uncertainty about market conditions such as the money market interest rate volatility (interest rate risk) is also added, as well as the interaction between this risk and the credit risk.

The abovementioned variables are fully explained in the following paragraphs.

6.3.2.1 *Monetary Policy Variables*

Interest Rate

Following Alessandri and Nelson (2015), Borio et al. (2017), Cruz-García et al. (2019) and Angori et al. (2019), among others, the three-month interbank market interest rate is used as a proxy for short-term interest rates (*Short-term interest rate*). The square of the variable is introduced in the estimates to capture a possible non-linear relationship between the level of interest rates and each of the dependent variables. Given that there exists an effective lower limit on the remuneration of deposits, it is not possible to transfer the decrease in interest rates to the interest rate of the deposits and, therefore, the net interest income is reduced. Therefore, a positive relationship between the level of interest rates and net interest income is expected.

The effect of the drop in level of interest rates on overall bank profitability will depend on whether or not the negative effect on the net interest margin is offset by other positive effects.

Slope of the Yield Curve

To proxy the slope of the yield curve (*Slope of the yield curve*), the difference between the interest rate on a ten-year bond and the three-month interbank market interest rate is used, following Aydemir and Ovenc (2016), Borio et al. (2017), Cruz-García et al. (2019) and Angori et al. (2019), among others. To capture a possible non-linear relationship between the slope of the yield curve and the alternative dependent variables, the square of the variable is included.

Analogously to the case of interest rates, the expected relationship between the slope of the yield curve and the net interest margin is positive. Once again, the effect of the slope of the yield curve in the bank's overall profitability will depend on whether or not the effect on the net interest margin is offset by other contrary effects.

6.3.2.2 Bank-Specific Variables

Market Power

As a proxy of market power the Lerner index (***Lerner index***) is used, defined as:

$$L_{it} = \frac{\left(P_{it} - MC_{it}\right)}{P_{it}} \tag{6.1}$$

where P_{it} is the average price of the output of bank i in year t and MC_{it} is the marginal cost. To calculate the Lerner index, the price of banking output (proxied by total assets) is measured as the ratio between total income and total assets.

Given that the traditional approximation of the Lerner index has the limitation that it disregards the risk faced by banks, following Cruz-García et al. (2018), the marginal cost is calculated based on the following translog cost function corrected by credit risk:

$$\begin{aligned} \ln C_{it} &= \alpha_0 + \alpha_1 lnTA_{it} + \frac{1}{2}\alpha_k\left(lnTA_{it}\right)^2 + \sum_{4}^{j=1}\beta_j \ln w_{jit} + \frac{1}{2}\sum_{4}^{j=1}\sum_{4}^{k=1}\beta_{jk} \\ &\ln w_{jit} \ln w_{kit} + \frac{1}{2}\sum_{4}^{j=1}\gamma_j lnTA_{it} \ln w_{jit} + \mu_1 Trend + \frac{1}{2}\mu_2 Trend^2 \\ &+ \mu_3 Trend\, lnTA_{it} + \sum_{4}^{j=1}\delta_j Trend \ln w_{jit} + v_i + u_{it} \end{aligned} \tag{6.2}$$

where C stands for the total costs (financial costs, operating costs and provisions [as an ex-post approximation of the cost of risk]), TA is total assets, *Trend* reflects the effect of technological change (which translates into displacements of the cost function over time), v_i are the fixed effects and u_{it} is a random disturbance. Lastly, w is the price of the production factors, which are measured as follows:

w_1: Price of labor = staff costs / total assets.[3]
w_2: Price of lendable funds = financial costs / lendable funds.
w_3: Price of capital = operating costs (except staff costs) / fixed assets.
w_4: Price of credit risk = financial asset impairment losses / volume of lending.

In line with common practice, Eq. (6.2) is estimated imposing conditions of symmetry and grade one homogeneity in input prices.[4]

The expected effect of the Lerner index on the net interest margin is positive, given that banks with more market power can establish wider margins. Therefore, as a consequence, the expected effect of the Lerner index on profitability will also be positive.

Credit Risk

Following Maudos and Fernández de Guevara (2004), Entrop et al. (2015), Altavilla et al. (2018), Cruz-García et al. (2019), among others, the credit risk is included as an explanatory variable. However, considering that a direct measure of the variation in the return on the lending portfolio associated with the risk of non-payment is unfortunately not available in the sources of data used, credit risk is approximated by the ratio between provisions for insolvencies and the net volume of credit granted, as it is to be assumed that the higher the default rate, the larger the provisions banks set aside.

The expected effect of credit risk on net interest margin is positive because banks charge an implicit risk premium in those operations with a higher default risk. The expected effect of credit risk on profitability will also be positive since riskier operations are usually the most profitable too.

[3] As there are no data in the databases used about the number of employees for the entire sample, the ratio of staff cost to total assets as a proxy for the price of labor has been used, instead of the ratio of staff cost to number of employees.

[4] Note that the cost function differs from the traditional one in that it includes, in addition to the financial and operational costs, the provisions that a bank sets aside each year (as a proxy ex-post of the cost of risk). Given that the cost is included in the dependent variable, it has been necessary to include the unit cost of this productive input that we can call "risk" as a determinant, approximating as a ratio between financial asset impairment losses and the volume of lending.

Bank Size

Following Mamatzakis and Bermpei (2016), Borio et al. (2017), Cruz-García et al. (2019) and Angori et al. (2019), among others, the bank size (*Size*), proxied by the logarithm of total assets, has been included. The expected effect of bank size on bank performance depends on whether or not economies of scope and scale take place.

Degree of Risk Aversion

Banks' degree of risk aversion (*Risk aversion*) is approximated by the ratio equity/total assets, following McShane and Sharpe (1985), Maudos and Fernández de Guevara (2004) and Cruz-García et al. (2019), among others.[5]

A positive relationship is expected between the degree of risk aversion and the interest margin, as banks that are more risk averse will set higher margins. The expected effect on profitability could be potentially positive or negative. The less risky operations carried out by the most risk-averse banks result in a lower profitability, since these operations are also the less profitable. However, the lower need for provisions associated with less risky operations could have a positive effect on profitability.

Operating Expenses

The operating expenses are proxied by the ratio of total operating costs (overheads, not including financial costs) to total assets, following Maudos and Fernández de Guevara (2004). Following theoretical models of the determination of the net interest margin (Maudos and Fernández de Guevara 2004), the expected effect of the operating expenses on the net interest margin is positive since net interest margin should at least cover operating costs. Therefore, the higher the operating costs the higher the net interest margin. Since operating expenses are a direct part (identity) of profitability, they are not included as a determinant of ROA.

Implicit Interest Payments

Deposits interest rate not only remunerates deposits, but it implicitly incorporates the remuneration (being a lower interest rate) of a wide array of services associated with them. As an approximation of the implicit

[5] Note that this ratio is a measure of capitalization and presents limitations as a measure of risk aversion, since it includes the minimum capital required by the regulation. However, unfortunately, there is no better proxy for this variable.

interest payment (*Interest payments*), the variable operating expenses net of non-interest revenues is used, expressed as a percentage of total assets, following Maudos and Fernández de Guevara (2004), Entrop et al. (2015), Cruz-García et al. (2019) and Angori et al. (2019), among others.

The implicit payments have an expected positive effect on net interest margin, since higher implicit payments imply higher operating costs, which need to be compensated by a higher margin.

Liquid Reserves

Liquid reserves represent an opportunity cost as they mean that these reserves cannot be invested in profitable assets. Since liquid reserves represent an opportunity cost of not investing funds held in more profitable assets, the expected effect of liquid reserves on profitability would be negative. However, the expected effect of liquid reserves on net interest margin is positive since banks set a higher margin to compensate this opportunity cost. Therefore, the net effect on profitability could also be positive if the effect on the net interest margin prevails.

This variable (*Reserves*) is approximated by the ratio between liquid reserves and total assets and it is included as an explanatory variable following Entrop et al. (2015), Mamatzakis and Bermpei (2016), Borio et al. (2017), Cruz-García et al. (2019) and Angori et al. (2019), among others.

Efficiency

To proxy the bank efficiency, the cost-to-income ratio (ratio of operating expenses to operating income) is used. The higher this ratio, the greater the operating inefficiency. This variable is included by other authors as Borio et al. (2017), Cruz-García et al. (2019) and Angori et al. (2019), among others.

The expected effect of the efficiency ratio on the net interest margin and profits is negative, since this variable is inversely proportional to management efficiency and better managed banks enjoy a greater margin.

6.3.2.3 Market Variables

Interest Rate Risk

Higher interest rate risk will imply that banks charge a higher implicit risk premium, so an indicator of the interest rate risk is included as a determinant of the net interest income and of profitability. The expected relationship between the interest rate risk and the interest margin is positive. The net effect of interest rate risk on bank profitability will depend on whether the effect on the margin or the other effects prevail.

Money market uncertainty is usually captured through the volatility of a representative interest rate. The coefficient of variation calculated with monthly data on the three-month interbank rate (*Interest rate risk*) is used to proxy the interest rate risk as in Borio et al. (2017), Cruz-García et al. (2019) and Angori et al. (2019), among others. As it is habitual in the literature of the determination of the net interest margin (see Angbazo 1997 or Maudos and Fernández de Guevara 2004), the interaction between credit risk and interest rate risk (*Risk interaction*) is included, proxied by the product of the measurement of credit risk and money market risk.

GDP Growth

Finally, in line with common practice in the literature, the annual rate of GDP growth (*GDPgrowth*) is included in order to control for the possible influence of the economic cycle.

Table 6.1 contains the average values of the variables used, and the number of observations per country. In the case of the net interest margin, the average ranges between a maximum value of 5.53% (Colombia) and a minimum value of 1.01% (Luxembourg). And for the case of the bank profitability, the average varies between a maximum value of 2.75% (Iceland) and a minimum value of 0.29% (Japan). Regarding the monetary policy variables, which are the focus of this chapter, the short-term interest rate varies between a maximum value of 8.79% (Russian Federation) and a minimum value of 0.29% (Japan), while in the case of the yield curve slope the variation ranges from 4.53% (Portugal) to −0.78% (Iceland). Therefore, although the interest rate does not vary across banks within a country, the sample comprises countries with different monetary contexts so that there are enough variations in interest rates.

6.3.3 Methodology

The empirical approach consists of regressing each dependent variable (net interest margin, loan loss provisions and ROA) against the determinants described in the previous section. In each regression the lagged dependent variable (one-year lag) is included as an explanatory variable to capture the inertia effects. The empirical estimation adopts the two-step

Table 6.1 Descriptive statistics (averages)

	Net interest margin/ total assets (%)	*ROA (profit before taxes) (%)*	*Short-term interest rate (%)*	*Slope of the yield curve (%)*	*Lerner index*	*Credit risk (%)*	*Volatility of market interest rates*	*Size*	*Risk aversion (%)*	*Operating costs (% total assets)*	*Implicit interest payments (%)*	*Reserves (% total assets)*	*Efficiency*	*GDP growth (%)*	*Number of obs.*
Austria	2.04	0.55	1.75	1.24	0.19	0.68	13.14	12.99	8.29	2.05	1.07	1.50	68.41	1.68	3,061
Australia	2.07	0.80	3.76	0.41	0.20	0.20	7.18	15.16	7.68	1.85	1.15	2.29	65.30	2.67	389
Belgium	2.02	0.90	2.10	1.46	0.22	0.46	12.86	15.45	7.05	2.08	0.92	1.60	66.76	1.63	269
Canada	2.02	0.76	2.24	1.19	0.22	0.25	10.27	14.95	7.19	2.14	1.12	2.70	71.49	2.52	567
Switzerland	1.37	0.59	0.74	1.17	0.22	0.44	24.32	13.35	6.84	1.65	0.54	4.16	65.47	1.75	4,008
Colombia	5.53	2.28	5.75	3.35	0.29	2.12	7.83	13.91	16.14	4.91	1.96	6.14	58.15	4.43	332
Czech Republic	2.12	1.14	1.72	1.41	0.31	0.65	11.05	15.17	8.31	1.70	0.65	5.14	51.62	2.60	184
Germany	2.40	0.50	2.25	0.99	0.16	1.31	12.44	13.35	6.77	2.33	1.41	2.20	70.13	1.38	21,238
Denmark	3.62	1.22	2.31	1.02	0.26	1.26	13.42	12.89	13.17	3.33	1.73	4.53	64.43	1.12	863
Spain	2.13	0.74	2.21	1.89	0.23	0.93	12.22	14.52	8.42	1.73	0.92	2.56	58.76	2.01	1,552
Finland	1.35	0.71	0.46	1.10	0.30	0.15	23.91	13.50	11.56	1.55	0.48	1.12	63.36	1.24	293
France	2.16	0.96	2.15	1.31	0.23	0.61	12.56	15.33	8.62	2.29	0.81	1.50	64.27	1.42	3,132
United Kingdom	1.79	0.70	2.58	0.92	0.21	0.52	9.30	14.13	9.78	1.61	0.85	4.36	63.92	1.71	882
Greece	2.33	0.87	2.59	3.38	0.22	0.89	11.97	15.26	11.41	2.05	0.81	2.77	59.53	1.41	146
Ireland	1.18	1.18	2.46	2.17	0.30	0.77	11.38	15.70	15.21	0.95	−0.25	3.05	30.34	5.03	55
Iceland	3.47	2.75	8.53	−0.78	0.28	1.97	9.96	12.34	15.18	3.58	−0.37	5.78	54.70	3.92	66
Italy	2.62	0.80	2.17	2.04	0.20	0.86	13.36	13.18	11.05	2.41	1.39	0.97	65.63	0.34	7,313
Japan	1.50	0.29	0.29	0.69	0.20	0.36	10.34	14.90	5.58	1.20	1.03	1.66	72.60	1.15	5,000
Luxembourg	1.01	0.85	2.07	0.88	0.23	0.79	12.56	14.68	7.00	1.36	0.00	3.23	55.87	3.72	394
Latvia	2.34	1.15	4.00	1.18	0.31	1.69	22.25	13.32	10.06	2.87	0.51	9.09	61.43	4.24	152

(*continued*)

Table 6.1 (continued)

	Net interest margin/ total assets (%)	*ROA (profit before taxes) (%)*	*Short-term interest rate (%)*	*Slope of the yield curve (%)*	*Lerner index*	*Credit risk (%)*	*Volatility of market interest rates*	*Size*	*Risk aversion (%)*	*Operating costs (% total assets)*	*Implicit interest payments (%)*	*Reserves (% total assets)*	*Efficiency*	*GDP growth (%)*	*Number of obs.*
Netherlands	1.56	0.78	2.09	1.18	0.23	0.57	12.44	15.68	7.83	1.41	0.51	5.08	55.39	1.58	85
Norway	2.11	1.04	2.85	0.49	0.25	0.22	10.88	13.14	9.90	1.52	0.92	2.57	55.93	1.49	1,233
New Zealand	2.41	1.02	4.04	0.74	0.22	0.25	7.18	14.58	10.31	1.96	1.22	3.43	59.20	2.53	139
Poland	2.85	0.99	3.76	0.82	0.23	0.95	7.98	13.49	10.54	2.80	1.29	3.23	65.23	3.75	476
Portugal	2.12	0.62	1.14	4.53	0.21	0.95	17.54	13.24	9.86	2.05	0.99	1.70	65.12	0.10	552
Russian Federation	5.08	2.23	8.79	0.20	0.32	3.19	23.44	11.50	18.68	5.14	1.37	10.13	59.62	5.32	2,376
Sweden	2.77	1.29	1.81	1.33	0.31	0.36	14.92	12.70	13.84	2.36	1.19	0.81	59.36	2.05	1,008
Slovenia	2.22	0.69	2.26	1.81	0.21	1.20	12.83	14.16	9.06	1.95	0.77	4.24	58.21	1.75	142
Slovak Republic	2.79	1.13	2.01	1.59	0.27	0.89	12.94	14.42	12.76	2.38	1.15	5.64	60.99	4.02	147
United States	3.21	1.29	2.33	1.56	0.30	0.52	14.16	14.58	10.12	2.77	1.57	3.44	62.88	2.07	11,743
South Africa	3.59	1.74	7.86	1.44	0.27	1.14	6.23	14.95	9.92	3.68	1.14	8.22	60.92	2.77	207

Source: BankScope, Orbis and authors' calculations.

system GMM (Generalized Method of Moments) dynamic panel estimator developed by Arellano and Bond (1991), Arellano and Bover (1995) and Blundell and Bond (1998). Both the endogeneity problem that comes from the inclusion of the lagged dependent variable as an explanatory variable and the potential endogeneity from the explanatory variables are corrected by estimating the model using the lagged variables in levels as instruments.

The consistency of the GMM estimator depends both on the assumption that the error term has no serial correlation and on the validity of the instruments used. To assess the first assumption, whether the differential error term is correlated in second-order series is tested. By construction, the error term will have first-order serial correlation. To assess the second assumption, the Hansen test of over-identifying restrictions is used, which tests the overall validity of the instruments.

The estimation also includes time effects to reflect the impact of particular shocks in each year affecting the dependent variables. The inclusion of time dummies is especially relevant for the period of analysis of this chapter, which comprises the pre-crisis sub-period, the crisis sub-period and the years of the subsequent economic recovery.

6.4 Results

Before discussing the results obtained from the regressions, the evolution of short-term interest rates and the slope of the yield curve over time for the sample of countries analyzed is examined. As Fig. 6.2 shows, from 2000 to 2017, the three-month interest rate in the interbank market fell sharply in 2009 and has remained low since then, in a context of accommodative monetary policy by the main central banks. There was also a significant fall in long-term interest rates (approximated by the yield on ten-year bonds). The difference between the long- and short-term rate increased considerably in 2009 (due to plummeting short-term rates) and then gradually came down.

Figure 6.3 shows the evolution, from 2000 to 2017,[6] of the short-term interest rate, the long-term interest rate and the slope of the yield curve for the euro area, the United States, Japan, the United Kingdom and the aggregation of the rest of countries in the sample. There are significant differences in the level of interest rates (both in short-term interest rates

[6] Unfortunately, the interest rates for Japan between 2000 and 2002 are not available.

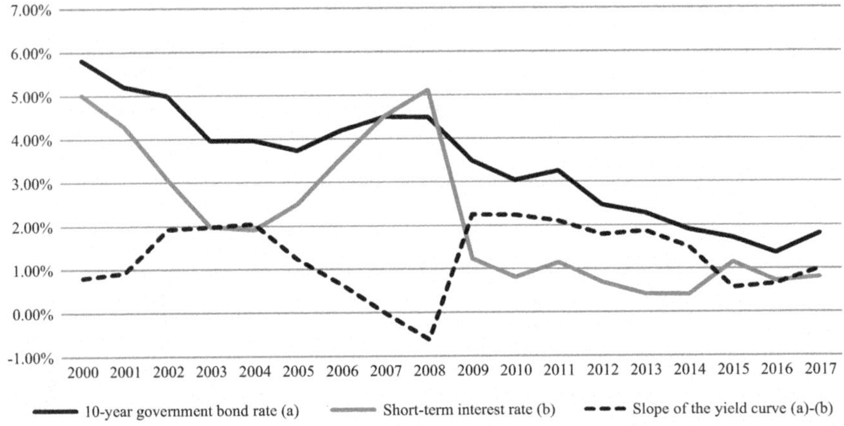

Fig. 6.2 Interest rates and slope of the yield curve. (Source: OECD [2019] database and authors' calculations)

and in long-term interest rates) and in the slope of the yield curve between countries/geographical regions and over time. In general, the interest rates are much higher in the group of other countries in the sample, being Japan that with the lowest interest rates. Regarding the slope of the yield curve, although the level was not similar in the initial years, it has converged in the United States, the United Kingdom and the group of other countries in the sample. For Japan, the slope of the yield curve has slightly decreased over the whole period, while in the euro area the differential between the ten-year bond interest rate and the three-month interbank rate increased from the outbreak of the crisis until 2012, and decreased thereafter.

Table 6.2 shows the results of the estimations for the net interest margin and profitability (ROA). All the estimations satisfy the statistical test that rejects the second-order serial correlation, as well as the Hansen test for over-identifying restrictions. Regressions also include time effects to control for specific particular shocks in each year affecting the dependent variable. The quadratic term of the monetary policy variables is included to test for a possible non-linear relationship between these variables and each of the dependent variables.

The first two columns show the results obtained with the net interest margin as dependent variable. In the first column, the interest rate is

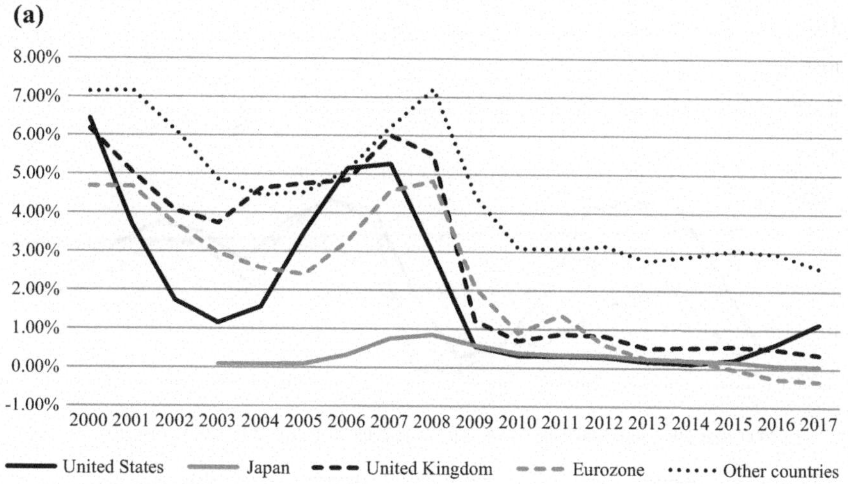

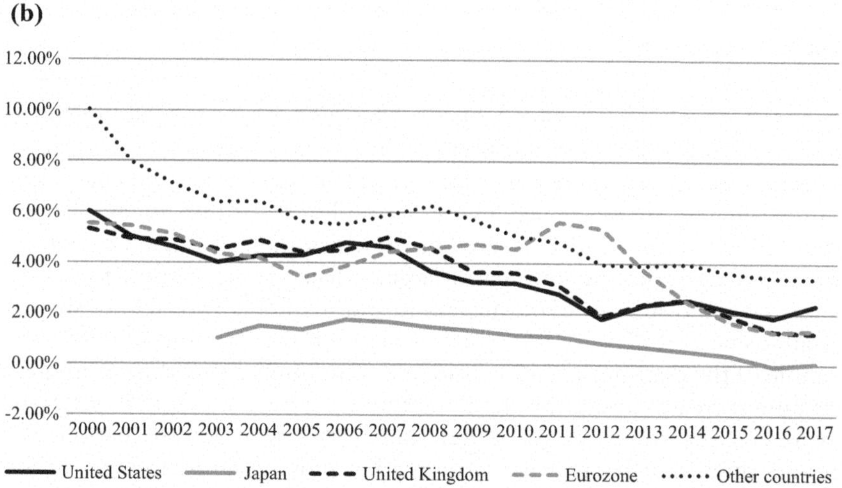

Fig. 6.3 Interest rates and yield curve by countries. (a) three-month interbank rates, (b) ten-year government bond rates, (c) slope of the yield curve. (Source: OECD [2019] database and authors' calculations)

(c)

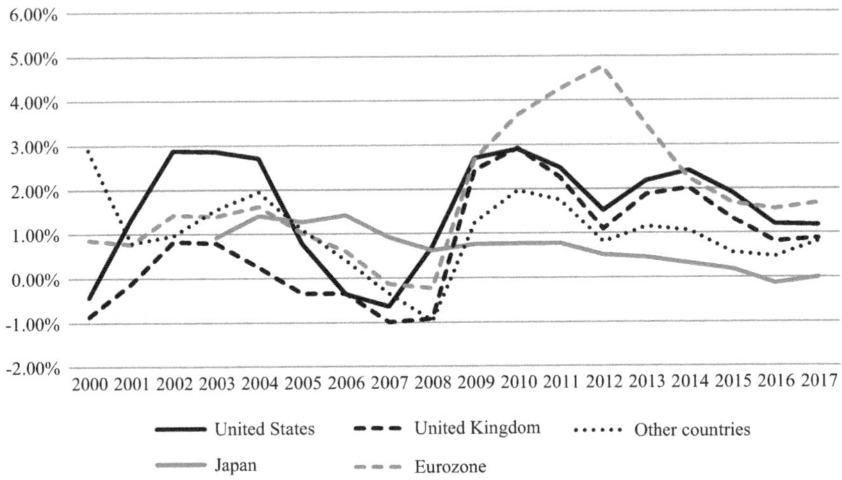

Fig. 6.3 (continued)

included as a monetary policy variable. The quadratic term is also included to capture a possible non-linear effect. The total effect of the short-term interest rate on net interest margins is positive. Given that the coefficient of the squared variable is negative and significant, the functional relationship follows an inverted U-shaped form, which indicates that a change in the short-term interest rate has a larger effect on the margin for lower levels of interest rates. The maximum point of this inverted U-shaped relationship is 0.075 (7.5%), which is between the 97th and the 98th percentile of the distribution of the variable. This implies that the net interest margin increases until this level of interest rate and then it starts to decrease. Regarding the other determinants of net interest margin, the results show that banks with more market power (approximated by the Lerner index) can set a higher interest margin. Considering risk, the impact is positive and statistically significant in the case of credit risk (approximated by the ratio of provisions to total assets), such that banks exposed to higher risk charge the corresponding premium. In the case of interest rate risk (approximated by the volatility of short-term interest rates), the resulting impact is negative. More risk averse banks set a higher interest margin.

Table 6.2 Results from the regressions

	Dependent variable:							
	Net interest income to total assets$_{it}$				*ROA$_{it}$*			
Dependent variable$_{i(t-1)}$	0.1488	***	0.2913	***	0.2489	**	0.3067	***
	(0.040)		(0.052)		(0.105)		(0.094)	
Short-term interest rate$_{it}$	0.0778	***	0.0768	**	0.1973	**	0.2335	***
	(0.022)		(0.031)		(0.093)		(0.088)	
Short-term interest rate$^2_{it}$	−0.5201	*	−0.2024		−1.8973	*	−0.3170	
	(0.275)		(0.285)		(1.015)		(0.860)	
Slope of the yield curve$_{it}$			0.0832	**			0.2670	***
			(0.036)				(0.073)	
Slope of the yield curve$^2_{it}$			−0.8064	**			−2.6798	***
			(0.351)				(1.028)	
Lerner index$_{it}$	0.0081	***	0.0031		0.0372		0.0427	***
	(0.003)		(0.003)		(0.029)		(0.009)	
Credit risk$_{it}$	0.0084	**	0.0472		0.0404		0.0077	
	(0.003)		(0.029)		(0.125)		(0.071)	
Interest rate risk$_{it}$	−0.0006	***	0.0000		−0.0003		−0.0008	
	(0.000)		(0.000)		(0.003)		(0.001)	
Risk interaction$_{it}$	0.0250	*	−0.0322	*	0.0780		0.0473	
	(0.014)		(0.017)		(0.149)		(0.034)	
Size$_{it}$	−0.0004		−0.0017	**	−0.0004		−0.0003	**
	(0.000)		(0.001)		(0.001)		(0.000)	
Risk aversion$_{it}$	0.0196	*	0.0522	***	0.0472	**	−0.0154	
	(0.011)		(0.012)		(0.019)		(0.011)	
Operating costs$_{it}$	0.3537	***	0.2107	***				
	(0.040)		(0.048)					
Implicit payments$_{it}$	0.8327	***	0.7885	***	−0.1103		−0.1900	**
	(0.050)		(0.073)		(0.360)		(0.083)	
Reserves$_{it}$	−0.0145	**	−0.0187	**	−0.0097		−0.0308	***
	(0.007)		(0.008)		(0.018)		(0.009)	
Efficiency$_{it}$	−0.0454	***	−0.0387	***	0.0013		0.0107	
	(0.003)		(0.003)		(0.011)		(0.007)	
GDP growth$_{it}$	0.0156	***	0.0037		0.0231		0.0241	**
	(0.006)		(0.007)		(0.030)		(0.011)	
Constant	0.0325	***	0.0440	***	−0.0044		−0.0108	*
	(0.007)		(0.009)		(0.008)		(0.006)	
Number of observations	48,858		48,858		48,858		48,858	

(*continued*)

Table 6.2 (continued)

	Dependent variable:			
	Net interest income to total assets$_{it}$		*ROA$_{it}$*	
Arellano-Bond test for AR(1) in first differences [p-value]	−2.87 [0.004]	−2.92 [0.003]	−1.66 [0.097]	−4.12 [0.000]
Arellano-Bond test for AR(2) in first differences [p-value]	−1.30 [0.193]	−0.69 [0.487]	0.48 [0.633]	1.42 [0.154]
Hansen test of overid. Restrictions [p-value]	48.53 [0.051]	36.55 [0.266]	1.94 [0.857]	43.10 [0.510]

Note: NIM, short-term interest rates and slope of the yield curve are in parts per unit. All estimations include time effects. Estimations are done using the Generalized Method of Moments (GMM) based on Arellano and Bond (1991), Arellano and Bover (1995) and Blundell and Bond (1998), where dependent variables are instrumented with their own second and third lags and other endogenous variables with their own second lag.

$^{*}p < 0.10$, $^{**}p < 0.05$, $^{***}p < 0.01$

The operating expenses have a positive, statistically significant coefficient, since net interest margin should at least cover operating costs and, therefore, the higher the operating costs the higher the net interest margin. The implicit payments also have a positive and statistically significant coefficient, suggesting that banks lowering the remuneration of liabilities and charging more implicitly for their services are more likely to set higher net interest margins. The bank's liquidity is also significant, and has a negative effect. The sign implies that banks investing a larger proportion of their assets in liquid assets have more reduced interest margin. This is logical bearing in mind the exiguous (or even zero) financial income from these assets. The results also show that better managed banks enjoy a greater margin, given the negative impact of the efficiency variable. GDP growth has a statistically significant coefficient and a positive sign. The rest of the explanatory variables have a non-significant coefficient. Finally, the lagged dependent variable shows a positive and significant coefficient, which confirms the high inertia in the determinants of the net interest margin.

In the second column, both the slope of the yield curve and its quadratic term are included. In this case, the quadratic term of the interest rates loses its significance, due to the collinearity with the yield curve, while the level of interest rates maintains its positive sign. The total effect of the slope of the yield curve on the net interest margin is positive. Given that the coefficient of the squared variable is negative and significant, the relationship has an inverted U-shaped form, indicating that a change in the yield curve slope has a bigger effect on the margin the flatter it is. The maximum point in this function is 0.052 (5.2%), which is well above the values observed in the sample. From the rest of the margin determinants, the results show that those banks with a larger size enjoy a smaller margin, possibly because economies of scope and scale are not taking place. The results also show that more risk averse banks set a higher interest margin. The operating expenses have a statistically significant coefficient and a positive sign, as net interest margin has at least cover the operating costs. The implicit payments also have a positive and statistically significant coefficient. The bank's liquidity is also significant, and has a negative effect. The results also show that better managed banks enjoy a greater margin, given the negative impact of the efficiency variable. Finally, the lagged dependent variable shows a positive and significant coefficient, which confirms the high inertia in the trend of the net interest margins.

The last two columns show the results obtained with ROA as dependent variable. The effect of the short-term interest rate on the bank profitability is again positive and non-linear (inverted U-shaped relationship), since the coefficient of the variable is positive and statistically significant and the coefficient of the quadratic term of the variable is negative and statistically significant. The maximum point of this inverted U-shaped relationship is 0.052 (5.2%), which is between the 92th and the 93th percentile of the distribution of the variable, implying that banks are increasingly profitable until the short-term interest rate hits this maximum value, after which profitability falls. This relationship also implies that a change in the short-term interest rate has a bigger effect on profitability the lower the level of interest rates.

In the fourth column, both the slope of the yield curve and its squared term are included. In this case, again the quadratic term of the interest rates loses its significance, due to the collinearity with the slope of the yield curve, while the level of interest rates maintains its positive sign. The total effect of the slope of the yield curve on the bank profitability is positive. Given that the coefficient of the squared variable is negative and significant, the relationship has an inverted U-shaped form, indicating that a change in the yield curve slope has a bigger effect on ROA the flatter it is.

The maximum point of the function is 0.05 (5%), which is above the values observed in the sample. Regarding the rest of the determinants of bank profitability, the results show that banks with more market power are more profitable. Results also show that larger banks have lower profitability, possibly as a consequence of failed economies of scope and scale. Implicit payments have a statistically significant coefficient and a negative sign, suggesting that higher implicit interest payments imply less profitability. Since liquid reserves represent an opportunity cost of not investing funds held in more profitable assets, a larger volume of liquid reserves means lower profitability. GDP growth has a statistically significant coefficient and a positive sign. Finally, the lagged dependent variable shows a positive and significant coefficient, which confirms the inertia in the trend of the bank profitability.

The chapter also quantifies the economic impact of each of the explanatory variables on the dependent variables. In doing so, the change (in basis points) in each dependent variable associated to an interquartile variation of the explanatory variables, i.e. a change from percentile 25th to 75th, is considered. Figure 6.4 ranks the variables from the largest to the smallest impact. For this purpose, the estimations of the second and fourth columns of Table 6.2 are used.

Figure 6.4 (a) displays the economic impact of each of the explanatory variables on the net interest margin, showing that the largest effect is that of the implicit interest payments. Specifically, the difference in net interest margin between a bank with an implicit payments level in the 25th percentile of the distribution and another with a level in the 75th percentile is 66 bp. The second variable in importance is efficiency, with a difference in net interest margin of 62 bp between two banks in the 25th and the 75th percentile, respectively. The third variable in the ranking is the bank size, for which a difference of 39 bp is associated to an interquartile variation, followed by the degree of risk aversion, which yields a 25 bp difference. The same impact is found for the short-term interest rate and the operating costs. Less meaningful are the estimated impacts for the slope of the yield curve (8 bp) and for the liquid reserves (3 bp).

Figure 6.4 (b) shows the economic impact of each of the explanatory variables on profitability. The biggest effect is that of the short-term interest rate variable, with an 82 bp impact associated to an interquartile variation. Slightly lower is the impact for the Lerner index (62 bp). Much more limited are the impacts found for the slope of the yield curve, the implicit

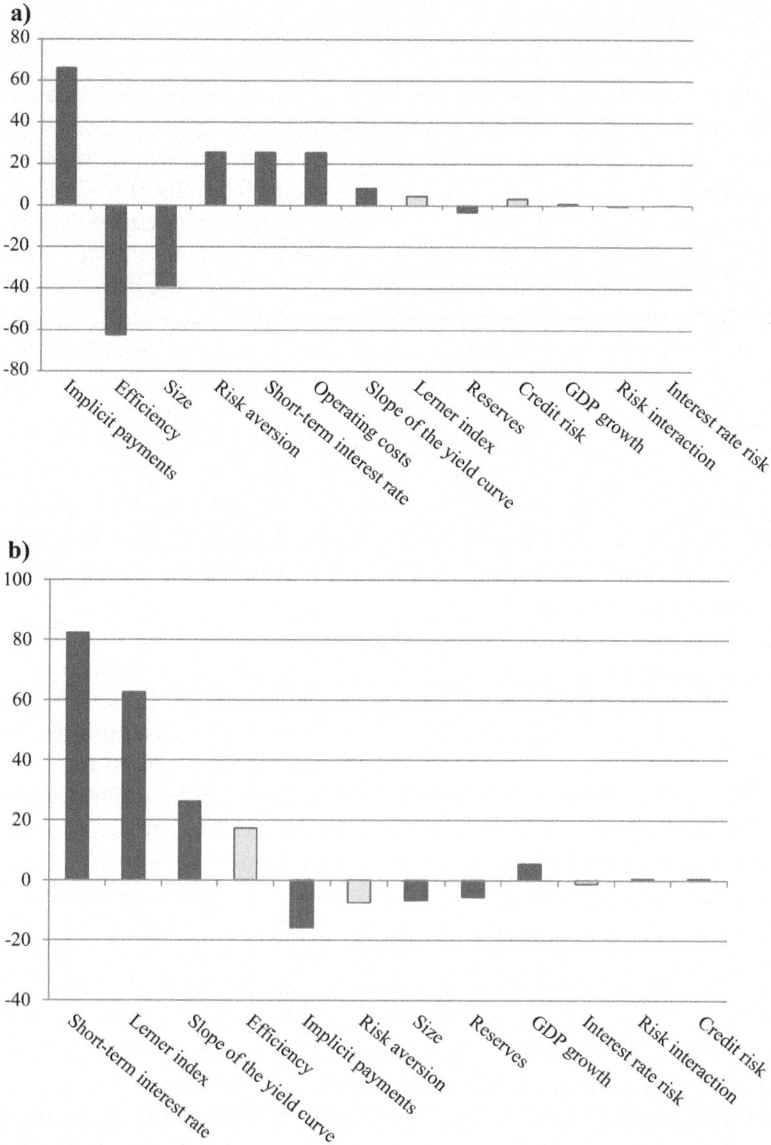

Fig. 6.4 Economic impact of the Lerner index determinants. Basis points. (a) net interest margin, (b) ROA. Note: The figure shows the effect on each of the dependent variables of a variation in each of the explanatory variables from the value of the bank located in the percentile 25th to 75th or, what is the same, the difference in each of the dependent variables between a bank that is in the 25th percentile of the distribution and another that is in the 75th percentile of each of the explanatory variables. The faint colored bars in the figure correspond to variables with no statistically significant effect. The variables are ordered from the highest to lowest relevance

payments, size, liquid reserves and GDP growth, with an impact of 26 bp, 16 bp, 7 bp, 6 bp and 5 bp, respectively.

Instead of considering interquartile variations, Table 6.3 shows the results for variations of the level of interest rates from 2000 to 2017. For this scenario, the drop in the net interest margin explained by decreased interest rates is 35 bp in the euro area, 35 bp in the United States, 38 bp in the United Kingdom, 0.22 bp in Japan and 37 bp in the group of other countries in the sample. Focusing on the drop in ROA, it is 115 bp in the euro area, 115 bp in the United States, 125 bp in the United Kingdom, 0.68 bp in Japan, and 123 bp in the group of other countries. In the case of the slope of the yield curve, the change in the net interest margin explained by changing the yield curve is 31 bp in the euro area, 15 bp in the United States, 17 bp in the United Kingdom, −7 bp in Japan, and −14 bp in the group of other countries in the sample. And the change in ROA is 102 bp in the euro area, 50 bp in the United States, 54 bp in the United Kingdom, −22 bp in Japan, and −43 bp in the group of other countries.

However, as the sharp reduction in the interest rates began in 2008 in most countries in the sample, the impact of interest rates on each dependent variable over the period 2008–2017 is estimated. Table 6.4 shows that the drop in the net interest margin explained by reduced interest rates is 34 bp in the euro area, 13 bp in the United States, 34 bp in the United Kingdom, 6 bp in Japan, and 31 bp in the group of other countries in the sample. Regarding ROA, the decline amounts 112 bp in the euro area, 41 bp in the United States, 112 bp in the United Kingdom, 18 bp in Japan, and 101 bp in the group of other countries. In the case of the slope of the yield curve, the sharp drop began in 2010 in the majority of countries in our sample, not in 2008 as for the level of interest rates. Hence, its impact on the net interest margin over the period 2010 to 2017 is also estimated. The results are also reported in Table 6.4. In this case, the flattening of the yield curve translates into a drop in the net interest margin of 6 bp for euro area banks, 12 bp in the United States, 14 bp in the United Kingdom, 6 bp in Japan, and 11 bp in the other countries. And the drop in ROA caused by the flattening of the yield curve is 19 bp in the euro area, 38 bp in the United States, 43 bp in the United Kingdom, 19 bp in Japan, and 35 bp in the group of other countries.

In this context and *ceteris paribus*, assuming that the interest rates recovered at 10 bp, 50 bp and 100 bp, the net interest margin would

Table 6.3 Observed changes in interest rates and yield curve slope, and predicted changes in net interest margin and profitability (2000–2017). Basis points

	Change in three-month interest rate, 2000–2017	*Predicted change in net interest margin, 2000–2017*	*Predicted change in ROA, 2000–2017*	*Change in yield curve slope, 2000–2017*	*Predicted change in net interest margin, 2000–2017*	*Predicted change in ROA, 2000–2017*
Euro area	−531	−35	−115	294	31	102
United States	−530	−35	−115	160	15	50
United Kingdom	−583	−38	−125	174	17	54
Japan	−3	−0.22	−0.68	−92	−7	−22
Other countries	−571	−37	−123	−204	−14	−43

Note: The change in three-month interest rate and the change in yield curve slope for the case of Japan is for 2003–2017 due to lack of available data.

Table 6.4 Observed changes in interest rates and yield curve slope, and predicted changes in net interest margin and profitability (2008–2017 and 2010–2017). Basis points

	Change in three-month interest rate, 2008–2017	*Predicted change in net interest margin, 2008–2017*	*Predicted change in ROA, 2008–2017*	*Change in yield curve slope, 2010–2017*	*Predicted change in net interest margin, 2010–2017*	*Predicted change in ROA, 2010–2017*
Euro area	−513	−34	−112	−79	−6	−19
United States	−181	−13	−41	−172	−12	−38
United Kingdom	−515	−34	−112	−205	−14	−43
Japan	−79	−6	−18	−77	−6	−19
Other countries	−463	−31	−101	−157	−11	−35

increase by 0.77 bp, 4 bp and 8 bp, respectively. Under these same assumptions, profitability would increase by 2 bp, 12 bp and 24 bp, respectively. Alternatively, *ceteris paribus*, assuming that the slope of the yield curve recovered at 10 bp, 50 bp and 100 bp, the net interest margin would increase by 0.84 bp, 4 bp and 9 bp, respectively. Under these same assumptions, profitability would increase by 3 bp, 14 bp and 29 bp, respectively.

6.5 Conclusions and Policy Implications

This chapter analyzes the changes on bank profitability and its main component, the net interest margin, due to the scenario of reduced interest rates and a flatter yield curve, both consequence of the expansionary monetary policy measures adopted by the main central banks to combat the crisis that erupted in 2008. To do so, a panel of data from 31 OECD countries covering the period 2000–2017 is used, which includes the pre-crisis, crisis and recovery sub-periods.

The results show the importance of expansionary monetary policy measures on bank's net interest margins and profitability. The relationship between the level of interest rates and bank profitability (measured by ROA) is positive. Therefore, lower interest rates reduce profitability. This effect is mainly due to the effect that low interest rates have on the net interest margin (the main component of ROA). Lower interest rates reduce the bank's net interest margin due to the difficulty for transferring interest rates to interest on deposits, which have a lower limit close to zero. The relationship between the slope of the yield curve and both net interest margin and profitability is also positive.

The relationship between interest rates and both net interest margin and bank profitability is non-linear. Among other things, this reflects that given that the deposit rate cannot be negative, the difference between the market rate and the deposit rate narrows when interest rates are low, being this reduction greater the lower the interest rates are. The same occurs for the case of the yield curve slope. The effect on the net interest margin and profitability is greater the more flattened the yield curve is.

In this context, the problem of low profitability that some banking sectors suffer—with profitability below the cost of capital in some countries—will persist as long as the current scenario of low interest rates remains. Low profitability could increase the likelihood that banks will assume a greater risk in order to compensate for that low profitability. In this scenario, financial stability could be compromised. Given this situation, the major challenge for those banks with low profitability is to increase efficiency by cutting costs and by finding sources of income other than interest.

Acknowledgments I am gratefully acknowledge financial support of the Spanish Ministry of Science and Innovation (research project ECO2017-84858-R) and Spanish Ministry of Education (FPU2014/00936).

References

Ahtik, M., B. Banerjee, and F. Remsak. 2016. Net Interest Margin in a Low Interest Rate Environment: Evidence for Slovenia. *The Journal for Money and Banking* 65 (11): 77–89.

Albertazzi, U., and L. Gambacorta. 2009. Bank Profitability and the Business Cycle. *Journal of Financial Stability* 5 (4): 393–409.

Albertazzi, U., M. Boucinha, and B. Becker. 2018. Portfolio Rebalancing and the Transmission of Large-Scale Asset Programmes: Evidence From the Euro Area. ECB Working Paper, 2125.

Alessandri, P., and B. Nelson. 2015. Simple Banking: Profitability and the Yield Curve. *Journal of Money, Credit and Banking* 47 (1): 143–175.

Altavilla, C., M. Boucinha, and J.-L. Peydró. 2018. Monetary Policy and Bank Profitability in a Low Interest Rate Environment. *Economic Policy* 33 (96): 531–586.

Angbazo, L. 1997. Commercial Bank Net Interest Margins, Default Risk, Interest-rate risk and Off-balance Sheet Banking. *Journal of Banking and Finance* 21: 55–87.

Angori, G., D. Aristei, and M. Gallo. 2019. Determinants of Banks' Net Interest Margin: Evidence from the Euro Area During the Crisis and Post-crisis Period. *Sustainability* 11 (14): 1–20.

Arce, O., M. García-Posada, S. Mayordomo, and S. Ongena. 2018. Adapting Lending Policies When Negative Interest Rates Hit Banks' Profits. Bank of Spain Working Paper, 1832.

Arellano, M., and S. Bond. 1991. Some Tests of Specification for Panel Data: Monte Carlo Evidence and an Application to Employment Equations. *Review of Economic Studies* 58: 277–297.

Arellano, M., and O. Bover. 1995. Another Look at the Instrumental-variable Estimation of Error-component Models. *Journal of Econometrics* 68 (1): 29–51.

Aydemir, R., and G. Ovenc. 2016. Interest Rates, the Yield Curve and Bank Profitability in an Emerging Market Economy. *Economic System* 40: 670–682.

Bikker, J.A., and T.M. Vervliet. 2018. Bank Profitability and Risk-taking Under Low Interest Rates. *International Journal of Finance & Economics* 23 (1): 3–18.

Blundell, R., and S. Bond. 1998. Initial Conditions and Moment Restrictions in Dynamic Panel Data Models. *Journal of Econometrics* 87 (1): 115–143.

Borio, C., and L. Gambacorta. 2017. Monetary Policy and Bank Lending in a Low Interest Rate Environment: Diminishing Effectiveness? *Journal of Macroeconomics* 54: 217–231.

Borio, C., L. Gambacorta, and B. Hofmann. 2017. The Influence of Monetary Policy on Bank Profitability. *International Finance* 20: 48–63.

Brunnermeier, M.K., and Y. Koby. 2018. The Reversal Interest Rate. NBER Working Paper, 25406.

Busch, R., and C. Memmel. 2015. Banks' Net Interest Margin and the Level of Interest Rates. Discussion Paper 16/2015, Deutsche Bundesbank Centre.

Claessens, S., N. Coleman, and M. Donnelly. 2018. Low-for-Long Interest Rates and Banks' Interest Margins and Profitability: Cross-country Evidence. *Journal of Financial Intermediation* 35: 1–16.

Cruz-García, P., J. Fernández de Guevara, and J. Maudos. 2018. Banking Concentration and Competition in Spain: The Impact of the Crisis and Restructuring. *Financial Stability Review* 34: 57–76.

———. 2019. Determinants of Bank's Interest Margin in the Aftermath of the Crisis: The Effect of Interest Rates and the Yield Curve Slope. *Empirical Economics* 56: 341–365.

Demiralp, S., J. Eisenschmidt, and T. Vlassopoulos. 2019. Negative Interest Rates, Excess Liquidity and Retail Deposits: Banks' Reaction to Unconventional Monetary Policy in the Euro Area. ECB Working Paper, 2283.

English, W.B. 2002. Interest Rate Risk and Bank Net Interest Margins. *BIS Quarterly Review*, December, 67–82.

Entrop, O., C. Memmel, B. Ruprecht, and M. Wilkens. 2015. Determinants of Bank Interest Margins: Impact of Maturity Transformation. *Journal of Banking & Finance* 54: 1–19.

Genay, H., and R. Podjasek. 2014. What is the Impact of a Low Interest Rate Environment on Bank Profitability? *Chicago Fed Letter* 324: 1–4.

Heider, F., F. Saidi, and G. Schepens. 2018. Life Below Zero: Bank Lending Under Negative Policy Rates. ECB Working Paper, 2173.

International Money Fund. 2016. *Global Financial Stability Report*, April.

Kohlscheen, E., A. Murcia, and J. Contreras. 2018. Determinants of Bank Profitability in Emerging Markets. BIS Working Papers n° 686. January.

Mamatzakis, E., and T. Bermpei. 2016. What is the Effect of Unconventional Monetary Policy on Bank Performance? *Journal of International Money and Finance* 67: 239–263.

Maudos, J., and J. Fernández de Guevara. 2004. Factors Explaining the Interest Margin in the Banking Sectors of the European Union. *Journal of Banking & Finance* 28 (9): 2259–2281.

McShane, R.W., and I.G. Sharpe. 1985. A Time Series/Cross Section Analysis of the Determinants of Australian Trading Bank Loan/Deposit Interest Margins: 1962–1981. *Journal of Banking & Finance* 9: 115–136.

Molyneux, P., A. Reghezza, and R. Xie. 2019. Bank Margins and Profits in a World of Negative Rates. *Journal of Banking & Finance* 107: 105613.

Pérez, C., and A. Ferrer. 2018. The Impact of the Interest Rate Level on Bank Profitability and Balance Sheet Structure. *Review of Financial Stability* 35: 123–152.

Rostagno, M., U. Bindseil, A. Kamps, W. Lemke, T. Sugo, and F. Vlassopoulos. 2016. Breaking Through the Zero Line: The ECB's Negative Interest Rate Policy. In *Presentation at Brookings Institutions, Washington, DC*, June 6.

Sääskilahti, J. 2018. Retail Bank Interest Margin in Low Interest Rate Environments. *Journal of Financial Services Research* 53 (1): 37–68.

Scheiber, T., M. Silgoner, and C. Stern. 2016. The Development of Bank Profitability in Denmark, Sweden and Switzerland during a Period of Ultra-low and Negative Interest Rates. *Focus on European Economic Integration*, Oesterreichische Nationalbank (Austrian Central Bank), 3, 8–28.

Turk Ariss, R.. 2016. Negative Interest Rates: How Big a Challenge for Large Danish and Swedish Banks? IMF Working Paper, 16/198.

Weistroffer, C. 2013. Ultra-low Interest Rates: How Japanese Banks have Coped. *Deutsche Bank Research*, June 10.

PART II

Frontiers in Financing: Instruments for Firms and Individuals

CHAPTER 7

The Value Drivers of the Italian Asset Management Industry: An Inquiry on the Systematic Risk Drivers

Andrea Ferrarin, Josanco Floreani, and Maurizio Polato

7.1 Introduction

This paper relies on a classical corporate finance theoretical model and aims to explore the drivers of the systematic risk exposure of Italian asset managers. Our study is motivated by two central aspects: first, the substantial growth of the asset management sector after the exacerbation of the global financial crisis and, second, by the significant lack of studies focused on the examination of the value drivers of the investment management industry.

Consequently, our chief objective is to provide an empirical investigation regarding the drivers of market betas of asset management firms. In fact, the correct pricing of the systematic risk exposure embodies a

A. Ferrarin • J. Floreani (✉) • M. Polato
Department of Economics and Statistics, University of Udine, Udine, Italy
e-mail: ferrarin.andrea@spes.uniud.it; josanco.floreani@uniud.it; maurizio.polato@uniud.it

C. Cruciani et al. (eds.), *Banking and Beyond*, Palgrave Macmillan Studies in Banking and Financial Institutions,
https://doi.org/10.1007/978-3-030-45752-5_7

fundamental as well as a tricky step for the accurate estimation of the cost of equity and hence of the value of asset management companies.

The idea of what the asset management industry represents nowadays has been totally questioned after the global financial crisis. Indeed, while before 2008 crisis asset managers were perceived mostly only as high operational leverage firms in which the ability of the company to manage the cost structure represented the main factor for the determination of the financial performance, after the global financial distress the industry has started to be subjected to huge profitability pressure from the market. Indeed, the peculiar business model of asset managers in which the market risk exposure is built into the fee generation process exhibits the necessity of companies to generate a high level of earnings (Scherer 2012).

Thus, our work contributes to the extant literature reflecting this renewed interest towards the investment management industry because of the necessity among scholars and practitioners to assess the dynamics of the main value drivers that have led the growth of the industry in recent years.

The significant expansion of the asset management sector is due to several causes: first, the regulatory response to the financial crisis, featured by the tightening of the regulatory constraints, which most affected the banking sector as it is traditionally considered to be the most exposed to both solvency and liquidity risks. Thus, the consequent increase of compliance costs and the constant deleveraging of banks' balance sheet (*see* Gropp et al. 2016) have shrunk the amount of funds intermediated by banks, allowing a growing role of asset managers, both in the collection of savings and in active investment choices to support the real economy (IMF 2015).

Secondly, the expansive monetary policy undertaken by the ECB, with a persistently low level of interest rates, has significantly contracted the interest margin of banks, making the traditional loans business less profitable and forcing institutions to change their business model by focusing on low-capital absorption businesses and considerably increasing the income deriving from non-interest activities. Thereby, the revenues from asset management have become a fundamental voice in banks' income statement, playing a crucial role in defining the financial performance of institutions (Landi and Venturelli 2017).

Finally, the demographic changes of the population and the transformation of the pension systems have significantly affected the investor's saving–investment decisions. Indeed, according to Walter (2016), in

Europe, national pension schemes are being reduced and people are highly encouraged to stipulate supplementary pension contracts. The primary significance of the social security issue is, therefore, one of the main factors that exploit the transformation of the intermediation circuits. Thus, the combination of these three crucial factors has provided a constant shift of the credit intermediation from the banking sector to the Am industry.

The disruptive growth of asset managers in industrialized countries entails different advantages. First, it encourages investors to diversify their financial portfolio and represents a fundamental tool capable of managing savings, and thus financing economic growth, even when banks are distressed. Furthermore, as highlighted by the IMF (2015), the asset management industry, from a financial stability prospective, has significant conveniences compared to the banking sector: while banks rely on deposits and generally short-term debt, investment funds have high cash flow generation ability and are generally highly capitalized. For these reasons the default risk is substantially lower compared to the banking sector (*see* October 2014 Global Financial Stability report).

The statistics show that the global value of asset under management (AuM) will almost double by 2025, from US$ 84.9 trillion in 2016 to US$ 111.2 trillion by 2020, and then to US$ 145.4 trillion in 2025. In Europe, the AuM level reached the record size of EUR 25.2 trillion at the end of 2017, and the AuM to EU GDP ratio is about 147%. The expected growth is 8.4% and 3.4% respectively for the two periods, with an increase of the AuM amount from EUR 25.2 trillion to 35.7 trillion (PWC 2017).

As of 2017 Europe represents the second largest market for asset management worldwide. Table 7.1 shows that the core of the asset management industry in Europe is localized in the UK where the AuM level at the end of 2016 reached a value of EUR 8 trillion. France and Germany follow with an AuM level of EUR 3.9 and 2 trillion respectively. Together these three countries, at the end of 2016, represented 62% of the total AuM value in Europe (EFAMA 2018). Thus, the asset management industry is confined to a limited number of EU countries and this high level of concentration mirrors the significant bond between the size of the population, the degree of development of the financial services and the level of domestic private savings. Table 7.1 also provides a distinction between investment funds and discretionary mandate. The former consists in a regulated fund (UCITS and non-UCITS) which manages savings of

Table 7.1 AuM in Europe by investment funds and discretionary mandates

			Discretionary mandates			*Investment funds*		
Total 2016	AuM/ GDP%	AuM	*AuM*	*Mkt share (%)*	*AuM/ GDP%*	*AuM*	*Mkt share (%)*	*AuM/ GDP%*
UK	338	8093	5533	50.40	231	2560	21.60	107
France	178	3971	1804	16.40	81	2167	18.30	97
Germany	67	2093	338	3.10	11	1755	14.80	56
Switzerland	272	1646	602	5.50	100	1044	8.80	173
Netherlands	189	1326	450	4.10	64	876	7.40	125
Italy	73	1229	826	7.50	49	402	3.40	24
Denmark	139	389	149	1.40	54	238	2.0	86
Spain	28	314	45	0.04	4	269	1.2	24
Belgium	71	301	156	1.40	37	146	1.2	34
Austria	37	132	n.a.	n.a.	n.a.	132	1.1	37
Portugal	40	73	51	0.05	27	22	0.2	12
Czech Republic	25	45	26	0.20	15	19	0.2	11
Hungary	25	28	9	0.10	8	19	0.2	16
Turkey	3	20	2	<0.1	0.30	18	0.2	2
Greece	5	10	4	<0.1	2	6	<0.1	<0.1
Romania	5	9	0.04	<0.1	0.02	9	<0.1	<0.1
Slovenia	6	3	1	<0.1	2	2	<0.1	<0.1
Bulgaria	1	1	n.a.	n.a.	n.a.	1	<0.1	<0.1
Rest of Europe	165	3172	988	9.00	51	2184	18.4	113
TOTAL	138	*22855*	10984	100	66	11867	100.0	72

Data from EFAMA (2018)

investors united by a similar target; conversely the latter represents an exclusive investment delegated to an asset manager by a specific investor with a defined investment aim.

This paper is organized as follows: Sect. 7.2 analyses the literature review, Sect. 7.3 presents the data and the methodology used, Sect. 7.4 contains the results and Sect. 7.5 discusses the implications and presents the conclusions.

7.2 Literature Review

7.2.1 *An Overview on the Peculiarities and the Valuation of Financial Firms*

The idea that financial firms differ significantly from other firms is well recognized among scholars and practitioners (*see* Kashyap et al. 2010; Damodaran 2013; Miles et al. 2013) and the literature concerned on the investigation of the value drivers of financial firms is mostly related to the banking sector, for three crucial reasons.

The first issue regards the pervasive regulatory context within which banks operate and that has declined along three different dimensions. Banks are primarily subjected to exogenous regulatory mechanisms, aimed at establishing minimum capital requirements (Basel regulatory framework) with the objective of absorbing losses, preventing insolvency and safeguarding depositors and claimholders (*see* Shrieves and Dahl 1992; Rochet 1992; Dewatripont and Tirole 1994; Milne and Jokipii 2011).

The objective of the second form of regulation is to set boundaries to the business activities with the purpose of limiting excessive risk-taking and moral hazard incentives, by ensuring the stability and the resilience of the financial system (*see* Barth et al. 2001, 2004; Laeven and Levine 2008).

Finally, regulators are in place to supervise the mergers and acquisitions, and authorities strictly monitor the access of new players within this sector in order to ensure that the fragile equilibrium that characterizes the financial intermediation segment is not threatened.

The second issue is the different role played by debt: while in non-financial companies debt is assumed essentially as a funding instrument used to make investments, in banks it serves as *raw material* (Damodaran 2013). Indeed, in the banking sector it is not possible to provide a clear distinction between financial debt, which is assumed as a source of value, and operational debt. In fact, as highlighted by Beltrame and Previtali (2016), the strong connection between funding policies and asset-side operations makes obtaining an estimation of different measures such as net working capital, capital expenditures and cost of capital (WACC) unrealistic in financial firms.

Finally, the third issue is related to the differences in the accounting principles which in the case of financial service firms diverge significantly compared to other companies. Indeed, financial firms' assets include essentially financial instruments which are mostly priced within regulated markets. Consequently, assets valuation is based on their market value instead of the original cost, causing several differences in the assessment of the value drivers (Damodaran 2013).

Focusing on the peculiar case of asset management firms, these provide consultancy advices and manage portfolios for clients, their earnings ensuing from advisory revenues and from management and sales fees for asset portfolios.

Even within the asset management industry investment firms are significantly different in several aspects—size, type of managed investment, investing policy and regulatory issues—and scholars argued that the differences compared to non-financial firms are much lower than in other financial companies (banks, insurance companies, etc.). Massari et al. (2014) support this idea from an operational perspective, highlighting that the financial statement of asset management companies is essentially similar to other non-financial service companies and in which finance-specifics items (loans and deposits) do not play a greater role. In particular, the role of debt is substantially equivalent to that of non-financial firms; indeed asset management firm's liabilities can be assumed at the same level of operating debts of non-financial firms.

Thus, while in the case of banks the literature has proved to be sceptic concerning the possible applicability of the Modigliani and Miller (1958) (M-M) theorem in relation to the liquidity provider function carried out by banks (Diamond and Rajan 2000) and the strong connection between deposits and short-term assets (Mehran and Thakor 2011), in the peculiar case of asset managers the M-M theorem seems to be applicable and the only limitations are related to the unrealistic baseline assumptions on which the M-M theorem is based (frictionless markets, absence of bankruptcy costs, etc.).

Therefore, it appears reasonable to consider that the systematic risk coefficient beta is able to capture the risk dynamics of the commonly used risk ratios in vogue in the non-financial sector (Scherer 2012).

Turning on the empirical literature concerned on the valuation of Am firms, this is relatively scant: Huberman (2004), relying on the assumption of infinite growth of the assets under management (under this assumption the amount of fees has no impact on the asset management firm's value) and applying a ***dividend discount model***, shows that the net present value of an asset management firm is a function of the market value of their AuM multiplied by the profit margin of the firm. Even though empirical results highlight that the operating margin of firms ranges between 20%

and 30%, the market capitalization is approximately only in the 3–8% margin of the AuM. This represents the so-called Huberman puzzle. Berk and Green (2004) overcome the limits of the Huberman model and investors are now rational and aware about the skills of the fund manager through the valuation of past performance. Therefore, in the Berk and Green (B-G) equilibrium model, managerial talent is a scarce resource and managers reflect different ability to manage the fund. Thus, the investment process is compromised by a significant level of diseconomies of scales. Moreover, Pastor et al. (2015) find strong empirical evidence of diseconomies of scale, pointing out a negative relation between industry size and fund performance, especially for funds with a higher turnover and volatility; the authors, therefore, emphasize the importance of the relative size within the Am industry, rejecting the hypothesis of significant return on scale in active management.

Finally, Joenväära and Scherer (2017), contrasting the Huberman model's assumption of infinite asset growth and exploiting the B-G model, demonstrate that the capacity to produce revenues is just as fundamental as the ability to convert them into earnings. This means that an asset management firm's valuation model must include both variables. On a sample of 33 U.S. Am firms, during the period 1998–2013, using different regression models, they show that the level of fees plays a significant role in explaining the ratio between market capitalization and AuM level.

7.2.2 Firms' Systematic Risk Drivers and Hypotheses Development

In the previous paragraph we have emphasized that a crucial point in the valuation of financial firms is the appropriate estimation of the cost of equity k_e and the cost of capital (WACC), which represent the discount factors of the discounted valuation models. The assessment of these measures necessarily involves the correct pricing of the systematic risk component.

In this regard, classical finance theory is based on the hypothesis that markets are efficient and the expected return by owners must be adequate to the level of risk they bear (Schall 1972). Risk is therefore defined as the possibility that the actual returns diverge from the expected returns (Watson and Head 2010; Schlegel 2015). Following the traditional Capital Asset Pricing Model (CAPM) by Sharp (1964), the risk held by shareholders can be fragmented into two components: the idiosyncratic and eliminable component (unsystematic risk), which is specific of the characteristics of the firm, and the systematic and non-eliminable component, which represents the portion of the stock's risk due to its correlation with the market portfolio. The CAPM affirms the investors are only compensated for the systematic and non-diversifiable risk component, which is measured by the beta factor that assesses the slope of the stock return to changes in total market return (Watson and Head 2010; Perold 2004; Schlegel 2015). Thus, the cost of equity can be expressed by the following formula:

$$k_e = r_f + \beta_e \cdot \left(r_m - r_f\right) \tag{7.1}$$

where r_f is the risk-free rate; β_e is the equity beta and r_m is the expected market return rate.

Thus, the cost of capital is a function of the market risk premium and the firm's beta which is extrapolated by regressing stock returns on market returns:

$$r_{i,t} = \alpha + \beta_e \cdot r_{m,t} + \varepsilon_{i,t} \tag{7.2}$$

where $r_{i,t}$ is the stock return rate at time t; β_e is the equity beta, $r_{m,t}$ is the market portfolio return rate at time t and $\varepsilon_{i,t}$ is the error term.

Several studies have assessed the determinants of firms' systematic risk exposure expressed by betas. Breen and Lerner (1973), Logue and Merville (1972) and Patel and Olsen (1984) show that profitability, financial structure, firm size and growth, liquidity, efficiency and macroeconomic conditions are the main factors which drive a firms' beta.

Beaver et al. (1970) highlight a negative relationship between firms' profitability and betas consistent with the hypothesis that more profitable firms reduce systematic risk exposure. Logue and Merville (1972) find a negative relationship between firms' betas and liquidity, demonstrating that the more the firm is liquid, the lower is its systematic risk exposure.

Conversely, Jensen (1984) provides empirical evidence of the positive impact of firms' liquidity on systematic risk due to moral hazard behaviour which increases agency costs of FCF. Gu and Kim (2002) evaluate the impact of operating efficiency on systematic risk, finding a negative relationship between the two, which suggests that firms that are more capable of generating revenues from their assets have a lower level of beta.

Arguably, beta determinants can largely vary across different industries since risk factors have a definite industry-specific nature. In the specific case of the financial sector, most of the studies which investigate the determinants of betas are typically focused on the banking and insurance segments; Borde et al. (1994) provide strong evidence regarding the positive impact of profitability on systematic risk exposure in the insurance sector. Rosenberg and Perry (1978) focused on the US banking sector between 1969 and 1977. They show that the main determinants of bank betas are size, level of capitalization the dividend yields and asset to long-term liabilities. Vander Vennet et al. (2005) explored the main factors which impact on banks' systematic and idiosyncratic risks in the EU banking system. They find confirmation on the results of Rosenberg and Perry (1978), highlighting that the capitalization level and the ratio between loans and core deposits in total assets are negatively correlated with banks' systematic risk. Agusman et al. (2008) examined the relationship between bank-specific factors and market measures of risk in the Asian banking sector. Profitability measured by ROA and the *non-performing* loans coverage ratios have a positive impact on banks' equity risks.

Das and Sy (2012) find a positive relationship between bank size and betas. Moreover, as predictable, they find a positive relationship between credit risk exposure and banks' betas. Di Biase and D'Apolito (2012) provide empirical evidence about the positive relationship between systematic risk exposure and size, business model expressed by the ratio of gross loans to total assets and intangible ratio (intangible assets to total assets) in the Italian banking system. Floreani et al. (2015) show using a sample of 59 European banks in the period 2006–2011 that financial performance does not affect banks' systematic risk component while risk measures have a positive impact on banks' systematic risk exposure.

Beltrame et al. (2018) investigate the relationship between banks' asset quality, leverage and banks' market risk. They show that the only book leverage ratio does not have a significant impact on banks' systematic risk, while the combined effect of leverage and NPLs is found to be significant on market risk.

In light of the literature outlined in the previous paragraph our work aims to provide empirical evidence regarding the determinants of the systematic risk exposure of Italian asset managers contributing to the extant literature concerning the investigation of main risk factors in the financial system.

Hull (2007, p. 372) states that "[f]or an asset manager the greatest risk is operational risk". Indeed before the global financial crisis the asset management industry was perceived mostly only as a high operational leverage industry (high ratio of fixed to variable costs) in which the ability of the asset managers to manage the cost structure represented the main factor which determined the financial performance of firms. High levels of operational leverage lead to what is defined as a "scalable business" in which the decreasing marginal cost of taking additional business in good times opens to potentially severe losses when the revenue collapses. Therefore, the first formal hypothesis we want to test is as follows:

H_1 : *As the asset management industry is characterized by a high level of operational leverage (high level of fixed-to-variables costs), the operational risk has a positive impact on market betas.*

After the global financial crisis, the assumption of Hull has been totally questioned; indeed asset managers began to be involved in acquisition processes and incorporated within bank groups. For these motives, the asset management industry started to be subjected to severe profitability pressures by the market. The reason originates from the fact that the business model of asset managers enables the direct market exposure to be generated into the fee contracts.

Indeed, the market betas of investments directly affect managers' fees through their impact on returns (Scherer 2012).

In other terms, market risk plays a primary role in the revenue volatility of asset managers, hence the risk borne by asset managers is directly reflected in fee contracts and is mostly related to market risk and not only operational risk.

Therefore, the peculiar business model of asset managers raises the issue of the relationship that occurs between the "fees at risk" and the market risk exposure of the companies.

Thereby, in this regard we can hypothesize the existence of a positive relationship between the amount of fees of asset managers and the systematic risk of the company. Therefore, the second formal hypothesis is as follows:

H_2 : *Given that the market risks of asset management firms are built through the revenues' generation process, we expect that the amount of fees is positively related to asset managers' systematic risk exposure.*

7.3 Data and Methodology

7.3.1 *Empirical Framework*

Our paper is built upon a sample of 44 Italian asset management firms spanning a period of 10 years, from 2006 to 2016, for which we collect yearly balance sheet data from firms' reports.

Given that only a small number of companies of the sample are listed, in order to estimate the betas properly, using the Bloomberg Intelligence Application, we identify a sample of 20 listed global asset managers as comparable firms.

Our methodology consists in a procedure conducted in three steps. The first two steps are addressed, on the one hand, to extrapolate and decompose unlevered betas of our comparable asset management firms and, on the other hand, to calculate the unlevered betas on our sample of study.

The third step is aimed at studying the main determinants of the betas using different regression specifications.

The levered beta can be expressed by the following traditional formula:

$$\beta_L = \beta_U \cdot \left(1 + \frac{D}{E} \cdot (1 - T_c)\right) \tag{7.3}$$

where β_L is the levered beta; β_U is the unlevered beta; D/E is the debt-to-equity ratio and T_c is the effective tax rate.

However, this formula assumes that the degree of operational leverage between comparable firms and our sample is similar and does not provide a valuation of the operational risk in relation with the degree of cyclicity of the revenues and the weight of the fixed costs within the structure of the operational costs.

For these reasons, in order to bring out the cost structure embedded by asset management firms, we follow Moschetta (2001) and by exploiting the additive property of betas we provide a factorization of the β_L as follows:

$$\beta_L = \beta_{VC} \cdot \left[1 + \frac{D}{E} \cdot (1 - T_c)\right] + \beta_{OL}\left[1 + \frac{D}{E} \cdot (1 - T_c)\right] \tag{7.4}$$

where β_{VC} is the ***variable costs beta***, which represents the exposition to systematic risk in the case that the only expenses that asset management firms bear are variables costs, hence the commissions and fees paid; β_{OL} conveys the major risk that the asset manager faces in relation with the weight of the fixed costs. This aspect represents a crucial issue in the asset management firms which traditionally presents a high level of operational leverage (high level of fixed to variable costs). In addition, according to the evaluation pattern proposed by Joenväära and Scherer (2017) for assessing the value of asset managers, the ability of the asset manager to transform revenues into earnings is as crucial as the capability to generate revenues from AuM.

Thus, in formula (7.4), starting with the assumption that the business risk of comparable firms is similar to that of Italian asset managers, and hence a similar level of β_{VC}, the differences in terms of systematic risk exposure are related to the degree of operational and financial leverage.

Given that the operating income of the asset manager is expressible as follows:

$$\text{Operating income} = \left(\text{revenues}_{+} - \text{revenues}_{-}\right) - \text{fixed costs} \tag{7.5}$$

By the formulas (7.4) and (7.5), given that the beta is defined as

$$\beta_i = \frac{\operatorname{cov}\left(r_i; r_m\right)}{\sigma^2 r_m} \tag{7.6}$$

And by exploiting the properties of the covariance we can write the following version of unlevered beta (*see* Appendix):

$$\beta_U = \frac{\text{Net Revenues}}{\text{Operating Income}} \cdot \frac{\text{Operating Income}}{\text{Gross Revenues}} \cdot \frac{\operatorname{cov}\left[\frac{\text{revenues}_{+}}{V_U}; r_m\right]}{\sigma^2 r_m} \tag{7.7}$$

where Net Revenues/Operating Income represents the degree of operational leverage; Operating Income/Gross Revenues represents the return on sales (ROS), and $\left(\operatorname{cov}\left[\frac{\text{revenues}_{+}}{V_U}; r_m\right]\right) / \left(\sigma^2 r_m\right)$ is the covariance index of cyclicity of the revenues (CICR) which expresses the degree of cyclicity of the revenues of the asset manager perceived by the market.

Thus, the unlevered beta of our sample being studied can be expressed as follows:

$$\beta_U = \text{Operational Leverage} \cdot \text{ROS} \cdot \text{CICR}_{\text{comparable}} \quad (7.8)$$

where the CICR refers to our comparable firms, by relying on the assumption that the cyclicity of the revenues of our sample is similar to that of our comparable firms.

7.3.2 Data and Regression Model

As we have specified in the previous paragraph, this study explores firm-specific and market measures which are related to the systematic risk exposure expressed by betas in the Italian Asset Management Industry. We gather annual financial data referring to our comparable asset managers from Bloomberg Professional Database, on a time frame spanning over a period of ten years, from 2006 to 2016. Instead, the data related to Italian Asset Managers are collected from firms' reports with the same time horizon.

This approach allows us to provide further insights into two crucial periods that characterized the last decade: the financial and sovereign debt crisis period of 2008–2012 and the post-financial crisis period. Table 7.2 provides further details about the main descriptive statistics of comparable firms; Table 7.3 shows the statistics of the key variables of Italian asset managers.

Built upon theory and previous literature concerning the financial service firms, we test different firm specifics and market predictors of asset managers' systematic risk exposure. We identify a limited number of variables as predictors of firms' systematic risk, as shown in Table 7.4.

The first three measures included in our study regard the operational efficiency of asset managers. The first considers the revenue generation ability of the asset manager, measured by the ratio of revenues, which represent the total amount of fee income collected by managing assets, to AuM (Joenväära and Scherer 2017).

Although one first branch of research shows that the operating efficiency in this approach is negative related to betas (Borde et al. 1994; Gu

Table 7.2 Descriptive statistics of comparable asset management firms

	Median values	*AuM (millions €)*	*(P/AuM) (%)*	*P/BV*	*CICR*	*(Revenues/AuM) (%)*	*(Income/ Revenues) (%)*	*Unlevered beta*
1.	AGF Management LTD	37312	2.96	1.10	5.89	1.20	18.04	1.46
2.	AllianceBernstein Holding LP	431800	1.46	3.15	3.76	0.41	12.93	1.16
3.	Artisan Partners Asset Management Inc	96224	2.53	19.00	2.60	0.74	10.16	0.89
4.	Azimut Holding Spa	17494	7.03	3.30	3.09	2.16	27.64	1.00
5.	Blackrock INC	717100	3.68	2.94	4.66	0.93	26.58	1.60
6.	CI Financial Corp	3791588	1.18	1.76	3.43	0.22	28.56	1.35
7.	Cohen & Steers INC	75720	8.83	4.24	1.56	1.78	26.32	0.56
8.	Eaton Vance Corp	45797	3.37	5.96	5.48	0.59	24.64	2.10
9.	Federated Investors Inc	199508	1.66	7.19	2.92	0.57	17.28	0.99
10.	Frenklin Resources Inc	369697	0.80	5.17	3.24	0.26	18.58	0.99
11.	Gamco Investors Inc	34354	3.81	1.50	2.41	0.93	25.46	1.08
12.	IGM Financial Inc	129484	9.01	2.56	1.88	2.01	29.20	0.79
13.	Invesco LTD	733200	1.75	1.48	5.88	0.59	18.20	1.63
14.	Lagg Mason Inc	701800	0.64	0.88	8.46	0.41	8.31	1.45
15.	Manning & Napier Inc	35442	0.37	0.88	4.77	0.80	2.71	1.22
16.	Och-Ziff Capital Management Group LLC	32552	12.20	1.46	1.37	2.54	22.25	0.52
17.	Pzena Investment Management Inc	24300	2.25	31.42	5.56	0.45	5.19	2.87
18.	Sprott Inc	7323	9.25	1.99	2.37	1.43	26.38	0.76
19.	T Rowe Price Group Inc	576800	2.96	4.29	3.26	0.53	29.20	1.48
20.	WisdomTree Investments Inc	81082	3.39	5.59	6.25	1.35	14.98	1.54
Total		*88653*	*2.92*	*3.18*	*3.63*	*0.80*	*19.40*	*1.22*

The table shows the descriptive statistics of comparable asset managers. AuM are the assets under management. P/AuM is the ratio between the stock price and the assets under management. P/BV is the Price-to-Book value. CICR is the ***covariance index of cyclicity of the revenues.*** Revenues/AuM is the ratio between gross revenues and the assets under management. Income/Revenues is the ratio between operating income and gross revenues

Table 7.3 Descriptive statistics of the sample being studied

	Median values	*AuM (millions €)*	*(Revenues/AuM) (%)*	*(Income/Revenues) (%)*	*Operational leverage*	*Unlevered beta*
1.	AcomeA SGR	719	1.74	12.24	4.69	2.27
2.	Agora Investments SGR	166	1.97	1.77	1.03	1.62
3.	Aletti Gestielle SGR	11600	1.62	7.96	1.33	0.93
4.	Allianz Global Investors SGR	33700	0.41	17.65	2.04	1.19
5.	Amundi SGR	6530	2.10	7.90	2.73	0.95
6.	Anima SGR	22900	1.07	25.28	1.44	1.19
7.	Aperta SGR	3630	0.10	22.76	2.96	3.36
8.	Arca SGR	21000	0.97	9.95	2.31	1.07
9.	Aureo Gestioni SGR	3660	1.50	8.24	3.78	1.26
10.	Azimut Capital Management SGR	3670	2.59	37.55	1.49	2.17
11.	Bancoposta Fondi SGR	33200	0.10	42.47	1.37	1.97
12.	BCC Risparmio&Previdenza SGR	3830	0.12	18.89	2.31	1.26
13.	BG SGR	3760	1.64	19.97	1.64	1.33
14.	BNP Paribas SGR	9800	1.26	4.98	5.89	0.99
15.	BPVI Fondi SGR	4190	0.36	12.72	3.66	1.54
16.	Carige Asset Management SGR	4430	0.93	10.03	2.13	0.85
17.	Consultinvent AM SGR	777	2.24	15.49	2.42	1.31
18.	Credit Suisse Asset Management SGR	498	0.31	7.11	4.23	2.37
19.	Duemme SGR	7240	0.44	8.26	4.20	1.50
20.	Epsilon Associati SGR	12800	0.28	44.18	1.36	2.12
21.	Ersel Asset Management SGR	2950	0.73	31.08	2.42	2.40
22.	Etica SGR	863	1.23	11.03	3.86	1.41
23.	Eurizon Capital SGR	113000	0.70	20.31	1.13	0.82
24.	Euromobiliare Asset Management SGR	13100	0.47	18.87	2.21	1.40

(*continued*)

Table 7.3 (continued)

	Median values	*AuM (millions €)*	*(Revenues/AuM) (%)*	*(Income/Revenues) (%)*	*Operational leverage*	*Unlevered beta*
25.	Fideuram SGR	22800	0.74	15.29	1.81	1.03
26.	Fondaco SGR	4730	0.13	21.41	3.16	2.42
27.	Genrali Investments SGR	133000	0.05	28.86	2.26	2.64
28.	Gesti-Re SGR	91	0.67	2.59	3.09	2.69
29.	Groupama SGR	32	16.31	19.91	2.50	1.66
30.	Investitori SGR	1020	0.86	15.04	2.14	2.60
31.	Kairos SGR	6010	0.97	36.48	2.50	2.55
32.	Leonardo SGR	1700	0.28	−3.13	2.14	2.22
33.	MC Gestioni Sgr	648	0.91	−7.51	−1.67	1.53
34.	Mediolanum Gestione Fondi SGR	16100	0.45	33.33	1.42	1.64
35.	Nextam Partners SGR	974	0.90	19.85	4.10	2.82
36.	Optima SGR	3050	0.34	26.74	1.95	1.73
37.	Pensplan SGR	1430	0.63	2.31	10.38	2.09
38.	Pioneer Investments SGR	34300	1.65	6.53	2.55	0.60
39.	Profilo SGR	59	1.18	−4.32	1.06	1.74
40.	Sella Gestioni SGR	1940	1.04	9.77	3.51	1.34
41.	Soprano SGR	471	1.15	6.65	3.31	2.31
42.	Symphonia SGR	4170	1.20	19.84	1.96	1.40
43.	UBI Pramerica SGR	31000	1.07	20.91	1.41	0.92
44.	Zenit SGR	361	1.26	−10.73	−2.16	2.41
	Total	*4540*	*0.91*	*10.75*	*2.31*	*1.58*

The table shows the descriptive statistics of the sample being studied. AuM are the assets under management. Revenues/AuM is the ratio between gross revenues and the assets under management. Income/Revenues is the ratio between operating income and gross revenues. Operating leverage is the level of operating leverage calculated as Net revenues/Operating Income

Table 7.4 Variables included in the study

	Variables	*Name*	*Measurement*
Firm-specific variables	Operating efficiency (1)	OPE1	(Revenues/Asset Under Management)
	Operating efficiency (2)	OPE2	(Operating Income/Gross Revenues)
	Operating efficiency (3)	OPE3	(Net Revenues/Operating Income)
	Profitability (ROE%)	PROF	(Net Income/Total Equity)
	Size	SIZE	(Natural Logarithm of AuM)
	Intangibles ratio	INT	(Intangibles/Total Assets)
Market variables	Δ% Vix Index	MKT 1	% variation rate of Vix Index
	Δ% Barclays Global Bond Index	MKT 2	% variation rate of Barclays Global Bond Index
	Δ% MSCI Global Equity Index	MKT 3	% variation rate of MSCI Global Equity Index
Dummy variable	Dummy Bank	DUMMY	The dummy takes on the value of 1 if the asset manager is of bank enactment, 0 otherwise

The table defines the variables included in the study

and Kim 2002), highlighting that firms that are more efficient or those that generate higher levels of revenues from their assets subtend a lower level of betas, given the specific business model of asset managers, in line with the study of Scherer (2012), we expect a positive relationship between this measurement and market betas. In fact, consistently with our *Hypothesis 1* we suppose that the systematic risk exposure of asset managers which is embedded within the fee generation process positively affects the market risk of the companies.

The second and the third variables of operating efficiency included in our study measure, on the one hand, the weight of the fixed costs on the whole cost structure by exploiting the theoretical model outlined in the previous section and, on the other hand, the ability of asset managers to transform the revenues in earnings as supported in the valuation model of Huberman (2004).

Even in this case, consistent with our *H2* the expected sign is positive: the more the asset manager is effective in generating earnings starting from the revenues, the greater is the operative risk (higher level of fixed to variables costs) and consequently the higher are the market betas.

We also investigate the role of profitability, measured by the return on equity (ROE). Logue and Merville (1972) underline that a higher level of profits improves the financial stability and consequently diminishes the market risk exposure of the firms; however, the study of Borde et al. (1994) which focuses on the peculiar case of insurance companies highlights a positive relationship between profitability and betas, suggesting that in the financial industry a higher value of profits subtend a higher level of risk taken into business. Relying on this study and given the particular profitability–risk profile that characterizes the asset management industry, we expect a positive relationship between ROE and market betas.

In line with previous studies focused on firms' systematic risk determinants, we include the size factor of asset managers captured by the natural logarithm of the assets under management. The literature has demonstrated that size is a key factor for the explanation of market risk, although the sign is ambiguous. On the one hand, larger institutions might benefit from competitive advantages embedding a lower level of market risk (Ben-Zion and Shalit 1975; Wessels and Titman 1988) while, on the other hand, especially in financial institutions, larger firms are more exposed to specific risk profiles as operating and exchange rate risks as well as market risk due to the negative effects of common financial distress (Vander Vennet et al. 2005). Consistently with this theory we expect the larger asset managers to present a higher level of systematic risk exposure, hence predicting a positive relationship between firm size and market betas.

The sixth explanatory variable includes the role of the intangibles, in line with the idea that, asset managers being basically like an empty box because the assets managed are diverse entities, goodwill and other intangibles assets have a direct impact on market risk, especially in relation to their link with growth opportunities and the transparency of balance sheets (Di Biase and D'Apolito 2012).

Moreover, we include three market variables: the variation rate of the Vix Index which reflects the degree of volatility of the market; the variation rate of the MSCI Global Equity Index; and the Barclays Global Bond Index, which represents a proxy of the equity and bond benchmark of asset managers.

Finally, with the aim of investigating such relationships across different typologies of firms we include a dummy variable "*bank dummy*" which takes on the value of 1 if the asset manager is of bank enactment and 0

Table 7.5 Descriptive statistics of the variables

Variables	*Symbol*	*Mean (%)*	*Median (%)*	*Standard deviation (%)*
Operating efficiency (1)	OPE1	1.37	0.92	2.54
Operating efficiency (2)	OPE2	15.36	16.61	22.03
Operating efficiency (3)	OPE3	2.47	2.26	22.16
Profitability	PROF	101.67	39.43	223.02
Size	SIZE	22.17	22.24	1.92
Intangibles ratio	INT	3.04	0.42	7.62
Δ% Vix Index	MKT1	0.28	14.38	5.72
Δ% Barclays Global Bond Index	MKT2	−1.44	19.29	8.82
Δ% MSCI Global Equity Index	MKT3	6.82	15.53	17.28

The table provides the descriptive statistics of the variables included in the regression model

otherwise. In this way we shed light on the recent phenomenon of incorporation of asset managers within structured bank groups.

Table 7.5 shows the descriptive statistics of the explanatory variables selected in our study.

Table 7.6 presents the Pearson pairwise correlations among the variables selected in our study.

The correlations among explanatory variables are generally low, lower than 0.4, which is considered the limit value above which multicollinearity problems become important (Kennedy 1985).

The determinants of equity betas in the Italian asset management industry are tested running the following linear regression model:

$$Beta_{jt} = \alpha + \gamma_1 OPE_{jt} + \gamma_2 PROF_{jt} + \gamma_3 SIZE_{jt} + \gamma_4 INT_{jt} + \gamma_4 MKT_{jt} + \theta_t + \varepsilon_t \quad (7.9)$$

where for firm $j = 1$ to N and time $t = 1$ to T, Beta are the betas estimated as outlined in Sect. 7.3.1.; OPE are the three configurations of operating efficiency as defined in the previous paragraph and in Table 7.4; PROF is the return on equity (ROE); Size is the natural logarithm of total assets under management, INT is the ratio between intangible assets and total assets; MKT are the three market variables as specified in the previous paragraph and in Table 7.4; θ_t are the time-fixed effects. Finally, we use the Modified-Wald test, which indicates the presence of cross-sectional heteroscedasticity. Therefore, we estimate Eq. (7.9) using Huber–White sandwich estimators in order to obtain standard errors that are robust to cross-sectional heteroscedasticity and within panel correlation.

Table 7.6 Pearson pairwise correlations

Variables	*OPE1*	*OPE2*	*OPE3*	*PROF*	*SIZE*	*INT*	*VIX*	*EQUITY*	*BOND*
OPE1	1.000								
OPE2	−0.013	1.000							
OPE3	−0.002	0.028	1.000						
PROF	−0.009	0.356	−0.009	1.000					
SIZE	−0.447	0.359	−0.026	0.231	1.000				
INT	−0.032	−0.046	−0.011	−0.054	0.000	1.000			
VIX	0.004	−0.129	0.073	−0.041	−0.010	0.014	1.000		
EQUITY	0.044	0.149	−0.094	0.102	0.051	0.040	−0.231	1.000	
BOND	0.012	0.175	−0.101	0.039	0.037	0.018	−0.814	0.353	1.000

The table provides the Pearson pairwise correlations among the explanatory variables

7.4 Empirical Results

In Table 7.7 we present the baseline results of Eq. (7.9). We choose fixed effects (FE) relative to random effects (RE) after the Hausman test.

In the first column of each model we consider only firm-specific variables while in the second we add market variables. The FE models show a significant positive relation between asset managers' market risk and the ratio between gross revenues and assets under management (OPE1). Thus, we find confirmation of *H2*, which is consistent with the valuation pattern proposed by Joenväära and Scherer (2017), and it supports the idea that the revenues of asset managers carry market risk of investments and positively impact on the systematic risk of firms, hence subtending a positive risk–return relationship (Borde et al. 1994; Scherer 2012).

We also find a significant and positive relationship between OPE2, that is the ratio between operating income and gross revenues, and market risk. Similarly, our results show a positive relationship between the operational leverage (OPE3), measured by the ratio between net revenues and operating income with asset managers' betas. The sign is positive, as expected; in fact, the higher the operational leverage, the greater is the impact of the fixed costs, relative to the contribution margin, hence subtending a higher level of operational risk and therefore of betas.

These results provide confirmation about our *H1* hypothesis suggesting that the costs structure is a crucial determinant of the risk perceived by the market. In fact, relying on Huberman's (2004) model, the ability of the asset manager to transform the revenues into earnings is a determinant variable for the correct pricing of the systematic risk exposure of the asset manager, and is therefore of value.

Our baseline results do not report a significant correlation between profitability (ROE) and betas, while the impact of the size, measured by the natural logarithm of AuM is negative. Although Bowman (1979) demonstrated the insistence of a theoretical relationship between market betas and firm size contrary to our expectations, our results are consistent with the vein of empirical literature which shows a negative relationship between size and systematic risk exposure (*see* Melicher 1974; Kim et al. 2002). Thus, despite Vander Vennet (2005) and Di Biase and D'Apolito (2012) showing a strong positive relationship between size and market betas in the financial sector, our results point in a different direction: larger asset managers might benefit from economies of scale and have the tendency to diversify the business more efficiently compared to small asset

Table 7.7 Determinants of equity betas—Baseline results

Variables	*Modell*	*Model 2*	*Model 3*	*Model 4*	*Model 5*	*Model 6*
Operating efficiency (1)	11.87***	10.19***				
	(3.441)	(2.993)				
Operating efficiency (2)			6.228***	5.434***		
			(0.514)	(0.607)		
Operating efficiency (3)					0.000789**	0.00215***
					(0.00103)	(0.000806)
Profitability	0.0785	0.0711	−0.0468	0.0147	0.0802	0.0714
	(0.0634)	(0.0565)	(0.0394)	(0.0136)	(0.0646)	(0.0569)
Size	−0.496***	−0.453***	−0.284***	−0.207***	−0.445***	−0.399***
	(0.110)	(0.112)	(0.0755)	(0.0517)	(0.123)	(0.123)
Intangibles ratio	0.0683	−0.219	−0.893	−0.838*	0.172	−0.119
	(1.167)	(0.863)	(0.673)	(0.463)	(1.143)	(0.796)
Δ% Vix Index		0.0183**		0.00828*		0.0176**
		(0.00855)		(0.00424)		(0.00830)
Δ% Barclays Global Bond Index		0.0117***		0.000957		0.0119***
		(0.00375)		(0.00173)		(0.00370)
Δ% MSCI Global Equity Index		0.0108***		0.00667***		0.0115***
		(0.00248)		(0.00157)		(0.00249)
Bank Dummy		0.285		0.0931		0.307
		(0.278)		(0.155)		(0.302)
Observations	309	309	309	309	307	307
Fixed Effects	Y	Y	Y	Y	Y	Y
Time-Fixed effects	Y	Y	Y	Y	Y	Y
R-Squared within	0.219	0.220	0.710	0.777	0.127	0.217
R-Squared between	0.673	0.685	0.804	0.848	0.544	0.605
R-Squared overall	0.423	0.430	0.696	0.750	0.320	0.383

This table shows the estimation of Eq. (7.8). See Table 7.4 for the definition of explanatory variables. Modified Wald test is a test of homoscedasticity. Robust standard errors are clustered at firm level and reported in brackets. *, ** and *** indicate statistical significance at 10%, 5% and 1% levels respectively management firms. Therefore, they are less exposed to default risk showing a lower level of market betas.

Moreover, we do not find a significant statistical relationship between intangibles and market betas. Turning on our market variables, our result show a strong positive relationship between the VIX index and betas as expected. This result suggests that the higher the volatility of the markets, the higher is the level of systematic risk exposure the asset managers face.

Finally, the results of our benchmark measures predictably show a strong positive relationship between the Bond and Equity indexes and market betas.

The bank dummy does not assume statistical significance, suggesting that it cannot subsist when there is considerable difference in the systematic risk exposure of asset managers of bank enactment.

The relationship between firm-specific variables and market betas may be endogenous, therefore, in order to deal with endogeneity concerns we run an instrumental variable regression with GMM estimator and instrumented firm-specific variables, using as instruments their own lagged values (Roberts and Whited 2012; Wooldridge 2015). The results are presented in Table 7.8.

The endogeneity issue appears to be absent; indeed, the meaningfulness of our baseline results remains valid.

7.5 Value Drivers in the Italian Asset Management Industry: Implications of Systemic Risk Exposures

Which are the main determinants of the market betas in the Italian asset management industry? To the best of our knowledge this paper is the first which addresses this question. Based on a sample of 44 Italian asset managers from 2006 to 2016, this study investigates the market beta determinants in the Italian asset management industry.

We focus primarily on the role of the operating efficiency as a crucial factor for the correct pricing of the systematic risk exposure of asset managers. In this regard we exploit three different measures of operational risk with the aim of evaluating the impact of both the ability of the asset manager to generate revenues from its assets under management and the cost structure on betas. Our empirical findings confirm our

Table 7.8 Instrumental Variable (IV) regression with GMM estimator

Variables	*Model 1*	*Model 2*	*Model 3*
Operating efficiency (1) *(Inst)*	11.83*** (2.273)		
Operating efficiency (2) *(Inst)*		3.170*** (0.500)	
Operating efficiency (3) *(Inst)*			0.00592** (0.00089)
Profitability (ROE%) *(Inst)*	0.355 (0.166)	0.243 (0.125)	0.373 (0.684)
Size *(Inst)*	−0.228*** (0.0712)	−0.0768 (0.0592)	−0.171** (0.0701)
Intangibles ratio *(Inst)*	0.632 (0.773)	0.880 (0.700)	0.629 (0.772)
Δ% Vix Index	0.00957 (0.00795)	0.0129** (0.00566)	0.0102 (0.00823)
Δ% Barclays Global Bond Index	0.00494*** (0.00187)	0.00378** (0.00165)	0.00636*** (0.00210)
Δ% MSCI Global Equity Index	0.00759*** (0.00287)	0.00547** (0.00220)	0.00913*** (0.00328)
Bank Dummy	−0.218 (0.149)	−0.264 (0.162)	−0.243 (0.167)
Observations	270	270	266
R-Squared	0.201	0.542	0.111
Sargan statistic	4.905 (0.297)	0.856 (0.930)	4.041 (0.400)
Hansen J statistic	4.014 (0.645)	5.285 (0.508)	3.778 (0.706)

This table shows the estimation of Instrumental Variable regression of formula (7.8) with GMM estimator. See Table 7.4 for the definition of the explanatory variables. *, ** and *** indicate statistical significance at the 10%, 5% and 1% level respectively. Robust standard errors are clustered at firm level and presented within parentheses

hypotheses and highlight that all the measures of operating efficiency are positively linked with market betas. As a result, given that the market risk of investments is carried into the revenue's generation process, we first argue that fees have a positive impact on firms' betas and second that a higher level of fixed-to-variable costs increases its exposure to systematic risk, as expected. Moreover, we provide empirical evidence that larger asset managers exhibit a lower level of betas, hence subtending lower exposure to market risk. Our findings are strengthened through different regression models and specifications.

Results from our analysis have important managerial and practical implications. First, since the market risk exposure is not currently hedged by asset managers, they necessarily need to rethink the risk management function, focusing on the hedging of the market risk and monitoring their risk fees, which negatively affect the systematic risk exposure of the company.

Therefore, firms need to evaluate the impact of the product strategy, the selected benchmark as well as the contract proposal on market risks.

From a shareholder's perspective this is startling; in fact, in this way they cannot properly select asset managers as their source of non-diversifiable risk exposure.

In addition, a further factor that should encourage asset managers to deal with the market risk exposure with attention concerns the macro-economic context and, in particular, the political uncertainties which increase the volatility in the market, impacting both bond and equity markets.

Second, from an operational point of view, it becomes essential for asset managers to act on the cost structure, targeting a significant containment of the fixed costs component, which represents a primary factor of market risk exposure. According to Barbagallo (2018) this is realizable only through a shift towards more value-added products and activities, in order to improve the operative efficiency and generate for clients a more effective risk–return profile. This results in a lower level of costs both for firms and clients, even in light of the latest introduction of the Mifid 2 regulatory framework, which establishes precise boundaries for the design and distribution of the investment products, putting in the spotlight transparency and protection towards investors. Thus, in such a context a crucial role is played by the potential disruptive technology (e.g. fintech), which might lead to a significant rationalization of the cost structure of asset managers as this might significantly impact on the different phases of the productive process: from the product design to the communication between the counterparts.

Acknowledgements We thank Riccardo Morassut and Assogestioni for providing Italian asset managers with financial data.

Appendix

Moschetta (2001) expresses the operating income of a generic firm as

$$OI = Q \cdot \left(P^{*} - Cvu^{*}\right) - FC$$

where P^* and Cvu^* are the medium price of selling and the unitary costs incurred by the firm respectively. Thus, the covariance of the operating income with the market, by exploiting the properties of the covariance, can be expressed as follows:

$$\frac{\left(P* - Cvu*\right)}{P*} \cdot \text{cov}\left[\frac{\text{sales}}{V_U}; rm\right]$$

The unlevered beta can be expressed as

$$\beta_U = \frac{\left(P* - Cvu*\right)}{P*} \cdot \frac{\text{cov}\left[\frac{\text{sales}}{V_U}; rm\right]}{\sigma^2 rm} = \%CM \cdot \frac{\text{COV}\left[\frac{\text{sales}}{V_U}; rm\right]}{\sigma^2 rm}$$

where %CM is the ratio between the contribution margin and total sales. $\left(\text{COV}\left[\left(\frac{\text{sales}}{V_U}\right); rm\right]\right) / \left(\sigma^2 rm\right)$ is the covariance index of the cyclicity of the revenues (CICR).

In the specific case of asset managers, the operating income can be expressed as

$$\text{Operating Income} = \left(\text{revenues}_{+} - \text{revenues}_{-}\right) - \text{fixed costs}$$

Therefore, $(P* - Cvu*)/P*$ in the specific case of asset management firms can be expressed as

$$\frac{\text{Net Revenues}}{\text{Operating Income}} \cdot \frac{\text{Operating Income}}{\text{Gross Revenues}}$$

- Net Revenues/Operating Income is the degree of *operational leverage*.
- Operating Income/Gross Revenues is the ratio between the operating income as defined earlier, and gross revenues (ROS).

Finally, the unlevered beta is as follows:

$$\beta_U = \text{Operational Leverage} \cdot \text{ROS} \cdot \text{CIC}$$

References

Agusman, A., G.S. Monroe, D. Gasbarro, and J.K. Zumwalt. 2008. Accounting and Capital Market Measure of Risk: Evidence from Asian Banks During 1998–2003. *Journal of Banking & Finance* 32 (4): 480–488.

Barbagallo, C. 2018. L'industria del risparmio gestito: la crescita degli anni recenti e le sfide del futuro AFB-Bocconi Academy Opening Conference Business Transformation in Asset/Wealth Management.

Barth, J.R., G. Caprio Jr., and R. Levine. 2001. Banking Systems Around the Globe: Do Regulations and Ownership Affect Performance and Stability? In *Prudential Supervision: What Works and What Doesn't*, ed. Frederic S. Mishkin. Chicago: University of Chicago Press.

Barth, J.R., G. Caprio, and R. Levine. 2004. Bank Regulation and Supervision: What Works Best? *Journal of Financial Intermediation* 13: 205–248.

Beaver, W., P. Kettler, and M. Scholes. 1970. The Association between Market Determined and Accounting Determined Risk Measures. *The Accounting Review* 45 (4): 654–682.

Beltrame, F., and D. Previtali. 2016. *Valuing Banks: A New Corporate Finance Approach*. Palgrave Macmillan Studies in Banking and Financial Institutions.

Beltrame, F., A. Sclip, and D. Previtali. 2018. Systematic Risk and Banks Leverage: The Role of Asset Quality. *Finance Research Letters* 27: 113–117.

Ben-Zion, U., and S.S. Shalit. 1975. Size, Leverage, and Dividend Record as Determinants of Equity Risk. *The Journal of Finance* 30 (4): 1015–1026.

Berk, J., and R.C. Green. 2004. Mutual Fund and Performance in Rational Markets. In *13th Annual Utah Winter Finance Conference.*

Borde, S.F., K. Chambliss, and J. Madura. 1994. Explaining Variation in Risk Across Insurance Companies. *Journal of Financial Services Research* 8 (3): 177–191.

Bowman, R.G. 1979. The Theoretical Relationship between Systematic Risk and Financial (Accounting) Variables. *The Journal of Finance* 34 (3): 617–630.

Breen, J., and M. Lerner. 1973. Corporate Financial Strategies and Market Measures of Risk and Return. *The Journal of Finance* 28 (2): 339–351.

Damodaran, A. 2013. Valuing Financial Service Firms. *Journal of Financial Perspectives* 1 (1): 59–74.

Das, S., and A.N.R. Sy. 2012. How Risky are Banks' Risk Weighted Assets? Evidence from the Financial Crisis. IMF working paper/12/36.

Dewatripont, M., and J. Tirole. 1994. A Theory of Debt and Equity: Diversity of Securities and Manager-Shareholder Congruence. *The Quarterly Journal of Economics* 109 (4): 1027–1054.

Di Biase, P., and E. D'Apolito. 2012. The Determinants of Systematic Risk in the Italian Banking System: A Cross-Sectional Time Series Analysis. *International Journal of Economics and Finance* 4 (11): 152–164.

Diamond, D.W., and R. Rajan. 2000. A Theory on Bank Capital. *Journal of Finance* 55: 2431–2465.

EFAMA. 2018. Asset Management in Europe: An Overview of the Asset Management Industry. 10th Edition Facts and Figures, September.

Floreani, J., M. Polato, A. Paltrinieri, and F. Pichler. 2015. Credit Quality, Bank Provisioning and Systematic Risk in Banking Business. In *Bank Risk, Governance and Regulation*, 1–34. Springer.

Gropp, R., T. Mosk, S. Ongena, and C. Wix. 2016. Bank Response to Higher Capital Requirements: Evidence from a Quasi-natural Experiment. SAFE Working Paper, Vol.156, Goethe University Frankfurt, SAFE—Sustainable Architecture for Finance in Europe, Frankfurt a.M.

Gu, Z., and H. Kim. 2002. Determinants of Restaurant Systematic Risk: A Re-examination. *The Journal of Hospitality Financial Management* 10 (1): 1–13.

Huberman, G. 2004. What is the NPV of Expected Future Profits of Money Managers? Working Paper, Columbia University.

Hull, J. 2007. *Risk Management and Financial Institutions.* Prentice Hall.

International Monetary Fund. 2015. *The Asset Management Industry and Financial Stability.* Global Financial Stability Report: Navigating Monetary Policy Challenges and Managing Risks. April.

Jensen, M.C. 1984. Agency Costs of Free Cash Flow, Corporate Finance, and Takeovers. *American Economic Reviews* 76: 323–329.

Joenväära, J., and B. Scherer. 2017. A Note on the Valuation of Asset Management Firms. *Financial Markets and Portfolio Management* 31 (2): 181–199.

Kashyap, A.K., J.C. Stein, and S. Hanson. 2010. *An Analysis of the Impact of Substantially Heightened' Capital Requirements on Large Financial Institutions.* Mimeo: Booth School of Business, University of Chicago.

Kennedy, P. 1985. *A Guide to Econometrics.* 2nd ed. Cambridge: The MIT Press.

Kim, H., Z. Gu, and A.S. Mattila. 2002. Hotel Real Estate Investment Trusts' Risk Features and Beta Determinants. *Journal of Hospitality &Tourism Research* 26 (2): 138–154.

Laeven, L., and R. Levine. 2008. Bank Governance, Regulation and Risk Taking. *Journal of Financial Economics* 93 (2): 259–275.

Landi, A., and V. Venturelli. 2017. Global Trend in Asset Management and Bank Business Models. *Bancaria*, 5.

Logue, L., and J. Merville. 1972. Financial Policy and Market Expectations. *Financial Management* 1 (3): 37–44.

Massari, M., G. Gianfrate, and L. Zanetti. 2014. *The Valuation of Financial Companies, Tools and Techniques to Value Banks, Insurance Companies and Other Financial Institutions*, Wiley Finance Series. Great Britain: Wiley.

Mehran, H., and A. Thakor. 2011. Bank Capital and Value in the Cross-Section. *The Review of Financial Studies* 24 (4): 1019–1067.

Melicher, R.W. 1974. Financial Factors Which Influence Beta Variations Within an Homogeneous Industry Environment. *The Journal of Financial and Quantitative Analysis* 9 (2): 231–241.

Miles, D., J. Yang, and G. Marcheggiano. 2013. Optimal Bank Capital. *The Economic Journal* 123 (567): 1–37.

Milne, A., and T. Jokipii. 2011. Bank Capital Buffer and Risk Adjustment Decisions. *Journal of Financial Stability* 7: 165–178.

Modigliani, F., and M.H. Miller. 1958. The Cost of Capital, Corporation Finance and the Theory of Investment. *The American Economic Review* 48 (3): 261–297.

Moschetta, E. 2001. Rischio operativo e Beta aziendale: la ciclicità del mercato e l'impatto dei costi fissi. *La valutazione Aziendale*. 23 (1): 27–33.

Pastor, L., R. Stambaugh, and L. Taylor. 2015. Scale and Skill in Active Management. *Journal of Financial Economics* 116 (1): 23–45.

Patel, R.C., and R.A. Olsen. 1984. Financial Determinants of Systematic Risk in Real Estate Investment Trusts. *Journal of Business Research* 12 (4): 481–491.

Perold, A.F. 2004. The Capital Asset Pricing Model. *Journal of Economic Perspectives* 18 (3): 3–24.

PWC. 2017. Asset & Wealth Management Revolution: Embracing Exponential Change. Report.

Roberts, M.R., and T.M. Whited. 2012. Endogeneity in Empirical Corporate Finance. Working paper.

Rochet, J.C. 1992. Capital Requirements and the Behaviour of Commercial Banks. *European Economic Review* 36: 1137–1170.

Rosenberg, B., and P.R. Perry. 1978. The Fundamental Determinants of Risk in Banking. NBER Working Paper, 265.

Schall, L.D. 1972. Asset Valuation, Firm Investment, and Firm Diversification. *The Journal of Business* 45 (1): 11–28.

Scherer, B. 2012. Market Risks in Asset Management Companies. *Quantitative Finance* 12 (10): 1547–1556.

Schlegel, D. 2015. *Cost-of-Capital in Managerial Finance, An Examination of Practices in the German Real Economy Sector*. Springer.

Sharpe, W. 1964. Capital Asset Prices: A Theory of Market Equilibrium Under Conditions of Risk. *The Journal of Finance* 19 (3): 425–442.

Shrieves, R.E., and D. Dahl. 1992. The Relationship between Risk and Capital in Commercial Banks. *Journal of Banking and Finance* 16 (2): 439–457.

Vander Vennet, R., L. Baele, and O. De Jonghe. 2005. Determinants of Systematic and Idiosyncratic Banking Risk in Europe. Working paper, Ghent University.

Walter, I. 2016. *The Industrial Organization of the Global Asset Management Business*. CFA Institute Research Foundation.

Watson, D., and A. Head. 2010. *Corporate Finance. Principles and Practice*. Harlow: Financial Times/Prentice Hall.

Wessels, R., and S. Titman. 1988. The Determinants of Capital Structure Choice. *The Journal of Finance* 43 (1): 1–19.

Wooldridge, J.M. 2015. *Introductory Econometrics: A Modern Approach*. South-Western Pub.

CHAPTER 8

Signaling Success Factors in Alternative Entrepreneurial Finance

Francesca Battaglia, Francesco Busato, and Maria Manganiello

8.1 Introduction

During a hearing of the Committee on Economic and Monetary Affairs of the European Parliament, Mario Draghi, President of the European Central Bank, in his introductory statement,[1] addressed the hot topics of Fintech and Block chain technology (Distributed Ledger Technology or DLT).

[1] https://www.ecb.europa.eu/press/key/date/2017/html/ecb.sp170529.en.html.

F. Battaglia
Department of Management Studies and Quantitative Methods, University of Naples "Parthenope", Naples, Italy
e-mail: francesca.battaglia@uniparthenope.it

F. Busato • M. Manganiello (✉)
Department of Economic and Legal Studies, University of Naples "Parthenope", Naples, Italy
e-mail: busato@uniparthenope.it; maria.manganiello@uniparthenope.it

C. Cruciani et al. (eds.), *Banking and Beyond*, Palgrave Macmillan Studies in Banking and Financial Institutions,
https://doi.org/10.1007/978-3-030-45752-5_8

While affirming his view that Fintech can provide more efficient and effective services for both individuals and businesses, Draghi stated that the rise of alternative finance may open up a host of concerns and "it is essential to assess and adapt the prudential framework to cater for the increased role of non-banks and financial innovation, in order to ensure a level playing field for both new and existing players and provide supervisors with adequate tools to address new risks".

It is clear that there is a widespread consensus on how new technologies are modifying entrepreneurial finance operations and on the huge impact they have on the financial services industry, by creating new challenges and new opportunities for entrepreneurs to raise seed capital.

This paper adds to prior studies on the determinants of funding success in the equity crowdfunding campaigns, by providing new evidence on the quality signal of the entrepreneur's social capital, the disclosure of financial information about start-ups and the share of equity retained by founders through a cross-platform analysis of the Italian scenario between January 2014 and November 2018. We specify that a common feature of previous research is that the data typically come from just one platform, while we explore all the Italian authorized equity crowdfunding platforms from the CONSOB registry, for which data are available. To our knowledge, only Piva and Rossi-Lamastra (2018) focus on the Italian context over the period 2010–2014 by analyzing the impact of human capital on entrepreneurs' success in equity crowdfunding through the platform SiamoSoci.[2]

Our results suggest that the disclosure of financial information, the share of equity retained by entrepreneurs and their social capital have a positive and significant impact on funding success and are interpreted as quality signals of crowdfunding campaigns by external investors.

The entrepreneur's social capital plays a key role in the setting of crowdfunding: it can reduce information asymmetries between entrepreneurs and investors, particularly severe in the equity crowdfunding context, by

[2] SiamoSoci was the first equity crowdfunding platform created in Italy. More than 2 years after its establishment, the Consob Regulation no. 18592 entered into force. This regulation included a set of rules and requisites for the managers of equity crowdfunding platforms aimed at reducing operational and legal risks and the risk of litigation and fraud. The regulation also established a register where platforms had to be included to be allowed to use the label "equity crowdfunding platforms". In light of the new Italian regulation, SiamoSoci could not use the label equity crowdfunding platform anymore and in 2014, it started changing its activity to become a marketplace for entrepreneurs searching funds for their activities, by creating the platform "Mamacrowd".

helping entrepreneurs to find a way to signal the quality of their project in order to receive financing and to close a crowdfunding campaign successfully.

Consequently, the recent literature on success factors for crowdfunding focuses on the role of investors' and proponents' social networks (Bollaert et al. 2019; Hervé et al. 2019; Ordanini et al. 2011; Mollick 2014; Colombo et al. 2015; Kromidha and Robson 2016; Vismara 2016; Angerer et al. 2017; Polzin et al. 2018). Some authors (Piva and Rossi-Lamastra 2018; Vismara 2016; Ahlers et al. 2015; Mollick 2014; Lin et al. 2013; Ordanini et al. 2011) find that a larger number of entrepreneurs' social network connections increases the probability of fundraising success. By focusing on reward and donation-based crowdfunding platforms, Colombo et al. (2015), Belleflamme et al. (2014), Mollick (2014) and Ordanini et al. (2011) show that the relationship between proponents' social capital and project outcome is positive, and by underlying that social network size should play a role in determining the success of projects. Vismara (2016) analyzes professional connections (e.g., LinkedIn), while other authors (Mollick 2014) use friendship connections (e.g., Facebook and Twitter). However, this is a field still relatively unexplored, as only some researchers (Piva and Rossi-Lamastra 2018; Lukkarinen et al. 2016; Vismara 2016; Ahlers et al. 2015) focus on the signals sent by projects' proponent to investors in the equity crowdfunding context.

The disclosure of financial information about start-ups (Epstein and Schneider 2008; Agrawal et al. 2013; Ahlers et al. 2015; Lukkarinen et al. 2016; Polzin et al. 2018) is an opportunity to provide financial information on the project and to include a disclaimer in the offering document describing the risks in detail. A high flow of financial information could potentially reduce the information asymmetry related to the project: investors have more financial knowledge to understand the key features, benefits and risks involved in the project.

Existing literature indicates that external investors consider the disclosure of financial information as a positive quality signal of the campaign success in equity and rewards-based crowdfunding. Ahlers et al. (2015) find that equity crowdfunding campaigns that do not provide financial forecasts or information collect significantly less funding. Also Mollick (2014) points out that the lack of financial information decreases the amount raised in rewards-based crowdfunding. Moreover, Blumberg and Letterie (2007) argue that the disclosure of information about financials and about the risk of the project can also reduce the perceived risk of moral hazard.

Also the entrepreneurs' willingness to invest in their own projects is perceived as a quality signal of the project itself (Block et al. 2018; Günther et al. 2018; Angerer et al. 2017; Piva and Rossi-Lamastra 2018; Vismara 2016; Hornuf and Neuenkirch 2017; Lukkarinen et al. 2016; Ralcheva and Roosenboom 2016; Vismara 2016; Vulkan et al. 2016; Agrawal et al. 2015; Ahlers et al. 2015); we turn to analyze the signaling role played toward external investors by the share of equity retained by founders. In this context, entrepreneurs can signal unobservable characteristics of their start-up by the amount of equity offered. The rationale is that it is costly for owners of low-quality firms to retain high proportions of equity because of high costs generated by the loss of wealth in the future: entrepreneurs, who are not confident in their company's project, tend to sell a higher amount of equity to investors (Barbi and Mattioli 2019; Block et al. 2018; Ralcheva and Roosenboom 2016; Vismara 2016; Ahlers et al. 2015; Busenitz et al. 2005). For this reason, a larger (lower) percentage of equity retained (offered) by founders should potentially increase (decrease) the investors' subscription to the offers and the probability of the campaign success. Hence, we expect that the share of equity retained by founders is able to reduce the information asymmetries and to drive entrepreneurs toward success in equity crowdfunding.

According to the signaling theory in the equity crowdfunding context, our testable hypotheses about the impact of our key variables (i.e., financial information, share of equity offered by founders and size of their social connections) on the project outcome are the following:

H1: The disclosure of financial information positively affects the probability of the campaign success.

H2: A lower (higher) percentage of equity offered (retained) by founders negatively (positively) affects the probability of the campaign success.

H3: A larger number of founders' social connections positively affect the probability of the campaign success.

To this end, we collect information about 191 successful and unsuccessful equity crowdfunding campaigns, over the period January 2014 to November 2018, posted on the main Italian platforms, namely Action Crowd, BackToWork 24 (ex Equinvest), Cofyp, CrowdFundMe, Idea Crowdfunding, Investi-RE, Leonardo Equity, Mamacrowd, Muum Lab, Next Equity, StarsUp, Two-Hundred Crowd and We Are Starting.

We decide to focus on the Italian context for two reasons. First of all, Italy is the first country in Europe to have a specific discipline on equity crowdfunding (Law 221/2012 and CONSOB Regulation of 26 June 2013 n. 18592, as further amended in 2016 by the CONSOB decision n. 19520). Moreover, although the growth of the Italian crowdfunding markets is marginal compared to that in countries like the United States or the United Kingdom, in recent years it has experienced a very strong increase: Crowdfunding Buzz shows that in 2018 the Italian equity crowdfunding platforms collected more than three times the amount gathered in 2017, with more than twice the number of successful campaigns. The overall volumes were well above expectations: total fundraising exceeded € 36 million in 2018 (11.7 million in 2017) and 114 companies were financed (50 in 2017). The number of investors also tripled, from around 3300 in 2017 to almost 9500 in 2018.

Consistently with previous studies (e.g., Colombo et al. 2015; Ahlers et al. 2015; Vismara 2016), we measure the campaign success (our dependent variable) by using the number of investors and the funding amount at the end of each campaign.

Following Ahlers et al. (2015) and Vismara (2016), we first run a Tobit regression for the amount of capital raised from a project and a negative binomial regression for the number of investors, and then we use year- and platform-fixed effects to account for unobserved heterogeneity between the projects' attractiveness due to, for example, varying degree of crowdfunding legitimacy over time or differing growth potentials between platforms. Robust standard errors are clustered at industry level.

As robustness checks, we first run a logistic regression by using a dichotomous measure of campaign success, equal to 1 for campaigns reaching or exceeding their capital (Ahlers et al. 2015; Colombo et al. 2015; Vismara 2016) and zero otherwise; second, because many of our variables have large positive outliers, to prevent extreme values from biasing the results of our study, without losing observations, we winsorize our variables at 2% and at 5%.

In line with previous research, we expect that founders' social capital, the share of retained equity by the entrepreneurs and the disclosure of financial information on the start-ups should increase the probability of fundraising success.

The rest of the paper is structured as follows. Section 8.2 describes our sample and introduces the variables used in the regression analyses. Section 8.3 reports our regression models and discusses the empirical results.

Section 8.4 shows the robustness checks. Conclusions are drawn in Sect. 8.5. Section 8.6 focuses on the limitations of our study by suggesting avenues for future research.

8.2 Sample and Variables

Our sample consists of 191 Italian equity crowdfunding campaigns posted in the period from January 2014 until November 2018. All data are gathered from the Italian platforms, where firms post their pitch, business plan and other documents. The list of Italian-authorized equity crowdfunding platforms is from the CONSOB registry. As of November 2018, there were 27 active platforms: Action Crowd, Back To Work 24, Club Deal, Cofyp, Concrete Investing, Crowd4capital, CrowdFundMe, Crowd Invest Italia, Ecomill, EuropaCrowd, Extrafunding, Fundera, House 4 crowd, Idea Crowdfunding, Investi-re, Leonardo equity, Life Seeder, Lita.co, Mamacrowd, Muum Lab, Next Equity, OpStart, Stars Up, The Best Equity, 200Crowd, Walliance, We are starting. Eleven of these platforms (Club Deal, Crowd4capital, Crowd Invest Italia, Ecomill, EuropaCrowd, Extrafunding, Fundera, Life Seeder, Lita.co, OpStart and The Best Equity) had no active campaigns at the collection date, while three of them (Concrete Investing, House 4 crowd and Walliance) are real estate crowdfunding platforms.

We collect data on the campaign outcomes, as well as different campaign and company characteristics at the time of the campaign. Table 8.1 reports the list of the investigated platforms. Table 8.2 provides an overview of the variables and their descriptions.

In our empirical analysis, we measure the campaign success (our dependent variable) through the number of investors (Number of Investors) and the funded amount at the end of each campaign (Amount Raised).

Alternatively, we look at the pitch success (Success), a dichotomous variable equal to 1 if the project reaches or exceeds its target capital. The amount raised is a more fine-tuned measure of success that depicts how close the pitch was to reaching its target. We also use the number of investors as a dependent variable because one of the main goals of crowdfunding is to accumulate a large number of backers. Table 8.3 shows that about 70% of the 191 pitches ended up being successful. The average project in our sample raised € 202,658.1 (154% raised) of its target amount and attracted 60 investors.

Table 8.1 Italian equity crowdfunding platforms

Platform	*Foundation year*	*Model*	*Sector*	*Status*
Action Crowd	2014	Equity	Generalist	Active
BackToWork (ex Equinvest)	2016	Equity	Generalist	Active
Cofyp	2016	Equity	Generalist	Active
CrowdFundMe	2015	Equity	Innovation	Active
Idea Crowdfunding	2017	Equity	Generalist	Active
Investi-RE	2014	Equity	Generalist	Active
Leonardo Equity	2018	Equity	Innovation	Active
Mamacrowd	2014	Equity	Generalist	Active
Muum Lab	2015	Equity	Generalist	Active
Next Equity	2015	Equity	Innovation	Active
StarsUp	2014	Equity	Generalist	Active
Two-Hundred – 200 Crowd	2015	Equity	Generalist	Active
We Are Starting	2015	Equity	Generalist	Active

Table 8.2 Variable definitions

Variable name	*Description*
	Dependent variables
Success	Dummy variable equal to 1, for campaigns reaching or exceeding their capital, and 0 otherwise
Amount raised (€)	The total amount raised at the end of the campaign
Number of investors	The number of investors at the end of the campaign
	Explanatory variables
Financial info	Dummy variable equal to 1 if financial information on the company is available on the platform, and 0 otherwise
Equity offered (%)	Percentage of equity offered
Social capital	Number of proponent's LinkedIn connections
	Control variables
Video	Duration of the video uploaded on the project page (measured in second)
Duration (days)	Duration of the campaign measured at the end of the pitch
Female founders	Dummy variable equal to 1, if the founder is a woman, and 0 otherwise
Female	Dummy variable equal to 1, if there is a female prevalence in the company, and 0 otherwise
Target capital (€)	Amount of target capital to be raised
Team qualification	Dummy variable equal to 1, if at least one of the team members hold high academic status, and 0 otherwise

This table shows the variables used in this paper, distinguishing by dependent explanatory and control variables

Table 8.3 Descriptive statistics

	Observation	*Mean Std. Dev.*		*Min*	*Max*
		Dependent variables			
Success	191	0.7068063	0.4564229	0	1
Amount raised	191	202,658.1	252,081.3	0	2,250,000
Number of investors	191	60.0226	75.21212	0	498
		Explanatory variables			
Financial info	191	0.548913	0.4989595	0	1
Equity offered	191	9.548308	12.02174	0.02	28.04
Social capital	191	267.4774	447.8383	1	3249
		Control variables			
Video	191	162.9249	82.21257	43	522
Duration	191	102.3782	58.61755	3	350
Female founders	191	0.35	0.5930227	0	2
Female	191	0.1213873	0.3275248	0	1
Target capital	191	149,886	122,474.2	18,000	710,000
Team qualification	191	0.3407821	0.4753017	0	1

This table shows the descriptive statistics for the sample of crowdfunding campaigns launched on the Italian platforms between January 2014 and the end of November 2018. ***Amount raised*** and ***Target capital*** are expressed in euros. ***Success***, ***Financial info***, ***Female Founders***, ***Female*** and ***Team qualification*** are binary variables that take the value of 1 if there is the presence of the qualitative attribute. ***Number of investors*** is expressed in absolute terms. ***Social capital*** is calculated as the average number of LinkedIn connections of all founders. ***Video*** is a variable that indicates the duration of the video uploaded on the project page and it is measured in seconds. ***Duration*** reports the duration of the campaign expressed in days. ***Equity offered*** is the percentage of equity offered

In order to test H1, H2 and H3, we use three explanatory variables: the disclosure of financial information about the start-up (Financial info), the equity offered (Equity offered) and the number of social network connections (Social Capital). To measure the effectiveness of the disclosure of financial information (Financial info), we check if it is explicitly mentioned in their campaign documents on the project page of the companies. The lack of availability of financial information, however, may discourage investors from pledging to the campaign. About 54% of the company made public financial information. The amount of equity offered (Equity offered) to investors is reported on the main page of each campaign. The average equity offered by companies in our sample equals about 10% and therefore about 90% of the equity is retained by the original owners of the firm. The social capital (Social capital) is calculated as the average number of the LinkedIn connections of all founders. The average entrepreneur in our sample has 267 LinkedIn connections.

We include a set of additional (control) variables in our analysis to account for other factors that might be driving success in equity-based crowdfunding. We control for campaign characteristics, such as the presence or the absence of a video on the project page (Video), the duration of the campaign (Duration) and the female presence in the start-up (Female). All start-ups posted on the platform feature rich content, including a video and the possibility to comment on their project. The presence of a product video may increase the campaign's success probability. For this reason, we include the duration of the video uploaded on the project page (measured in seconds). The duration of the video uploaded on the project page is, in mean, 163 seconds. Equity crowdfunding campaigns have a limited duration and so we control for the number of days elapsed between the launch and the conclusion of the crowdfunding campaign. The duration of the campaign ranges from 3 to 350 days, with an average of 102 days.

We take into account several company characteristics as the board composition of each start-up (Female Founders), which may positively influence investors' decisions. In mean, only 35% of founders are women and there is a low female presence in the companies (about 12%). We also control for the impact of a team members' education (Team qualification), because people who hold high academic status are more likely to get funded by venture capital investors. In our sample, about 35% of the team members have a high level of education.

In designing their pitch, entrepreneurs make choices regarding the amount they want to raise and the percentage shares they make available to investors in exchange. We, therefore, control for target amount (Target capital) in our analysis. Campaign goals tend to be higher on equity crowdfunding platforms (the average target amount in our sample is € 149,886 ranging between € 18,000 and € 710,000). Given that we might not have controlled for all relevant explanatory variables, in all empirical analyses, we first include year-fixed effects to capture the time of investments; second, we include platform-fixed effects to remove any time-invariant heterogeneity from the focal campaign. Tables 8.3 and 8.4 report, respectively, the summary statistics and the correlation matrix.

Table 8.4 Correlation matrix

#1 Success 1	*#1*	*#2*	*#3*	*#4*	*#5*	*#6*	*#7*	*#8*	*#9*	*#10*	*#11*	*#12*
#2 Amount Raised 0.4602	1											
#3 Number of Investors	0.4130	0.7026	1									
#4 Financial info 0.1210	0.0697	0.1341	1									
#5 Equity Offered −0.1084	−0.0355	−0.2306	−0.1889	1								
#6 Social capital 0.2042	0.1349	0.2382	0.0871	−0.1339	1							
#7 Video 0.0502	0.1395	−0.0210	0.1117	0.1614	−0.0354	1						
#8 Duration −0.2437	−0.0818	−0.2640	0.0101	0.1885	−0.1141	−0.190	1					
#9 Female Founders	−0.042	0.0142	0.023	−0.0378	0.0551	−0.1095	0.1364	−0.0558	1			
#10 Female −0.0167	−0.0118	−0.0791	0.0256	0.039	−0.1120	0.1400	−0.082	0.4035	1			
#11 Target capital −0.1568	0.3676	−0.0220	−0.0816	0.3567	0.0199	0.2093	0.2723	−0.0714	−0.0797	1		
#12 Team qualification	−0.0263	0.0454	0.0446	−0.0437	0.0289	0.1211	−0.0214	0.1746	0.0505	−0.1140	0.1071	1

The table shows the correlations between variables related to funded crowdfunding campaigns launched on the Italian platforms between January 2014 and the end of November 2018

We first conduct our analysis in a univariate setting by comparing successful and unsuccessful campaigns, in order to gain some initial insights into the dynamics of equity crowdfunding. After this, we turn to a more detailed multivariate analysis to account for the simultaneous effect of multiple drivers of success.

Table 8.5 presents the difference in means between successful and unsuccessful campaigns. This test provides the difference between two means (one of which is a value against which the mean of an observed variable is tested) of two groups. It allows us to state if there is a statistical difference between successful and unsuccessful projects.

Successful pitches raise 210% of their target and have 78 backers on average, while unsuccessful ones seem to fail by a large margin (17% raised) with only 18 backers on average. Successful campaigns are able to attract investors who pledge significantly higher amounts of funds (€ 277,182 as compared to € 23,001).

Concerning our independent variables, Table 8.5 shows that higher equity offerings negatively affect funding success. The original owners of successful pitches also retain significantly more equity. Moreover, successful companies are more often the ones that have more social network connections and that explicitly made public their financial information on the project page. These univariate results present initial evidence that signaling theory is crucial in the context of equity crowdfunding.

Table 8.5 Difference in means between successful and unsuccessful campaigns

	Successful	*Unsuccessful*	*Difference in means*
Amount raised	277,182.4	23,001.43	−25,4180.9***
Number of investors	78.10606	6.977778	−71.12828***
Equity offered	8.714143	11.57193	2.857787***
Social capital	318.5169	104.7027	−213.8142***
Financial info	0.5851852	0.4489796	−0.1362056*
Video	165.4365	156.1915	−9.245019
Duration	95.5748	132.1724	36.59761***
Female founders	0.3484848	0.3541667	0.0056818
Female	0.1181102	0.1304348	0.0123245
Target capital	137,507.5	179,505.9	41,998.36**
Team qualification	0.3333333	0.3617021	0.0283688

This table represents the difference in means between successful and unsuccessful campaigns. ***, ** and * denote statistical significance at the 1%, 5% and 10% level, respectively. See Table 8.1 for variable definitions

Considering the set of control variables, we observe that successful campaigns have lower targets and more often upload an exhaustive video on the project page (although the latter difference is not significant). Moreover, successful companies have a lower duration. The difference in means between successful and unsuccessful campaigns relating to the female presence in the company, to the female founders, and the level of education of team members doesn't seem to be significant.

8.3 Empirical Analysis and Results

Table 8.6 shows the results of the main econometric analyses with dependent variables measuring crowdfunding campaign success. Following Piva and Rossi-Lamastra (2018), we first run a Tobit regression for the amount of capital raised from a project (model 1) and then, following Ahlers et al. (2015) and Vismara (2016), we run a negative binomial regression (model 2), as the number of investors is measured as a count variable. Moreover, as a robustness check (see Sect. 8.4), we run a logistic regression by using a dichotomous measure of campaign success (model 3), equal to 1 for campaigns reaching or exceeding their capital (Ahlers et al. 2015; Colombo et al. 2015; Vismara 2016) and zero otherwise.

Since many of our investigated variables have large positive outliers (for a similar approach, see Ahlers et al. 2015; Vismara 2016; Vulkan et al. 2016; Piva and Rossi-Lamastra 2018), in all our model specifications, we winsorize at the 3rd and 97th percentiles. We use year- and platform-fixed effects to account for unobserved heterogeneity between the projects' attractiveness due to, for example, varying degrees of crowdfunding legitimacy over time or differing growth potentials between platforms. Robust standard errors are clustered at the industry level.

By using all three alternative dependent variables, the empirical analysis supports our hypotheses. We find consistent evidence for the strong positive impact of the disclosure of financial information (Hypothesis 1), social network connections (Hypothesis 3) and a negative (positive) impact of the equity offered (retained) (Hypothesis 2).

More specifically, according to some studies in equity and rewards-based crowdfunding (Ahlers et al. 2015; Mollick 2014; Lukkarinen et al. 2016), the disclosure of financial information (Financial info) positively affects the amount raised, the number of investors and the probability of equity crowdfunding campaign success (model 1, coefficient = 0.419, significant at 5%; model 2, coefficient = 0.500, significant at 1%; model 3,

Table 8.6 Determinants of the amount raised, number of investors and success

	Model 1	*Model 2*	*Model 3*
Variables	*Amount raised*	*Number of investors*	*Success*
Financial info	0.419**	0.500***	0.800*
	(0.147)	(0.121)	(0.398)
Equity offered	−0.985***	−0.329***	0.341
	(0.0692)	(0.0858)	(0.515)
Social capital	0.0457***	0.0669***	0.0469**
	(0.00111)	(0.000956)	(0.00839)
Video	0.152*	−0.155	0.556*
	(0.0702)	(0.0970)	(0.258)
Duration	−0.00443*	−0.0000506	−0.0102
	(0.00329)	(0.00162)	(0.00560)
Female founders	−0.0157	0.0788	−0.00344
	(0.236)	(0.175)	(0.649)
Female	0.0342	−0.218	0.266
	(0.365)	(0.339)	(1.604)
Target capital	0.279	0.459*	−0.962
	(0.344)	(0.179)	(0.892)
Team qualification	0.171	−0.111	0.735
	(0.209)	(0.149)	(0.687)
Constant	8.281*	−4.076	10.53
	(3.755)	(2.422)	(8.695)
lnalpha		−0.373***	
		(0.129)	
Observations	115	115	115
Year-fixed effect	Yes	Yes	Yes
Platform-fixed effect	Yes	Yes	Yes
Adj. R-squared	0.3810	0.0498	0.3403

The table reports the coefficients of our empirical analysis with all variables winsorized at the 3rd and the 97th percentiles. Model 1 reports the coefficient of a Tobit regression of *Ln(Amount Raised)*, that is the natural logarithm of the amount raised by the company at the end of the campaign, on the chosen explanatory variables. Model 2 reports the coefficients of a negative binomial regression of *Number of Investors*, on the chosen explanatory variables. Model 3 reports the coefficient of a logit regression in which the dependent variable is *Success*, a binary variable that identifies the success of equity crowdfunding projects. In each analysis we include independent variables referring to the financial information (*financial info*), the equity offered (*equity offered) the* social network information (*social capital*), the duration of the video uploaded on the project page (*video*), the duration of the campaign (*duration*), the number of female founders of the company (*female founders*), the female prevalence in the company (*female*), the level of education of the team members (*team qualification*) and finally information related to the amount that founders seek to raise using crowdfunding (*target capital*). The variables *equity offered*, *social capital*, *video* and *target capital* are standardized. All the specifications include year- and platform-fixed effects. Standard errors (in brackets) are clustered at industry level (the several sectors are defined by the NACE codes). The asterisks ***, ** or * denote significance at the 1%, 5% and 10% levels, respectively coefficient = 0.800, significant at 10%); hence, in line with prior research, our study shows that equity crowdfunding campaigns without financial forecasts or a disclaimer collect significantly less funding. The disclosure of financial information is an important quality signal for investors and creditors in order to evaluate a company's financial performance. The inclusion of a disclaimer in the offering document provides a more accurate and comprehensive overview of the firm's risks; moreover, it is helpful both in reducing information asymmetries and in increasing the total funded amount.

According to Ahlers et al. (2015), Vismara (2016) and Ralcheva and Roosenboom (2016), a larger percentage of equity offered (Equity offered) is associated with a smaller amount of capital raised (model 1, coefficient = −0.985, significant at 1%). We also observe a negative and significant influence with respect to the number of investors (model 2, coefficient = −0.329, significant at 1%). According to this evidence, unobservable characteristics of the start-up can be signaled by entrepreneurs through the amount of equity that they retain after an offering. In this sense, following our hypothesis, the amount of equity retained is a signal of quality, which is actively set by the founders.

Our results also show that the founders' LinkedIn connections (Social capital) significantly affect the amount raised, the number of investors and the campaign success probability (model 1, coefficient = 0.0457; and model 2, coefficient = 0.0669, both significant at 1%; model 3, coefficient = 0.0469, significant at 5%). According to Ordanini et al. (2011), Belleflamme et al. (2014), Mollick (2014), Ahlers et al. (2015), Vismara (2016) and Agrawal et al. (2015), in the equity crowdfunding context, campaigns in which founders have a large number of connections are more likely to be successful.

Among our control variables, the female presence in the company as well as the female founders (Female Founders) don't seem to be related to the campaign success. According to Vismara (2016), Piva and Rossi-Lamastra (2018) and Barbi and Mattioli (2019), female founders are not different from male founders in terms of the ability to attract investors.

We also find that the duration of the video uploaded on the project page (Video) and the target capital amount (Target capital) have a positive impact on the equity crowdfunding campaigns. In detail, the video has a significant impact on the amount raised and on the success of the crowdfunding campaign, while the target capital significantly affects the number of investors. These findings are in line with those of Ahlers et al. (2015) and Vismara (2016).

According to Vismara (2016) and Lukkarinen et al. (2016), the duration of the campaign (Duration) is negatively associated with the number of investors. Shorter campaigns may convey a message of decisiveness and ability to deliver, moreover they may also encourage prospective investors to act fast, rather than postpone decision-making.

Finally, conversely to Piva and Rossi-Lamastra (2018) and Barbi and Mattioli (2019), our results show that the education of the team members (Team qualification) does not have a significant impact on the campaign success.

8.4 Robustness Checks

In this section, we discuss the results from a set of robustness checks. In particular, we test the robustness of our findings by using a different econometric specification and different levels of winsorization.

First, we run a logistic regression by using a dichotomous measure of campaign success (model 3), equal to 1 for campaigns reaching or exceeding their capital (Ahlers et al. 2015; Colombo et al. 2015; Vismara 2016) and zero otherwise. Again, as mentioned earlier, the results support our hypotheses (see Sect. 8.3).

Second, because many of our variables have large positive outliers, to prevent extreme values from biasing the results of our study, without losing observations, we winsorize our variables at 2% and at 5%.

In detail, winsorizing at 2% involves assigning a value equal to the value of the 2nd or 98th percentile to outliers beyond the 2nd and 98th percentiles in order to limit the influence of outliers on the empirical analyses. To make sure that the results do not depend on the specific treatment of the outliers, in Table 8.7, we report the estimates obtained when winsorizing at 2% and 5%.

In all cases, we use year- and platform-fixed effects to account for unobserved heterogeneity between the projects' attractiveness due to, for example, varying degrees of crowdfunding legitimacy over time or differing growth potentials between platforms. Robust standard errors are clustered at the industry level.

Table 8.7 presents the estimation results of Tobit regressions for Model 1, negative binomial regressions for Model 2 and logit regressions for Model 3. The standard errors are reported in column 3.

Table 8.7 Determinants of the amount raised, number of investors and success

Dependent variables	*Model 1*						*Model 2*						*Model 3*					
	Winsorization 2%			*Winsorization 5%*			*Winsorization 2%*			*Winsorization 5%*			*Winsorization 2%*			*Winsorization 5%*		
Model 1: Amount raised Model 2: # of investors Model 3: Success	*Coefficients (1)*	*Sig (2)*	*Robust standard errors (3)*	*Coefficients (1)*	*Sig (2)*	*Robust standard errors (3)*	*Coefficients (1)*	*Sig (2)*	*Robust standard errors (3)*	*Coefficients (1)*	*Sig (2)*	*Robust standard errors (3)*	*Coefficients (1)*	*Sig (2)*	*Robust standard errors (3)*	*Coefficients (1)*	*Sig (2)*	*Robust standard errors (3)*
Key independent variables																		
Financial info	0.419	**	0.147	0.360	*	0.141	0.500	***	0.121	0.502	***	0.121	0.800	*	0.398	0.768	*	0.396
Equity offered	−0.985	***	0.0692	−0.986	***	0.0556	−0.329	***	0.0858	−0.333	***	0.0812	0.341		0.515	0.307		0.459
Social capital	0.0457	***	0.00111	0.0442	***	0.00108	0.0669	***	0.000956	0.0666	***	0.000935	0.0469	**	0.00839	0.0467	***	0.00861
Control variables																		
Video	0.152	*	0.0702	0.148	*	0.0657	−0.155		0.0970	−0.156		0.0944	0.556	*	0.258	0.545	*	0.246
Duration	−0.00443	*	0.00329	−0.00440	*	0.00199	−0.0000506		0.00162	−0.0000633		0.00161	−0.0102		0.00560	−0.0102		0.00549
Female founders	−0.0157		0.236	−0.105		0.260	0.0788		0.175	0.117		0.184	−0.00344		0.649	−0.0562		0.682
Female	0.0342		0.365	0.0973		0.373	−0.218		0.339	−0.243		0.329	0.266		1.604	0.360		1.614

Target capital	0.279		0.344	0.278		0.309	0.459	*	0.179	0.471	**	0.172	−0.962		0.892	−0.911		0.882
Team qualification	0.171		0.209	0.162		0.199	−0.111		0.149	−0.118		0.149	0.735		0.687	0.762		0.690
Cons.	8.281	*	3.755	8.291	*	3.385	−4.076		2.422	−4.220		2.337	10.53		8.695	9.902		8.683
lnalpha							−0.373	***	0.129	−0.376	**	0.131						
Observation	115			115			115			115			115			115		
Year-fixed effect	Yes			Yes			Yes			Yes			Yes			Yes		
Platform-fixed effect	Yes			Yes			Yes			Yes			Yes			Yes		
Adj. R-squared	0.3810			0.3904			0.0498			0.0501			0.3403			0.3366		

The table reports the coefficients of our empirical analysis with all variables winsorized at the 2nd and the 98th percentiles and at 5th and 95th percentiles. Model 1 reports the coefficient of a Tobit regression of ***Ln(Amount Raised)***, that is the natural logarithm of the amount raised by the company at the end of the campaign, on the chosen explanatory variables. Model 2 reports the coefficients of a negative binomial regression of ***Number of Investors***, on the chosen explanatory variables. Model 3 reports the coefficient of a logit regression in which the dependent variable is *Success*, a binary variable that identifies the success of equity crowdfunding projects. In each analysis we include independent variables referring to the financial information (***financial info***), the equity offered (***equity offered) the*** social network information (***social capital***), the duration of the video uploaded on the project page (***video***), the duration of the campaign (***duration***), the number of female company's founders (***female founders***), the female prevalence in the company (***female***), the level of education of the team members (***team qualification***) and finally information related to the amount that founders seek to raise using crowdfunding (***target capital***). The variables ***equity offered***, ***social capital***, ***video*** and ***target capital*** are standardized. All the specifications include year- and platform-fixed effects. Standard errors are clustered at industry level (the several sectors are defined by the NACE codes). The asterisks ***, ** or * denote significance at the 1%, 5% and 10% levels, respectively

When we consider the 2% winsorization, the R-square is 0.3810 in Model 1, 0.0498 in Model 2 and 0.3403 in Model 3. The estimates of all three models show a positive and significant impact on the disclosure of financial information and social network connections. Furthermore, the results point out a negative effect of equity offered on the amount raised (model 1) and on the number of investors (model 2). In detail, the disclosure of financials, such as income statements or financial forecasts of the company, in the pitch is positively associated with the amount raised, the number of investors and the success of the campaigns.

Conversely, we can argue that external investors negatively evaluate the unavailability of financial information on the company. Again, a larger percentage of equity offered is associated with a smaller amount of capital raised and a smaller number of investors. Hence, entrepreneurs can signal the quality of campaigns by offering a smaller percentage of equity and so by retaining a higher percentage of it in their company. Then, we find a positive and significant coefficient for the founders' LinkedIn connections.

Turning to our control variables, we find significant and positive coefficients for the video variable in Model 1, and for the success of campaigns in Model 3, while the duration of campaign is negatively associated with the amount raised, but it is not significantly related to the number of investors and to the success. Finally, the funded target is positively associated with the number of investors (model 2), while it is not significantly related to the amount raised and to the likelihood of successful funding.

When we consider the 5% winsorization, the R-square is 0.3904 in Model 1, 0.0501 in Model 2 and 0.3366 in Model 3. The empirical evidence shows that our results do not change by using different winsorization levels, as the significance of our variables remains still unchanged.

8.5 Conclusions

Crowdfunding is an innovative and relatively new concept that connects investors to entrepreneurs. It is a new Internet-based method of fundraising, based on the ability to pool money from potential investors. Crowdfunding is presently growing very fast because it has the potential to foster innovation by offering new sources of capital, thereby reducing the funding gap for innovative start-ups.

Our paper adds to prior studies on the determinants of funding success in the equity crowdfunding campaigns, by providing new evidence on the quality signal of the entrepreneurs' social capital, the disclosure of financial information about start-ups and the share of equity retained by founders through a cross-platform analysis of the Italian scenario between January 2014 and November 2018. Overall, our results are consistent with our theoretical arguments: we provide suggestive evidence that the disclosure of financial information, the equity offered by founders and the entrepreneurs' social connections are perceived as signals of quality by external investors.

Our paper has several practical implications for both entrepreneurs and crowdfunding platforms. More specifically, the disclosure of financial information provides a more precise overview of the risks and it can help to reduce asymmetric information between entrepreneurs and potential investors. The availability of financial information increases the probability of campaign success, as shown by Epstein and Schneider (2008), Ahlers et al. (2015), Mollick (2014) and Lukkarinen et al. (2016).

Second, the share of equity offered by founders plays a key role in the setting of equity crowdfunding. In line with Ahlers et al. (2015) and Vismara (2016), our results point out that a higher percentage of equity offered by entrepreneurs negatively affects the probability of funding success. According to this evidence, we can assume that unobservable characteristics of the start-up can be signaled by entrepreneurs also through the amount of equity they retain.

Finally, entrepreneurs' social connections influence company finance decisions (Shane and Cable 2002). Our empirical analyses highlight the importance of these connections to attract more investors and capital.

Our results indicate also that this new form of financing requires research of its own, as its dynamics differ from those of traditional financing mechanisms and other forms of crowdfunding.

8.6 Limitations and Future Research

The results of our study have limitations that open up avenues for further research. First, the limited number of observations in the sample requires further investigation in the future to provide more information on the role of individual investors. In particular, from the study of larger samples, it is possible to derive benefits by exploiting information at the individual level.

Another concern is the unobserved heterogeneity. We cannot entirely rule out the possibility that unobserved factors affect our conclusions, in spite of our setting mitigating this concern. According to this evidence, we test our research hypotheses through a cross-platform analysis and we use year- and platform-fixed effects to account for unobserved heterogeneity between the projects' attractiveness due to varying degrees of crowdfunding legitimacy over time or differing growth potentials between platforms. As highlighted by some studies (Cumming et al. 2019; Rossi et al. 2019), we recognize that the success of the campaign can be influenced by the different features of the platform. To this end, we believe we can improve the contribution of our study by analyzing in depth the characteristics of the platforms in order to investigate their impact on our key independent variables and the success of the campaigns.

Furthermore, it would be interesting to investigate the post-offering lives of equity-crowdfunded companies, by answering the following research questions: Is there a higher survival rate for firms with disclosure of financial information/higher percentage of equity retained/larger number of founders' social connections? Are they more successful in attracting further funding? Or do they have a higher chance of successful exit? Unfortunately, concerning this issue, as the growth of the equity crowdfunding in Italy occurred later than in other countries, we don't have enough historical data to monitor post-offering lives of equity-crowdfunded companies and to analyze what happened to firms after a successful campaign.

References

Agrawal, A., C. Catalani, and A. Goldfarb. 2013. *Some simple economics of crowdfunding*. NBER Working Paper no. 19133.

———. 2015. Crowdfunding: Geography, Social Networks, and the Timing of Investment Decisions. *Journal of Economics and Management Strategy* 24 (2): 253–274.

Ahlers, G.K., D. Cumming, C. Günther, and D. Schweizer. 2015. Signaling in Equity Crowdfunding. *Entrepreneurship: Theory and Practice* 39 (4): 955–980.

Angerer, M., A. Brem, S. Kraus, and A. Peter. 2017. Start-up Funding via Equity Crowdfunding in Germany – a Qualitative Analysis of Success Factors. *The Journal of Entrepreneurial Finance* 19 (1): 1–34.

Barbi, M., and S. Mattioli. 2019. Human Capital, Investor Trust, and Equity Crowdfunding. *Research in International Business and Finance* 49: 1–12.

Belleflamme, P., T. Lambert, and A. Schwienbacher. 2014. Crowdfunding: Tapping the Right Crowd. *Journal of Business Venturing* 29 (5): 585–609.

Block, J., L. Hornuf, and A. Moritz. 2018. Which Updates During an Equity Crowdfunding Campaign Increase Crowd Participation? *Small Business Economics* 50 (1): 3–27.

Blumberg, B.F., and W.A. Letterie. 2007. Business Starters and Credit Rationing. *Small Business Economics* 30 (2): 187–200.

Bollaert, H., G. Leboeuf, and A. Schwienbacher. 2019. The Narcissism of Crowdfunding Entrepreneurs. *Small Business Economics* 1–20.

Busenitz, L.W., J.O. Fiet, and D. Moesel. 2005. Signaling in Venture Capitalist-New Venture Team Funding Decisions: Does It Indicate Long-Term Venture Outcomes? *Entrepreneurship Theory and Practice* 29 (1): 1–12.

Colombo, M.G., C. Franzoni, and C. Rossi Lamastra. 2015. Internal Social Capital and the Attraction of Early Contributions in Crowdfunding. *Entrepreneurship Theory and Practice* 39 (1): 75–100.

Cumming, D., M. Meoli, and S. Vismara. 2019. Investors' Choices Between Cash and Voting Rights: Evidence from Dual-Class Equity Crowdfunding. *Research Policy* 48 (8): 103740.

Epstein, L.G., and M. Schneider. 2008. Ambiguity, Information Quality and Asset Pricing. *The Journal of Finance* 63 (1): 197–228.

Evidence on Entrepreneurs, Investors, Deals and Taste-Based Discrimination. SSRN. https://ssrn.com/abstract=2442954 or https://doi.org/10.2139/ssrn.2442954.

Günther, C., S. Johan, and D. Schweizer. 2018. Is the Crowd Sensitive to Distance? How Investment Decisions Differ by Investor Type. *Small Business Economics* 50 (2): 289–305.

Hervé, F., E. Manthé, A. Sannajust, and A. Schwienbacher. 2019. Determinants of Individual Investment Decisions in Investment-Based Crowdfunding. *Journal of Business Finance & Accounting* 46 (5–6): 762–783.

Hornuf, L., and M. Neuenkirch. 2017. Pricing Shares in Equity Crowdfunding. *Small Business Economics* 48 (4): 795–811.

Kromidha, E., and P. Robson. 2016. Social Identity and Signaling Success Factors in Online Crowdfunding. *Entrepreneurship and Regional Development* 28 (9–10): 605–629.

Lin, M., N.R. Prabhala, and S. Viswanathan. 2013. Judging Borrowers by the Company They Keep: Friendship Networks and Information Asymmetry in Online Peer-to-Peer Lending. *Management Science* 59 (1): 17–35.

Lukkarinen, A., J.E. Teich, H. Wallenius, and J. Wallenius. 2016. Success Drivers of Online Equity Crowdfunding Campaigns. *Decision Support System* 87: 26–38.

Mollick, E. 2014. The Dynamics of Crowdfunding: An Exploratory Study. *Journal of Business Venturing* 29 (1): 1–16.

Ordanini, A., L. Miceli, M. Pizzetti, and A. Parasuraman. 2011. Crowd-Funding: Transforming Customers into Investors Through Innovative Service Platforms. *Journal of Service Management* 22 (4): 443–470.

Piva, E., and C. Rossi-Lamastra. 2018. Human Capital Signals and Entrepreneurs' Success in Equity Crowdfunding. *Small Business Economics* 51 (3): 667–686.

Polzin, F., H. Toxopeus, and E. Stam. 2018. The Wisdom of the Crowd in Funding: Information Heterogeneity and Social Networks of Crowdfunders. *Small Business Economics* 50 (2): 251–273.

Ralcheva, A., and P. Roosenboom. 2016. *On the Road to Success in Equity Crowdfunding*. SSRN Working Paper, No. 2727742. SSRN. https://papers.ssrn.com/sol3/papers.cfm?abstract_id=2727742.

Rossi, A., S. Vismara, and M. Meoli. 2019. Voting Rights Delivery in Investment-Based Crowdfunding: A Cross-Platform Analysis. *Journal of Industrial and Business Economics* 46 (2): 251–281.

Shane, S., and D. Cable. 2002. Network Ties, Reputation, and the Financing of New Ventures. *Management Science* 48 (3): 364–381.

Vismara, S. 2016. Equity Retention and Social Network Theory in Equity Crowdfunding. *Small Business Economics* 46 (4): 579–590.

Vulkan, N., T. Astebro, and M. Sierra Fernandez. 2016. Equity Crowdfunding: A New Phenomenon. *Journal of Business Venturing Insights* 5: 37–49.

CHAPTER 9

Business Models in the Lending-Based Crowdfunding Industry

Stefano Cosma, Francesco Pattarin, and Daniela Pennetta

9.1 Introduction

The gradual change in the organization of social relations and the growing connection between individuals, families and economic units allowed by new technologies have enabled new forms of financial intermediation. Now, the credit function involves new actors as well as traditional banks and specialized intermediaries, which also operate by means of new processes.

S. Cosma (✉)
Department of Communication and Economics, University of Modena and Reggio Emilia, Reggio Emilia, Italy
e-mail: stefano.cosma@unimore.it

F. Pattarin
"Marco Biagi" Department of Economics, University of Modena and Reggio Emilia, Modena, Italy
e-mail: francesco.pattarin@unimore.it

D. Pennetta
"Marco Biagi" Foundation, University of Modena and Reggio Emilia, Modena, Italy
e-mail: daniela.pennetta@unimore.it

C. Cruciani et al. (eds.), *Banking and Beyond*, Palgrave Macmillan Studies in Banking and Financial Institutions,
https://doi.org/10.1007/978-3-030-45752-5_9

Lending-Based Crowdfunding (LBCF) facilitates the matching of credit demand and supply through a specific marketplace, managed through online platforms. However, the creation of a digital, geographically scattered credit marketplace on which lenders and borrowers can conclude financial exchanges is not a solution for the problems and risks generated by information asymmetry and the limited rationality of individuals (Freedman and Jin 2008; Herzenstein et al. 2011); it is only a new way of overcoming and managing financial market imperfections. Therefore, LBCF companies' activities are important in managing the risks that arise from investment decisions, as well as in supporting the efficiency and development of financial intermediation.

In recent years, the LBCF phenomenon has been analysed from different perspectives. In particular, many studies focus on lenders' and borrowers' behaviour, companies' operating mechanisms and network effects, since these are widely considered to be critical points for the growth and stability of market operators (Chen et al. 2014; Serrano-Cinca et al. 2015; Maier 2016; Yan et al. 2018; Yoon et al. 2019). However, there has been little discussion about the strategies and business models adopted by LBCF companies. As a consequence, we still only have an unclear, incomplete overview of LBCF companies' business models, often identified simply on the basis of the kind of intermediation they undertake (Kirby and Worner 2014), which is actually just one of the several features of a business model (Ansoff 1965; Porter and Strategy 1980; Osterwalder and Pigneur 2004).

The aim of this study is to arrive at a more insightful categorization of LBCF companies' business models by simultaneously considering, in addition to their intermediation function, their strategic choices concerning customer segments (borrowers and lenders) and the additional services they provide. Specifically, we identify four main business models in the LBCF industry: diversified, business-specialized, consumer-specialized and peer-to-peer. This classification provides a more effective, realistic description of LBCF companies' strategies at a global level and can be a useful tool for future analysis on the performance of LBCF companies, as well as for their market positioning and for benchmarking their activities.

The article is structured as follows: in Sect. 9.2 we present a literature review of the existing LBCF business model classification and the business model concept in the management literature, together with our research question. In Sect. 9.3 we present our sample and we describe the variables in our dataset. In Sect. 9.4 we present our data analysis and propose a new classification scheme for the LBCF industry based on business models. In Sect. 9.5 we discuss our results; and in Sect. 9.6 we present our conclusion.

9.2 Literature Review

In recent years, LBCF has attracted many researchers from different backgrounds who study this topic from different perspectives. In particular, the most common theoretical frameworks concern information asymmetry, through which they try to explain the determinants of borrowers' and lenders' behaviour and risk assessment (Martínez-Climent et al. 2018). The way in which the information gap between lenders and borrowers drives adverse selection is discussed by Freedman and Jin (2008) and Emekter et al. (2015), who show that often loan interest rates are low and inadequate with respect to borrowers' risk. Consequently, lenders tend to adopt a herding behaviour, as shown by Herzenstein et al. (2011), Lee and Lee (2012) and Käfer (2018). In some articles, authors discuss the role of social networks and "soft" information (e.g. group membership, friend endorsement, textual statements and other voluntary information) in mitigating information asymmetry and herding behaviour (Iyer et al. 2010; Michels 2012; Everett 2015; Ge et al. 2017). In particular, their results show that the inclusion of this kind of information in the risk assessment process can reduce the overall probability of default and improve investments' performance. On the other hand, borrowers can take advantage of soft information disclosure, because it can reduce loans' interest rates and increase the likelihood of fundraising.

Another key topic in LBCF literature concerns factors that affect fundraising success and borrowers' default probability, as well as the factors affecting lenders' investment decisions. Many researchers agree that hard information about borrowers, such as credit scoring, purpose of the loan, income, home ownership, credit track record and leverage are strongly predictive of default probability and affect the likelihood of fundraising success (Serrano-Cinca et al. 2015; Emekter et al. 2015). Other social-demographic variables that affect the probability of loans' success are borrowers' age, gender, job and ethnicity; if these characteristics are shared by lenders and borrowers, then investors tend to be more generous (Pope and Sydnor 2011; Duarte et al. 2012; Chen et al. 2016). Fundraising can also depend on herding behaviour, in fact there is some evidence that investors lend to borrowers with a higher number of bids or with positive feedback from other lenders (Herzenstein et al. 2011; Lee and Lee 2012; Xu and Chau 2018).

A smaller number of contributions focus on the activities of LBCF companies and their *modus operandi*, with particular attention to these factors' impact on their performance. Regarding the borrowers of LBCF companies, if both consumers and enterprises can apply for loans, then the number of transactions can grow rapidly; in fact, a higher number of investment opportunities can attract a larger pool of investors (Jiang et al. 2018). On the contrary, if the company is specialized in the business segment, then lenders may perceive a higher risk, because business loans involve larger amounts and have longer maturity than consumer loans, and thus retail investors may not be willing to invest, which may have a negative impact on total transactions (Serrano-Cinca et al. 2015; Maier 2016; Jiang et al. 2018). Similarly, if both retail and institutional lenders can invest through the company, then the volume of loans originated may increase; furthermore, investments made by institutional investors can be seen as a signal of borrowers' creditworthiness, so they can be useful in directing investments towards quality borrowers and, consequently, in stabilizing the network and reducing the company's default probability. On the other hand, the opposite effects can occur if an LBCF company only accepts investments from retail investors: since they do not have to satisfy knowledge and competence requirements, the average quality of investment decisions on the platform may decrease. If lenders adopt a herding behaviour, this negative effect can be worse.

The intermediation model depends on many factors, such as the company's willingness to bear credit and liquidity risk and to adopt an active role in financial intermediation. The main implication concerns lenders' inclination to invest through the platform: the less an LBCF company undertakes risks, the higher will be the lenders' exposure to credit and liquidity risk and the less likely they will be to invest. In other words, in choosing their intermediation model, LBCF companies are faced with a trade-off between increasing the volume of investments and originated loans and decreasing their default risk (Yoon et al. 2019). The choice of the intermediation model is also affected by the specific regulatory framework in force in the country where a company is based (Sciarrone Alibrandi et al. 2019).

The decision to provide additional services to lenders or borrowers derives from the different incentives they have to interact with the LBCF company (Maier 2016). Borrowers pay attention to experience factors, that is speed, transparency and simplicity of services, while lenders mostly decide to invest through a company on the basis of risk factors, in particular credit and liquidity risks. Given the same kind of product, experience factors for borrowers tend to be very similar across companies and are therefore equally attractive; the risk factors for lenders, on the other hand, are perceived in different ways across companies, even if the investment products are similar. The different perception of risks is influenced by the kind of risk management services that LBCF companies offer with the aim of attracting a larger number of lenders and of increasing their willingness to invest (Chen et al. 2014; Borello et al. 2015; Dibrova 2016; Yan et al. 2018; Lee et al. 2017; Yoon et al. 2019). In particular, lenders' perception of risk is lower if they can rely on credit risk mitigation services, such as the opportunity to invest in secured loans, the existence of a lender protection fund and the presence of automatic investment diversification on the platform (Chen et al. 2014; Yan et al. 2018; Lee et al. 2017; Yoon et al. 2019). The same positive effect can be obtained if liquidity risk mitigation services, such as the establishment of a secondary market, are provided (Borello et al. 2015; Dibrova 2016).

However, there has been little discussion about the business models adopted by companies and often researchers who deal with this issue provide an unclear and incomplete overview of LBCF companies' business models. In 2014, a (if not the only) general classification was introduced by IOSCO which proposed three main LBCF business models: client-segregated account, notary and guaranteed return; a brief description of these models is provided in Table 9.1.

Table 9.1 Business models in the LBCF industry defined by IOSCO (2014)

	Client-segregated account model	*Notary model*	*Guaranteed return model*
Borrowers' contractual counterpart	Lenders	Partner bank	LBCF Company
Lenders' contractual counterpart	Borrowers	LBCF Company	LBCF Company
Intermediation between parties	Direct	Indirect	Indirect
Lenders' risk exposure	Credit risk Liquidity risk	Credit risk Liquidity risk LBCF Company's default risk	LBCF Company's default risk

Source: Our elaboration

In the first model, LBCF companies have a narrow role in the financial exchange between lenders and borrowers and their main function is to facilitate the matching of parties on the basis of their preferences in terms of maturity, risk and amount. Companies do not assume any risk, so that contractual obligations are borne by the parties and the lenders bear all credit and liquidity risk. If a company defaults, obligations between lenders and borrowers are still valid, and if the borrower defaults, the lender is not reimbursed by the company. Companies' revenue consists of fees paid by borrowers (as a percentage of loan amount) and lenders (as a percentage of investment amount).

In the notary model, the financial exchange between lenders and borrowers is indirect: once the loan request on the marketplace is fully funded, a loan is originated by a partner bank; after a few days, the company purchases the loan by transferring the funds invested by lenders, usually collected through payment accounts provided by the company. Then, the company issues debt notes and assigns them to lenders according to their participation in the loan financing. As in the client-segregated account model, notary LBCF companies do not assume any risk and lenders bear all credit and liquidity risk. Furthermore, they could also be exposed to the company's own default risk, because LBCF companies are their contractual counterpart. Companies' revenue comes from fees paid by borrowers (as a percentage of loan amount) and lenders (as a percentage of investment amount).

In the guaranteed return model, LBCF companies are licensed as banks, so they can collect deposits from lenders (usually a guaranteed fixed return is paid) and provide loans to borrowers. Therefore, the financial exchange between parties is indirect and their contractual counterpart is the company, which plays a strong role in the definition of contractual terms on both sides. As companies of this kind bear credit and liquidity risk, they are similar to traditional financial intermediaries and lenders are exposed to the companies' default risk. Company's revenue is the interest margin, which should be sufficient to cover operating expenses and to establish a guarantee fund to cover delay or non-payment of arrears by borrowers.

As this outline reveals, the classification of LBCF companies' business models provided by the IOSCO is based only on the intermediation model and does not consider other important aspects of their activity, such as customer selection or additional services offered. Some contributions describe the business model of LBCF companies (see, for example, Wang et al. 2009; Zhao et al. 2017) and without providing a generalization of business models in the LBCF industry. Other authors identify differences between LBCF companies in terms of operating and strategic choices; usually each choice is examined individually, without an analysis of their possible combinations and the resulting business model. For instance, Davis and Murphy (2016) show that platforms differ in terms of pricing system, which can be based on an online auction or on interest rates set by the platforms for each risk category, and in terms of diversification strategy, which can be directly managed by the lender or by an automatic investment system. Kirby and Worner (2014), EBA (2015), Lenz (2016), Havrylchyk and Verdier (2018) and CONSOB (Sciarrone Alibrandi et al. 2019) show that platforms can also differ in terms of presence or absence of a secondary market and presence or absence of further credit risk management services, such as the request for collateral on loans or the establishment of a provision fund that covers lenders' losses when default occurs.

We argue that a deeper and more complete classification of business models in the LBCF industry can be achieved by considering the theoretical definitions provided by the management literature. Amongst the copious theoretical studies on business models, we refer to the IT and e-business stream and the strategy stream.

In the IT and e-business stream, classification by business model has become a way of analysing firms' competitive behaviour and of explaining their performance; these environments are very competitive, because they are characterized by intensive use of IT in both production and distribution processes and because of the growing importance of stakeholder networks in value creation (Zott et al. 2011). Here, a business model can be defined by means of the set of enterprises' choices and activities, as well as through the relations between them (Osterwalder and Pigneur 2004), which determine how value is generated ('value proposition'), how cost–revenue structures can be optimized ('value capture') and how the interactions with the stakeholder network enterprises (suppliers, customers, delivery channels, partners, competitors) can be enhanced. The business model framework is a means for understanding what enterprises do and how they do it, so that it becomes a focus of analysis which puts emphasis on the activities through which firms create and capture value. In this context, business models could also become drivers of competitiveness, which contribute to enterprises' performance: innovative, specific ways of organizing activities and processes can contribute to value creation and can be a source of competitive advantage over competitors, strengthening the ability to pursue strategic objectives (Amit and Zott 2001).

In agreement with the theoretical strategy stream, we believe that value creation comes from a strategy (or combination of strategies) able to create and defend a competitive advantage and the related market positioning, with respect to internal (within the firm) and external (within the environment) changes that require an adequate capacity to react and forecast.

Strategy involves a different set of activities and choices about how an enterprise should compete. In particular, the strategy concept can be split into two levels: corporate strategy and business strategy (Porter and Strategy 1980). The first refers to the long-term choice of an enterprise's business portfolio or, in other words, to the definition of the various Strategic Business Areas (SBAs) in which the firm will compete (Ansoff 1965); these include choices related to integration, internationalization, growth and capital and resource allocation. On the other hand, business strategy identifies how to compete and how to achieve and defend the competitive advantage in each SBA through a combination of customer, product and internal resources. The business model concept may seem to be very similar to that of strategy, but it is not. A business model can be defined as the specific choices that derive from the actual business strategy in SBAs and from the diverse variables and activities involved (e.g. price, costs, customers, distribution channels, technology) which represent *de facto* managerial choices for creating and capturing value. Therefore, a business model is not a strategy but is the direct result of a firm's realized strategy (Casadesus-Masanell and Ricart 2010).

We are aware that a business model can be insufficient to ensure sustainable competitive advantage, because many elements of a business model are easy to imitate (Magretta 2002; Grant 2005). However, the recognition and study of business models in the LBCF industry is really useful and efficient for studying the strategies and competitive plans of action of LBCF companies.

Therefore, the aim of our study is to arrive at a deeper and more complete classification of business models in the LBCF industry, in order to provide an effective, realistic representation of LBCF companies' strategies at a global level.

9.3 Sample and Data

In order to test our hypotheses, we collected qualitative information about 30 companies worldwide (Table 9.2) for which an English version of the website is available (the Appendix provides a full list of the LBCF companies analysed). We created a qualitative dataset containing LBCF companies' choices concerning customer segments, intermediation models and the risk management services provided.

Table 9.2 Geographical percentage composition of the sample

	Number of LBCF companies	*LBCF companies in total (%)*
UK	9	30
USA	7	23.3
Italy	6	20
Latvia	3	10
Germany	1	3.3
France	1	3.3
Canada	1	3.3
Ireland	1	3.3
Singapore	1	3.3

9.3.1 *Choice of Customer*

By 'choice of customer' we refer to the customer types allowed access to the financial products and services provided by an LBCF company. In some cases, LBCF companies may specialize in offering loans only to consumers or to businesses, while in other cases they may operate in an undifferentiated way and accept loan requests from both segments. This choice has a strong impact on credit risk assessment and the selection processes, as well as on the litigation and credit recovery management skills required. The categorical variable 'borrowers' has three categories:

- *Consumer*, if on the borrower side the company is specialized in the consumer segment
- *Business*, if on the borrower side the company is specialized in the business segment
- *All*, if on the borrower side the company is diversified and accepts loan requests from the business and consumer segments

With regard to investment products, LBCF companies may specialize in the retail investor segment or the institutional investor segment, which consists of banks, financial intermediaries, enterprises and other accredited investors. The possibility of including institutional investors as lenders is subject to regulatory constraints and requirements that often affect companies' intermediation model and legal form. The categorical variable 'lenders' has three categories:

Table 9.3 Distribution of lenders (rows) and borrowers (columns) for LBCF companies in the sample (% of total observations)

	All	*Business*	*Consumer*	*Tot Lenders*
All	23.3	33.3	6.7	63.3
Business	3.3	0	13.3	16.7
Consumer	3.3	3.3	13.3	20
Total borrowers	30	36.7	33.3	100

- *Consumer*, if on the lender side the company is specialized in the retail investor segment
- *Business*, if on the lender side the company is specialized in the institutional investor segment
- *All*, if on the lender side the company is diversified and accepts investments from retail and institutional investors

Descriptive sample statistics for these variables and their combinations are shown in Table 9.3.

9.3.2 *Intermediation Model*

'Intermediation model' refers to the way in which LBCF companies act and facilitate financial exchanges between lenders and borrowers. The intermediation model is the reflection of the company's willingness to bear risks and its contribution to overall marketplace risk (i.e. if it introduces platform default risk, as described in Table 9.1). Therefore, we propose a new definition of intermediation model, which considers the role and risk position of LBCF companies, translates into direct versus indirect intermediation between parties and goes beyond the mere functional schema of intermediation introduced by IOSCO in 2014.

The variable 'intermediation model' has two categories:

- *Indirect*, if there is an indirect financial exchange between lenders and borrowers. In this case, LBCF companies play an active role in transactions and bear the credit risk.
- *Direct*, if there is a direct financial exchange between lenders and borrowers. In this case, LBCF companies play a passive role in transactions without themselves being exposed to credit risk.

Table 9.4 Descriptive sample statistics of intermediation model variable (% of total observations)

Intermediation model	*LBCF companies (%)*
Indirect	43.3
Direct	56.7

Table 9.4 shows the percentage composition of the two variables just explained.

9.3.3 *Additional Risk Management Services Provided to Lenders*

When maturity transformation is not carried out directly by LBCF companies, lenders' investments tend to be illiquid because it is impossible to disinvest funds before loans' maturity. LBCF companies can supply loans on their own and transform maturities through their balance sheets but they can only match the demand and supply of funds. In order to mitigate the prospective liquidity risk, the main additional service provided by companies is the creation of an internal secondary market, through which lenders can sell their investments to other investors before maturity—usually after paying a fee.

When lenders are exposed to borrowers' default risk, it is important to attract them by supplying credit risk management services. In the LBCF industry, there are two main types of such services: investment fractioning, carried out by the company, which allows lenders to reduce their portfolio concentration; and credit risk mitigation mechanisms, which can include the opportunity to invest in secured loans and the establishment of a lender protection fund that investors can access if borrower default occurs—usually this fund is fed by a specific fee paid by borrowers (or even lenders) when the loan is originated. The categorical variable 'risk management services' has three categories:

- *Absent*, if the company does not provide any additional risk management service
- *Partial*, if the company provides a liquidity OR credit risk management service
- *Complete*, if the company provides a liquidity AND credit risk management service

Table 9.5 Descriptive sample statistics of additional risk management services variable (% of total observations)

Additional risk management services	*Percent of LBCF companies*
Absent	16.7
Partial	43.3
Complete	40

In Table 9.5 the percentage composition of the 'additional risk management service' variable is shown.

9.4 Data Analysis: Methodology and Results

The aim of our research is to analyse LBCF companies' strategic choices and provide a more effective, realistic description of their business models. We argue that grouping companies by using information apart from their intermediation model can maximize homogeneity within groups and heterogeneity between groups.

In particular, we use a clustering algorithm to form groups of companies by simultaneously considering strategic choices concerning target customers, intermediation model and additional risk management services provided. More precisely, we implement a partitioning and exclusive algorithm called PAM (Partitioning Around Medoids), so that each observation in the sample has a unique group membership, which is determined on the basis of the distance between the observation and a representative point in the cluster. After an iterative process, observations are grouped around a medoid, which is itself an observation in the sample (Kaufman and Rousseeuw 1990). Compared to alternative algorithms, PAM tends to be more robust to outlier observations, because medoids are not set according to averages of observed features but are chosen amongst units of each cluster. We use the Manhattan distance to evaluate the homogeneity of each case in the sample with respect to any cluster, as it is the most common choice when dealing with qualitative variables like those in our sample.

We evaluate the goodness of fit of PAM results through the average of the silhouette width of all clusters. The silhouette value of a case measures the degree of confidence in its clustering assignment; it can assume any value between −1 and 1, where 1 corresponds to the highest confidence level. For any case i, the silhouette value is defined as

$$S(i) = \frac{b_i - a_i}{\max(b_i, a_i)}$$

where a_i is the average distance between case i and all other cases in the same cluster and b_i is the average distance between case i and the cases in the neighbouring clusters, as measured by the Manhattan distance:

$$b_i = \min_{C_k \in C \setminus C_i} \sum_{i \in C_k} \frac{\text{dist}(i, j)}{n_k} s$$

where C is the set of all clusters, C_i is the cluster containing observation i, dist(i, j) is the Manhattan distance between cases i and j, and n_k is the cardinality of cluster C_k. Then, the silhouette width of the generic cluster $k = 1, 2, \ldots, K$:

$$S_k = \frac{1}{n_k} \sum_{i \in C_k} S(i)$$

Finally, the average silhouette width of C is

$$\bar{S} = \frac{1}{K} \sum_{k=1}^{K} S_k$$

which is also in the $[-1, 1]$ range.

We use average silhouette width as a criterion to (1) select the best-fitting clustering outcome of PAM for different values of $K \in \{2, 3, 4, 5\}$, and (2) compare it to existing alternative classification schemes. Specifically, we focus on IOSCO's 2014 intermediation-based classification because it is the most common benchmark in the existing literature on LBCF.[1]

Table 9.6 shows the features of companies by IOSCO classification: client-segregated account model, notary model and guaranteed return model. We can observe that if LBCF companies' business models are defined only on the basis of their intermediation model, then homogeneity of features within groups is very low. In fact, there is no strong dominant orientation for any of the strategic choices.

[1] We performed all data analyses in the R environment (R Core Team 2019); we used package cluster (Schubert and Rousseeuw 2019) for the PAM algorithm.

Table 9.6 Features of companies by IOSCO classification

		Client-segregated account model (16 obs) (%)	*Guaranteed return model (5 obs) (%)*	*Notary model (9 obs) (%)*
Lenders	All	62.5	20	88.9
	Business	12.5	40	11.1
	Consumer	25	40	0
Borrowers	All	12.5	40	55.6
	Business	56.25	0	22.2
	Consumer	31.25	60	22.2
Additional risk management services	Absent	25	0	11.1
	Partial	18.75	80	55.6
	Complete	56.25	20	33.3

The silhouette plot in Fig. 9.1, shows the silhouette values of each company; in any of the three classes values are plotted as a horizontal bar. It is apparent that, for any class, at least one third of cases have negative silhouette values, meaning that potentially significant features of LBCF companies are not well represented by looking at intermediation models only.

The client-segregated account model has an average silhouette width of −0.08, the notary model has a value of 0.11 and the guaranteed return model has a value of −0.01. The average silhouette width over all classes is 0.006, so we can conclude that a classification of LBCF based only on intermediation models leads to low homogeneity within groups.

We compute Fisher's statistics for each variable in our sample to test whether the three IOSCO groups are statistically different from each other. Table 9.7 shows that differences are not significant for every variable we considered (p value > 0.05). These results suggest that the intermediation-based classification of LBCF companies introduced by IOSCO does not account for the type of customer they attract or the different kinds of additional risk management that they offer. Because customer type is likely to be related to risk management services, apart from the distinction arising from the kind of intermediation, these results suggest that the IOSCO classification could be improved upon.

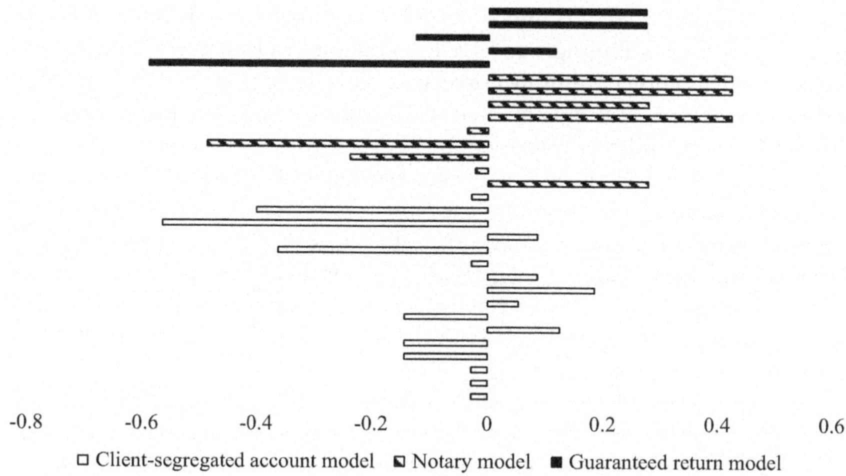

Fig. 9.1 Silhouette plot of IOSCO classification. Note: the client-segregated account model has an average silhouette width of −0.08, the notary model of 0.11 and the guaranteed return model of −0.01. The overall average silhouette width is 0.006

Table 9.7 Fisher's exact tests of heterogeneity between groups of LBCF companies sharing similar intermediation model (IOSCO classification)

Features	*IOSCO classification*
Lenders	0.076
Borrowers	0.0514
Additional risk management services	0.1377

We simultaneously consider strategic choices concerning target customers (borrowers and lenders), intermediation model and additional risk management services. We run different trials of the PAM algorithm to partition our sample into $K = 2, 3, 4, 5$ clusters and choose $K = 4$ as it is the result with the best average silhouette width and the least overlapping of the business models identified.

Furthermore, it appears sensible to introduce a new definition of intermediation model, which considers only the direct/indirect financial exchange between lenders and borrowers, arguing that this definition can better reflect the willingness of LBCF companies to bear credit and liquidity risk. As this choice is highly correlated with the supply of additional risk management services, cluster analysis results can further improve if we consider direct/indirect intermediation as a grouping variable.

The features of the four clusters are synthetized in Table 9.8, and seem to be quite homogeneous within each cluster; in fact, every class is denoted by a dominant feature. The average silhouette width for each cluster is positive and fairly high—0.49, 0.59, 0.83 and 0.61 respectively—especially if compared to IOSCO classes; the average overall silhouette width is 0.6, compared to zero for IOSCO (Fig. 9.2). It is remarkable that silhouette width is positive for all the observations.

Moreover, the classes are quite different, so heterogeneity between clusters also improves; indeed, as shown in Table 9.9, the classes are statistically different in terms of lenders (p value < 0.001), borrowers (p value < 0.001), intermediation model (p value < 0.001) and additional risk management services (p value < 0.001). So, features apart from the intermediation role improve business model–based classification in terms both of sensitivity (as many cases are clearly classified) and of specificity (as few cases are of uncertain classification).

Table 9.8 Cluster analysis results with direct/indirect intermediation model: features of LBCF companies in each cluster

		Cluster 1 (9 obs) (%)	*Cluster 2 (11 obs) (%)*	*Cluster 3 (4 obs) (%)*	*Cluster 4 (6 obs) (%)*
Lenders	All	77.8	100	25	0
	Business	11.1	0	75	16.7
	Consumer	11.1	0	0	83.3
Borrowers	All	100	0	0	0
	Business	0	90.9	0	16.7
	Consumer	0	9.1	100	83.3
Intermediation model	Direct	22.2	81.8	0	100
	Indirect	77.8	18.2	100	0
Additional risk management services	Absent	0	27.3	0	33.3
	Partial	77.8	9.1	100	0
	Complete	22.2	63.6	0	66.7

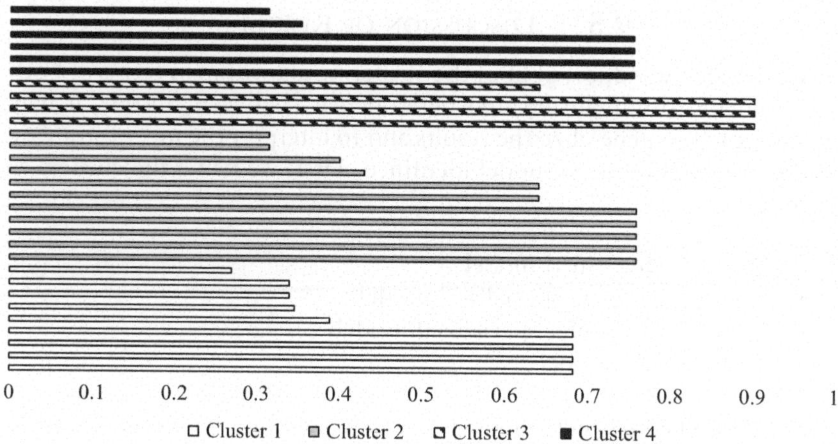

Fig. 9.2 Silhouette plot of the cluster analysis results with direct/indirect intermediation model. Note: the average silhouette width for the four clusters is 0.49, 0.59, 0.83 and 0.61 respectively. The average silhouette width for the entire dataset is 0.6

Table 9.9 Fisher's exact tests of heterogeneity between groups (cluster analysis–based classification versus IOSCO classification)

Features	*IOSCO classification*	*Cluster analysis–based classification*
Lenders	0.076	>0.0000
Borrowers	0.0514	>0.0000
Intermediation model	NA	0.0004
Additional risk management services	0.1377	0.0006

In order to compare and test our results fairly, we also ran a trial of the PAM algorithm considering the IOSCO classification as 'intermediation model' variable (client-segregated account, notary and guaranteed return), together with target customers (borrowers and lenders) and supply of additional risk management services. The comparison confirms that our results are better, in terms of both homogeneity within clusters and heterogeneity between clusters (results are available from the authors upon request).

9.5 Discussion of Results

Given the high goodness of fit of the clustering algorithm in terms of both homogeneity within clusters and heterogeneity between clusters, it may be interesting to generalize the results and to interpret the mix of strategic choices for each business model identified. First, we name the clusters as follows:

- *Cluster 1*: Diversified model
- *Cluster 2*: Business-specialized model
- *Cluster 3*: Consumer-specialized model
- *Cluster 4*: P2P model

The diversified business model is characterized by a high diversification of customer segments. In fact, investment products are offered to all types of lenders, accepting funds without distinction from retail, institutional and accredited investors. At the same time, financing products are also offered to all types of borrowers, accepting loan requests from both consumers and enterprises. Companies that adopt this business model choose indirect intermediation, meaning they make use of a partner bank and issue debt notes, or they provide loans on their own. The active role in financial exchange between parties facilitates the transformation of lenders' and borrowers' preferences and, consequently, the transformation of amounts, maturities and risk of closed operations. This means that this business model includes companies that directly manage and partially reduce credit and liquidity risk. As a result, in most cases the risk management service offered to lenders is partial, in particular with regard to credit risk management.

The business-specialized model includes companies that only offer their financing product to enterprises, and thus specialize in the business loan market. However, their investment products are offered to all types of lenders. These customer segment choices are rational: business loans usually have a higher amount and a longer maturity, so collecting funds from a wide range of investors can increase the probability of operations' funding success. Companies that adopt this business model choose direct intermediation, so they assume a passive role in financial exchanges between lenders and borrowers, limiting their activity to facilitation of demand and supply matching the marketplace. The direct consequence of this strategic choice is the full exposure of lenders to credit and liquidity risk. For this reason, in order to attract more lenders and to gain a satisfactory market positioning, these companies tend to offer a complete risk management service.

The consumer-specialized model includes LBCF companies specialized in the consumer loan market. They offer their financing products only to consumer borrowers, usually in the form of personal loans. Loan purposes are numerous: car purchase, debt consolidation, travel expenses, medical expenses and so on. They also specialize in the supply of investment products; in fact, only institutional investors can invest through the platform. Companies that adopt this business model choose indirect intermediation, meaning that they make use of a partner bank and issue debt notes, or they provide loans on their own. As explained for the first business model, the decision to play an active role in financial exchanges between parties arises from the desire to facilitate the transformation of lenders' and borrowers' preferences, in order to make the matching of demand and supply in the marketplace more effective in terms of amounts, maturities and risk. Consequently, companies directly manage and partially reduce credit and liquidity risk, and thus they usually offer a partial risk management service. This is also reasonable, since they only work with institutional investors.

Like the previous model, the P2P business model includes LBCF companies that only offer their financing products to consumers, so they are specialized in the consumer loan market. They also specialize in offering investment products, but unlike the previous business model only retail investors can invest through the platform. The financial exchanges between parties are direct, so the company plays a passive role in transactions. Consequently, lenders bear all credit and liquidity risk. In order to be competitive and to attract more lenders, companies in this group usually offer a complete risk management service. The completeness of the risk management service is fundamental in terms of network stability, since they only work with retail investors.

9.6 Conclusion, Limitations and Future Research

Within the growing literature on LBCF, this paper introduces a new categorization of the business models of LBCF companies. It reflects these companies' main strategic choices and proves more effective than the common classification schemes that only consider their intermediation models. In particular, it considers strategic choices concerning target customers (borrowers and lenders), intermediation model and additional risk management services supplied.

The analysis points out four prevalent business models: diversified model, business-specialized model, consumer-specialized model and peer-to-peer model. The classification is better than the previous one not only in statistical terms of homogeneity within and heterogeneity between groups of LBCF companies, but above all in terms of economic and strategic explanatory meaning. In fact, it improves on the existing classifications as it is both more sensitive and specific, and provides a clearer picture of LBCF companies' business models.

It allows us to understand companies' strategy and market positioning in the LBCF industry. Our categorization of LBCF business models can be an important tool for future analysis of the performance of lending-based crowdfunding companies, as well as for their market strategy and for benchmarking their activities. Since economic and financial information was not available for every company, we were unable to compare the four business models in terms of evolution, growth, sustainability and performance. This will be the next step of our research.

Appendix

List of analysed companies:

1. Atom Bank	16. MoneyThing
2. Avant	17. MoolahSense
3. Bitbond	18. Motus Quo
4. Borsa del Credito	19. October
5. CircleBack Lending	20. OctopusChoice
6. Earnest	21. Patch of Land
7. FinanceIt	22. Prestiamoci
8. Funding Circle	23. Prosper
9. Funding Knight	24. Smartika
10. Groupeer	25. Soisy
11. Lendbay	26. StreetShares
12. Lending Club	27. Thincats
13. Lendinvest	28. Twino
14. Lenndy	29. Unilend
15. LinkedFinance	30. Zopa

References

Amit, R., and C. Zott. 2001. Value Creation in e-Business. *Strategic Management Journal* 22 (6–7): 493–520.

Ansoff, H.I. 1965. *Corporate Strategy*. New York: McGraw Hill.

Borello, G., V. De Crescenzo, and F. Pichler. 2015. The Funding Gap and the Role of Financial Return Crowdfunding: Some Evidence from European Platforms. *The Journal of Internet Banking and Commerce* 20 (1): 1–20.

Casadesus-Masanell, R., and J.E. Ricart. 2010. From Strategy to Business Models and onto Tactics. *Long Range Planning* 43 (2–3): 195–215.

Chen, D., F. Lai, and Z. Lin. 2014. A Trust Model for Online Peer-to-Peer Lending: A Lender's Perspective. *Information Technology and Management* 15 (4): 239–254.

Chen, X.H., F.J. Jin, Q. Zhang, and L. Yang. 2016. Are Investors Rational or Perceptual in P2P Lending? *Information Systems and e-Business Management* 14 (4): 921–944.

Davis, K.T., and J. Murphy. 2016. Peer to Peer Lending: Structures, Risks and Regulation. *JASSA: The Finsia Journal of Applied Finance* 3: 37–44.

Dibrova, A. 2016. Analysis of Crowdfunding in European Union: Performance and Perspectives. *Contemporary Issues in Finance: Current Challenges from Across Europe* 98: 37–48.

Dong, X., and U.K. Lee. 2017. A Study on Lenders' Perceived Uncertainty and Willingness to Bid in Online P2P lending. *2017 International Conference on Service Systems and Service Management*, 1–5.

Duarte, J., S. Siegel, and L. Young. 2012. Trust and Credit: The Role of Appearance in Peer-to-Peer Lending. *The Review of Financial Studies* 25 (8): 2455–2484.

Emekter, R., Y. Tu, B. Jirasakuldech, and M. Lu. 2015. Evaluating Credit Risk and Loan Performance in Online Peer-to-Peer (P2P) Lending. *Applied Economics* 47 (1): 54–70.

European Banking Authority. 2015. *Opinion of the European Banking Authority on Lending-based Crowdfunding*. Discussion paper EBA/Op/2015/03.

Everett, C.R. 2015. Group Membership, Relationship Banking and Loan Default Risk: The Case of Online Social Lending. *Banking and Finance Review* 7 (2).

Freedman, S., and G.Z. Jin. 2008. Do Social Networks Solve Information Problems for Peer-to-Peer Lending? Evidence from prosper.com.

Ge, R., J. Feng, B. Gu, and P. Zhang. 2017. Predicting and Deterring Default with Social Media Information in Peer-to-Peer Lending. *Journal of Management Information Systems* 34 (2): 401–424.

Grant, R.M. 2005. *Contemporary Strategy Analysis*. 5th ed. Oxford: Blackwell.

Havrylchyk, O., and M. Verdier. 2018. The Financial Intermediation Role of the P2P Lending Platforms. *Comparative Economic Studies* 60 (1): 115–130.

Herzenstein, M., U.M. Dholakia, and R.L. Andrews. 2011. Strategic Herding Behavior in Peer-to-Peer Loan Auctions. *Journal of Interactive Marketing* 25 (1): 27–36.

Iyer, R., A.I. Khwaja, E.F.P. Luttmer, and K. Shue 2010. Screening in New Credit Markets: Can Individual Lenders Infer Borrower Creditworthiness in Peer-to-Peer Lending?. *SSRN Electronic Journal.*

Jiang, Y., Y.C. Ho, X. Yan, and Y. Tan. 2018. Investor Platform Choice: Herding, Platform Attributes, and Regulations. *Journal of Management Information Systems* 35 (1): 86–116.

Käfer, B. 2018. Peer-to-Peer Lending–A (Financial Stability) Risk Perspective. *Review of Economics* 69 (1): 1–25.

Kaufman, L., and P.J. Rousseeuw. 1990. Partitioning around Medoids (Program Pam). *Finding Groups in Data: An Introduction to Cluster Analysis* 344: 68–125.

Kirby, E., and S. Worner. 2014. Crowd-Funding: An Infant Industry Growing Fast. *IOSCO Research Department.*

Lee, E., and B. Lee. 2012. Herding Behavior in Online P2P Lending: An Empirical Investigation. *Electronic Commerce Research and Applications* 11 (5): 495–503.

Lee, Y.W., S.H. Chen, and T. Yu. 2017. *Analysis of the Impact of Collateral on Peer-to-Peer Lending.* 2017 IEEE/SICE International Symposium on System Integration (SII), 77–82.

Lenz, R. 2016. Peer-to-Peer Lending: Opportunities and Risks. *European Journal of Risk Regulation* 7 (4): 688–700.

Magretta, J. 2002. Why Business Models Matter. *Harvard Business Review.*

Maier, E. 2016. Supply and Demand on Crowdlending Platforms: Connecting Small and Medium-Sized Enterprise Borrowers and Consumer Investors. *Journal of Retailing and Consumer Services* 33: 143–153.

Martínez-Climent, C., A. Zorio-Grima, and D. Ribeiro-Soriano. 2018. Financial Return Crowdfunding: Literature Review and Bibliometric Analysis. *International Entrepreneurship and Management Journal* 14 (3): 527–553.

Michels, J. 2012. Do Unverifiable Disclosures Matter? Evidence from Peer-to-Peer Lending. *The Accounting Review* 87 (4): 1385–1413.

Osterwalder, A., and Y. Pigneur. 2004. An Ontology for e-Business Models. *Value Creation from e-Business Models* 1: 65–97.

Pope, D.G., and J.R. Sydnor. 2011. What's in a Picture? Evidence of Discrimination from Prosper. com. *Journal of Human resources* 46 (1): 53–92.

Porter, M.E., and C. Strategy. 1980. Techniques for Analyzing Industries and Competitors. *Competitive Strategy.* New York: Free Press.

Schubert, E., and P.J. Rousseeuw. 2019. Faster k-Medoids Clustering: Improving the PAM, CLARA, and CLARANS Algorithms. In *International Conference on Similarity Search and Applications*, 171–187.

Sciarrone Alibrandi, A., G. Borello, R. Ferretti, F. Lenoci, E. Macchiavello, F. Mattassoglio, and F. Panisi. 2019. Marketplace Lending. Verso nuove forme di intermediazione finanziaria?, CONSOB, Quaderni Fintech Luglio 2019.

Serrano-Cinca, C., B. Gutiérrez-Nieto, and L. López-Palacios. 2015. Determinants of Default in P2P Lending. *PLoS One* 10 (10).

R Core Team. 2019. R: A Language and Environment for Statistical Computing (Version 3.5.3) [software].

Wang, H., M. Greiner, and J.E. Aronson. 2009. People-to-People Lending: The Emerging e-Commerce Transformation of a Financial Market. In *SIGeBIZ Track of the Americas Conference on Information Systems*, 182–195. Berlin, Heidelberg: Springer.

Xu, J.J., and M. Chau. 2018. Cheap Talk? The Impact of Lender-Borrower Communication on Peer-to-Peer Lending Outcomes. *Journal of Management Information Systems* 35 (1): 53–85.

Yan, Y., Z. Lv, and B. Hu. 2018. Building Investor Trust in the P2P Lending Platform with a Focus on Chinese P2P Lending Platforms. *Electronic Commerce Research* 18 (2): 203–224.

Yoon, Y., Y. Li, and Y. Feng. 2019. Factors Affecting Platform Default Risk in Online Peer-to-Peer (P2P) Lending Business: An Empirical Study Using Chinese Online P2P Platform Data. *Electronic Commerce Research* 19 (1): 131–158.

Zhao, H., Y. Ge, Q. Liu, G. Wang, E. Chen, and H. Zhang. 2017. P2P Lending Survey: Platforms, Recent Advances and Prospects. *ACM Transactions on Intelligent Systems and Technology (TIST)* 8 (6): 72.

Zott, C., R. Amit, and L. Massa. 2011. The Business Model: Recent Developments and Future Research. *Journal of Management* 37 (4): 1019–1042.

CHAPTER 10

The Italian Minibonds Experience in Triveneto

Nicola Carta and Caterina Cruciani

10.1 Minibonds: Expanding the Toolkit for Firm Financing

10.1.1 Introduction and Normative Framework

In 2012 the Italian government started introducing a new and more favourable regulatory framework for bond issuance by non-listed small and medium enterprises (SMEs) in order to create an attractive alternative to bank debt. In the aftermath of the financial crisis, this move was explicitly targeted to expanding the financing opportunities of SMEs traditionally heavily reliant on bank debt. The Italian legislator voluntarily excluded micro-enterprises, as well as banks and insurance companies, from the advantages of the new regulatory framework. Financial experts and commentators have devised the term "minibonds" to define such bonds issues by SMEs (Grasso and Pattarin 2019; Accornero et al. 2015). Minibonds

N. Carta • C. Cruciani (✉)
Department of Management, Ca' Foscari University of Venice, Venice, Italy
e-mail: nicola.carta@unive.it; cruciani@unive.it

C. Cruciani et al. (eds.), *Banking and Beyond*, Palgrave Macmillan Studies in Banking and Financial Institutions,
https://doi.org/10.1007/978-3-030-45752-5_10

are fixed-income securities with a medium–long term expiration date, issued by listed or non-listed SMEs (Caratelli and Fattobene 2018; Broccardo et al. 2014), firms with strictly less than 250 employees, annual turnover below €50 million and whose statute explicitly provides for the possibility to raise external financing through debt obligations.

Minibonds, as fixed-income securities, guarantee debtholders the right to receive the principal at maturity, which can occur in a single solution (bullet-type) or progressively up to the final deadline (amortizing type), and the right to receive a return in the form of fixed or floating periodic interest payments. The inclusion of a call or put option is common; in fact, only 14.1% of all minibonds considered by the Osservatorio Minibond up to 2018 include no option. Additionally, issuers can put into force collateral in order to offer a guarantee to investors and to reduce the cost of capital. However, most of the issues (71%) are generally unsecured and the company prefers to provide a list of covenants, binding itself to the compliance with some management good practices or certain financial ratios (Osservatorio Mini-bond 2018). The interest rate, the principal and provisions of minibonds are generally discussed during the issuing phases, taking into account the characteristics of the issuer, their financing needs and the investors' requests.

Abdulsaleh and Worthington (2013) include government assistance and initiatives as one of the ways in which SMEs can see their access to external funding improved. Such programmes build upon the recognition that SMEs have been more credit-constrained than other subsets of the productive structure of countries. The introduction of minibonds regulation is an expression of the willingness of the Italian government to contribute to the further diversification of funding sources, which started in 2012 in the aftermath of a significant credit crunch due to the combined effects of the global financial crisis and the introduction of more stringent Basel III requirements.

Regulatory amendments that eased and promoted the access to bond financing by Italian SMEs are contained in the Law-Decree No. 83/2012 (called "Decreto Sviluppo") and in the subsequent Law-Decree No. 179/2012 (called "Decreto Sviluppo-Bis"), Law-Decree No. 145/2013 (called "Decreto Destinazione Italia") and Law-Decree No. 91/2014 (called "Decreto Competitività").

It should be emphasized that the possibility of using debt securities as a source of financing by SMEs was possible even before the aforementioned regulatory interventions. The legislator did not introduce a radically new form of financing but simply removed some obstacles that made this channel too little attractive for SMEs compared to the traditional bank financing.

The previous regulatory framework maintained two main limitations that hindered SMEs from financing through the issuance of bonds. The first limitation referred to art. 2412 of the Italian Civil Code, which set the limits for the issuance of bonds by joint-stock companies. The first paragraph of art. 2412 stipulates that joint-stock companies can issue bonds for a total amount that does not exceed twice the corporate equity capital. Only companies with shares listed on regulated markets were exempt from the previous rule. Therefore, the issuance of bonds was precluded and extremely difficult for most of the Italian SMEs, which are generally undercapitalized and opaque (Caratelli and Fattobene 2018). For this reason, the Law-Decree No. 83/2012 ("Decreto Sviluppo") modified paragraph five of article 2412, stating that the previous limit also does not apply to the issuance of bonds intended to be listed on regulated markets or on multilateral trading facilities.

The second regulatory limitation referred to the fiscal dimension. The previous tax legislation applied a particularly unfavourable tax regime both to the SMEs issuers and to the SMEs bond subscribers, discouraging recourse to the debt capital market by this kind of firms.

Regarding the issuers side, interest expenses paid to the subscribers were subject to the regime of ordinary deductibility if the issuer was a listed company or a large-sized issuer (art. 96 TUIR), while they were subject to a regime of partial non-deductibility for all other issuers (art. 3 par. 115 of Law 549/1995). The legislator had introduced this difference on the assumption that debt securities could be used by unlisted issuers for tax avoidance purposes as a substitute for contributions of own capital or other forms of shareholder financing (Broccardo et al. 2014). Law-Decrees No. 83/2012 ("Decreto Sviluppo") and No. 179/2012 ("Decreto Sviluppo-Bis") removed the differences between listed and non-listed firms in the tax treatment of coupon expenses paid on bonds. They provided for the appliance of the regime of ordinary deductibility (art. 96 TUIR) for both listed and non-listed companies on the condition that the securities are traded on regulated markets or multilateral trading facility in the European Union or the securities are held by qualified investors (according to Art. 100 of the Italian Financial Code), not directly by shareholders of the issuing company.

Regarding the investors' side, interest incomes were subjected to a favourable tax regime if the issuer was a listed company (Law-Decree No. 239/1996) while they were subjected to the ordinary tax rate of 26% if the issuer was a non-listed company (art. 26 par. 1 of Law 600/1973). These differences discouraged investors, particularly institutional investors, from investing in bonds issued by unlisted SMEs. Law-Decree No. 83/2012 ("Decreto Sviluppo") and subsequent Law Decree No. 91/2014 ("Decreto Competitività") stipulated that the favourable tax regime on interest income received by investors applies both to bond issued by listed firms and to bond issued by unlisted SMEs, on the condition that the securities are traded on regulated markets or multilateral trading facility in the European Union or the securities are held by qualified investors (according to art. 100 of the Italian Financial Code), not directly by shareholders of the issuing company, when their investment in such securities is equal to at least 50% of the fund's total assets.

Law-Decrees No. 83/2012 ("Decreto Sviluppo") and No. 179/2012 ("Decreto Sviluppo-Bis") therefore tried to eliminate the main civil and fiscal limits for the issuance of bonds by SMEs. Another important innovation introduced by these two decrees was the possibility for the issuing company to deduct from the taxable income of the year all the costs incurred for the issuance of bonds. These costs include, for instance, consultancy expenses, rating fees and placement costs. Osservatorio Mini-bond (2018) provides ranges for these costs that may also vary according to firm size.[1]

Subsequently, the Law-Decree No. 145/2013 ("Decreto Destinazione Italia") presented further important changes. Firstly, it introduced the opportunity for credit funds to receive a partial guarantee from the government fund ("Fondo Centrale di Garanzia") on investments in minibonds, both on individual and portfolio subscriptions. Secondly, it simplified securitization procedures and made it possible for minibonds to be included in the securitized assets. Thirdly, it provided banks with the possibility of structuring covered bonds with minibonds as collateral. Lastly, it opened up the option for insurance companies to use minibonds,

[1] Costs for issues below €50 million include balance sheet certification (€5000–15,000), adviser and arranger costs (between 0.5% and 1.5% of the issue) and other costs related to the preparation of the proper documentation by an accredited legal firm (between €15,000 and €25,000). These costs do not include listing costs for the ExtraMotPro and rating costs. All issue costs are tax-deductible (Osservatorio Mini-bond 2018).

asset-backed securities and funds investing in minibonds to cover technical reserves.

The most recent Law-Decree No. 91/2014 ("Decreto Competitività") introduced two main innovations. Firstly, it authorized insurance companies and securitization vehicles to lend directly to firms. Secondly, it provided withholding tax exemptions on minibond coupons, even if not listed, for professional investors, foreign credit funds and insurance companies.

The process that leads to the issue and placement of minibonds generally lasts from 3 to 10 months, depending on the complexity of the structured transaction and on the characteristics of the issuance. Placement can take place either through a public offering or through a private placement. Furthermore, the investment in minibonds is currently reserved for professional investors such as banks, insurance companies, asset management companies and private debt funds (subjects who possess the necessary experience and knowledge to make conscientious investment decisions with an adequate risk assessment).

In February 2013, Borsa Italiana (the market management company of Italian stock exchange) decided to launch ExtraMOT Pro, the Professional Segment of ExtraMOT market, in order to ensure that SMEs have a flexible, simple and cost-effective national market for listing their bonds, commercial papers and project bonds. According to the MiFID directive (2004/39/EC), the ExtraMOT Pro is not a regulated market, but a 'multilateral trading facility' (MTF). The cost to list a minibond in this market is relatively small compared to the overall costs of bond issuance: in case of traditional placement the admission fee is €2500 (or €500 in case of dual listing on another exchange) despite the investment horizon and no additional payments are due during the life of the instrument. If the instrument is an asset-backed security (ABS), where the underlying bonds are all already listed on Borsa Italiana markets, a 20% discount on the listing fees of each underlying debt security is applied. If the security has a maturity of less than 12 months, the fee is €2500 up to five securities issued in the same calendar year and €500 starting from the sixth security issued in the same year. Conversely, in case of placement through the ExtraMOT PRO platform, the fee is equal to a digressive percentage of the placement value (between 0.0025% and 0.01%), with a minimum amount of €4500.

The only bond listing requirements for companies (including SMEs) are publishing the annual financial statements of the past two years, with the last one being audited, and providing an information document compliant with the guidelines of the Italian Exchange. Publication of a listing prospectus, in accordance with Directive 2003/71/EC, is not mandatory. The issuer must also apply for an ISIN code for security. Subsequent to the listing of minibonds, the issuer is require to publish on the company website: the audited annual financial statement (within six months from the end of the corresponding financial year); the public ratings if available; any information related to any change in the rights of bondholders; any technical information such as payment dates, coupon amounts and repayment schedules.

The minibond market can be compared with similar initiatives in Germany, where the Schuldschein market was launched (Schweizer et al. 2015; Feihle and Lawrenz 2017), in France with the Euro PP and in the US with the USPP. According to a recent report by Global Capital, the market for private debt has blossomed thanks to the combined credit crunch by banks and the stimuli towards debt provided by central banks: Schuldschein raised $27 billion in 2017 and the USPP raised $75 billion (Global Capital 2018).

10.1.2 The Backdrop for the Minibond Introduction

Minibonds can be defined as a particular form of corporate bond issued by a specific subset of Italian enterprises, namely SMEs. The population of SMEs in Italy is mainly characterized by micro-enterprises, which account for almost 95% of the total number of SMEs; nevertheless, they have been excluded by the benefits of the new regulatory framework. Conversely, small (10–49 employees) and medium-sized SMEs (between 50 and 249 employees), which may raise capital through minibonds, account for about 5% of total Italian SMEs.

SMEs accounted for almost half of the value-added generated by non-financial firms in Europe in the post-crisis time frame (2008–2017), generating 52% of the increase in employment in the area. The number of SMEs in Europe is constantly growing, due also to the relatively high mortality of this type of enterprises, some of which manage to achieve very high growth levels: Italy accounts for 7.6% of approximately 180,000 high-growth SMEs, defined as "firms with a three year-average growth rate in employment of at least 10%" (Muller et al. 2018)

In the Italian non-financial business economy SMEs play an even larger role than in Europe and are responsible for 67.1% of the value-added generated, compared to a European average of around 56%. A similar result is found for employment, with Italian SMEs generating 78.5% of the employment, over 12 percentage points above the European average (EC 2019).

Despite their economic relevance, SMEs in Europe, and in Italy in particular, have traditionally been particularly reliant on bank financing (Thompson et al. 2018). Consequently, they have also been more credit-constrained than larger firms in the aftermath of the financial crisis, as banks and banking groups ensured compliance with the more stringent Basel III requirements (Altman et al. 2018).

Alternative funding sources beyond bank financing are equity financing and debt financing. While the former refers to any financing invested in the business that does not contractually require a specific repayment date or any interest payment, the latter refers to any loans provided by different types of creditors such as lending institutions or even private investors (Ou and Haynes 2006).

Reviewing the theoretical literature on the existence of an optimal leverage ratio in capital structure decisions would be beyond the scope of this article. Much more pertinent to the discussion regarding the choice to raise debt through minibonds is the literature regarding debt composition. The empirical literature suggests that there are specific features that lead firms to enter the bond market. Accornero et al. (2015) suggest that a decrease in the availability of external funds increases the likelihood of resorting to debt financing. SMEs qualify in the category of firms that have suffered most from the credit crunch following the financial crisis. Moreover, Berger and Udell (1998) suggest that SMEs are much more likely to resort to debt financing due to their inherent opacity and the willingness to reduce the risk of diluting ownership compared to raising funds through equity.

Given the nature of minibond potential subscribers—institutional investors—the minibond market qualifies as a market for private debt. Private markets are restricted to a specific set of investors, often turn out to be less liquid and transparent, and may involve different disclosure requirements compared to public markets, where all investors are allowed to trade (Thompson et al. 2018).

The literature has looked at the choice between public and private debt at different levels. Denis and Mihov (2003) show that firms work towards building a strong credit reputation borrowing from banks first; once the good reputation is established, they are likely to move to the public bond market, where such reputation can be banked upon. Kale and Meneghetti

(2011) provide a survey of the empirical literature on capital structure, organizing it into two broad groups: information-based model of the choice between public and private debt and models that assume that banks are better at managing firm distress. The former group basically assumes that relying on public debt is informationally more costly, as banks already have access to firms' accounts and are more cost-efficient in gathering the necessary information. Thus, there exists an empirically significant positive relationship between firm size and the share of public debt on total debt. The second strand of literature suggests that banks can be more financially flexible in the renegotiation or liquidation of distressed firms; in particular, Johnson (1997) shows that the level of public debt is negatively related to a firms' credit risk, a result supported by Denis and Mihov (2003), who find the same relationship using debt rating and Altman's Z-score.

Resorting to private debt may be a more suitable choice for SMEs that issue securities and for their subscribers (Thompson et al. 2018). A related question is how SMEs choose between bank and non-bank private debt. According to Kale and Meneghetti (2011), just a handful of papers distinguish between these two sources, with mixed results. For instance, Denis and Mihov (2003) find no clear pattern when it comes to the choice of private non-bank debt, showing no significant relationship between fixed assets and the likelihood to choose non-bank debt, but showing that safer firms tend to prefer bank debt. Johnson (1997) echoes this latter finding showing that non-bank financial institutions tend to serve riskier firms.

The evidence presented so far corroborates the idea that the expansion of financing sources for relatively larger SMEs towards new forms of private debt is a suitable avenue to help support SMEs' development.

10.1.3 Empirical Evidence on the Minibond Market

Several empirical papers have already been published on the minibond market despite its relatively young age. Earlier papers set out to discuss the features of the new instrument and derive some inferences on the outlook for the related ExtraMotPro market. For example, Minnetti (2015) looks at the conditions that may favour the further diffusion of minibonds, looking at the role that the intermediaries involved in the process may play to support the diffusion of minibonds. The minibonds market featured a slow start, with volumes starting to pick up slowly. This is documented by Riccio (2016), who presents an empirical investigation of the first year of minibonds to address the issues that initially emerged, showing that larger companies were the first movers but have progressively left room for smaller ones.

Thomadakis (2017) frames minibonds as part of a broader shift towards capital markets as an alternative to bank credit for SMEs and highlights the key aspects that may hinder their future diffusion—low liquidity and increasing transaction costs.

Caratelli and Fattobene (2018) recognize the role that minibonds may play to reframe the investment landscape of SMEs, while Altman et al. (2018) look at the creditworthiness of minibond issuers using the z-score and show that a significant lingering information asymmetry needs to be overcome to increase the number both of potential investors and of businesses deploying this new financing tool.

10.2 Research Design

10.2.1 The Triveneto Region

Due to the complexities in collecting the relevant information for non-listed issues, this research project provisionally focuses on a particular area in the north-east of Italy, commonly known as "Triveneto", which comprises the Italian regions Friuli-Venezia Giulia, Trentino-Alto Adige and Veneto. This area is characterized by a high concentration of small and medium-sized companies and by a diversified manufacturing output, ranging from the manufacture of textiles, leather products and shoes to the production of mechanical components or from the manufacture of jewellery to the production of chemicals. It is the birthplace of great industrial excellence and it is amongst the most eminent industrial districts within the Italian industrial firmament. Osservatorio Mini-bond (2018) reports that Veneto and Trentino represent respectively the second and the fourth region by number of issuers in Italy. Overall, Triveneto comprises 23.5% of all Italian minibond issuers.

The most recent reports by the Bank of Italy show that the regions that comprise the *Triveneto* area have managed to continue sustaining economic growth, in some cases even beating the national average. Veneto continues on in its expansive phases, although preliminary data show a slowdown in the first quarter of 2019 (Banca d'Italia 2019b). GDP growth in Trentino Alto Adige beats the national average, reaching almost 1% (Banca d'Italia 2019c). Friuli-Venezia Giulia has shown a decrease in industrial production, coupled with an increase in investment in productive activities (Banca d'Italia 2019a).

10.2.2 The Database

Our dataset comprises 143 minibond issues (84 listed issues + 59 non-listed issues) carried out by 104 Italian non-financial SMEs belonging to the regions of Friuli-Venezia Giulia, Trentino-Alto Adige and Veneto over the period 2013–2018. The total number of emissions varies across the years and totals 143 issues. The only financial company[2] included in the sample has been dropped.

The dataset was constructed from the Italian minibond industry reports released by Politecnico di Milano School of Management every year. As a consequence, our dataset adopts the same requirements identified by Politecnico di Milano School of Management to define debt security as a minibond.[3]

Listed bonds' technical data were collected parsing the admission documents to the Italian SME's Bond Market (ExtraMot PRO segment) owned by Borsa Italiana or to other European SME's Bond Markets.

Non-listed bonds' technical data are not always publicly available, as the issuers often withhold some data (such the coupon rate) in order to protect their privacy from other market players or because of mere reluctance to disclose information. In order to complete the database with respect to this important subset of minibond issues, the press releases by the issuing firm or by the arranger have been carefully analysed in order to

[2] Finanziaria internazionale is the only firm with NACE Rev.2 code identifying a strictly financial company.

[3] The research conducted by Politecnico di Milano School of Management considers debt securities complying with the following requirements:

(a) The issuer is an Italian company (or with operations carried out mainly in Italy), which is not interested by bankruptcy events or arrangements with creditors.
(b) The issuer is not a banking or insurance company, nor an asset management company supervised by market authorities, nor a "shell company" owned by an investor just to carry out an acquisition or a securitization deal.
(c) The issue amount is strictly below €500 million (considering the cumulated value of any issue from the same company in the same month).
(d) The minibond is not convertible into equity capital and is not listed on a regulated exchange open to retail investors.

fill the information gaps, parsing the original note to the financial statements (available on AIDA database).

Figure 10.1 shows the distribution of minibond new issues over time by regional location, distinguishing between unlisted and listed securities. The number of unlisted new issues has increased over time in all these regions, in particular in Veneto, starting from 2016.

Figure 10.2 shows the distribution of minibond new issues over time by business activity, distinguishing between unlisted and listed securities. We defined three sectors[4]: (1) manufacturing, which comprises all manufacturing activities; (2) services, which comprise accommodation activity, communication, holding activity, professional activity and other services; and (3) others, which comprise a residual category. As Fig. 10.2 shows, all sectors exhibit an important fraction of non-listed minibonds.

Tables 10.1 and 10.2 report the distribution of fixed coupon rate by year for listed and unlisted bonds. Since the dataset comprises issues and

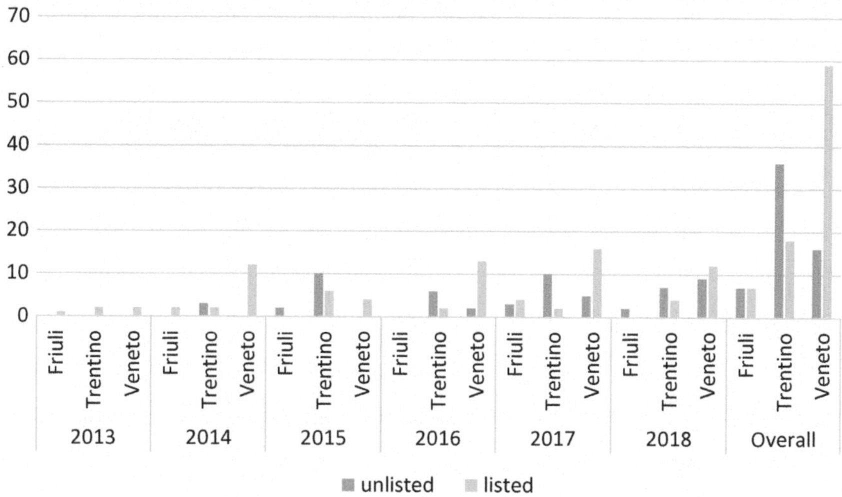

Fig. 10.1 Unlisted and listed minibond new issues by regional location

[4] Manufacturing refers to NACE Rev.2 code X, while services includes activities registered with NACE Rev.2 codes I, J, M and S; Others includes activities with NACE Rev.2 codes D-H, L, N, Q and R.

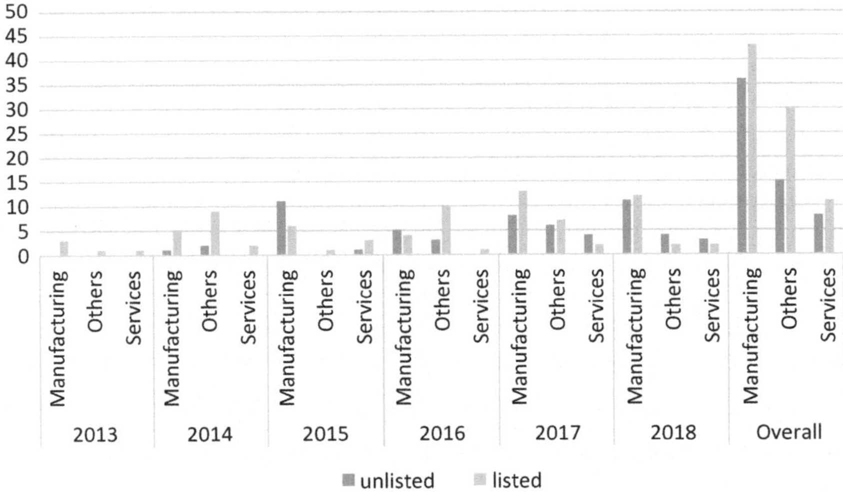

Fig. 10.2 Unlisted and listed minibond new issues by business activity over time

Table 10.1 Distribution of minibond new listed issues by fixed coupon rate

Year	*Fixed coupon rate %*					
	Minimum	*Quartile I*	*Median*	*Mean*	*Quartile III*	*Maximum*
2013	3.75	5.06	6.69	6.41	8.03	8.50
2014	0.00	4.20	4.20	4.77	5.99	6.50
2015	4.30	5.00	5.08	5.28	5.56	6.50
2016	3.90	3.95	4.30	4.42	4.68	5.75
2017	2.60	3.33	3.95	3.99	4.30	6.50
2018	2.47	4.13	4.50	4.48	4.99	6.00
2013–2018	0.00	3.99	4.33	4.59	5.24	8.50

issuers with very different characteristics, the range between the maximum value and the minimum value is remarkably wide; nonetheless, it has shrunk over time.

Table 10.2 Distribution of minibond new unlisted issues by fixed coupon rate

Year	*Fixed coupon rate %*					
	Minimum	*Quartile I*	*Median*	*Mean*	*Quartile III*	*Maximum*
2013	–	–	–	–	–	–
2014	3.99	4.67	5.35	5.11	5.68	6.00
2015	3.25	3.94	4.13	4.26	4.51	5.50
2016	4.25	4.38	4.75	4.90	5.25	5.85
2017	1.65	3.64	4.30	3.69	4.35	4.50
2018	3.00	3.00	3.00	3.37	3.55	4.10
2013–2018	1.65	4.00	4.30	4.29	4.88	6.00

10.3 Exploring the Minibond Market in the North East

10.3.1 Minibonds' Outlook and Prospects Down Less-Travelled Avenues

Despite its relatively young age, the minibond market has attracted the interest of an increasing number of scholars due to the potentiality it may hold for a segment of credit-constrained SMEs in Italy. We believe that the evidence collected and interpreted so far is now sufficient to explore at least two neglected dimensions regarding the outlook and prospects of the minibond markets.

The first dimension focuses on the current state of the market and regards the difference between issues and issuers choosing to list minibonds in the ExtraMotPro or opting for private placement (thus, not listing). More specifically it looks at how these two options shape the potential demand of minibonds.

The second dimension looks instead at the prospects of the markets and explores whether the empirical evidence suggested so far is correctly capturing the potential of this market, focusing on the criteria used to gauge the potential supply of minibonds.

10.3.2 *Beyond the ExtraMotPro: Implications for the Demand of Minibonds*

Previous research has focused on the determinants of the key elements of the minibonds market. Most of the previous research focuses on minibonds listed in the ExtraMotPro platform, but the choice to trade on this market is technically not compulsory.

Since its inception the performance of listed minibonds in the ExtraMotPro market was the dimension that attracted the most interest, as continues to be the case even in recent empirical studies (Rossi 2014; Broccardo et al. 2014; Riccio 2016; Altman et al. 2018; Grasso and Pattarin 2019).

The Annual report on Minibonds (Osservatorio Mini-bond 2018) is a notable exception looking at both listed and non-listed issues, but the report does not elaborate on the differences between these two types of issues or the reasons behind the issuers' choice. Notably the Fifth Annual report of the Osservatorio Minibond highlights a "tendency towards a reduction in the share of listed issues (…) partly due to introduction of the new European legislation on Market Abuse Regulation (MAR, European Regulation 596/2014) that tightens formal requirements also for non-regulated markets like the ExtraMotPro in a way that seems disproportionate with respect to the features of the minibond market" (own translation, page 46, Osservatorio Mini-bond 2018).

Angelini et al. (2019) look at "the 246 Italian companies that made, between 2012 and 2016, the 285 minibonds issues, of which 245 under 50 mln/€ of value" (Page 8), drawing the list from the Osservatorio minibond. Thus, they look at both listed and non-listed issues although they do not distinguish between them in the analysis.

From a purely technical point of view, both the choice to list on the ExtraMotPro and the choice to opt for a private placement have strengths and weaknesses. The way in which the legislation is devised allows for some tax exemptions in case of listing for what concerns investors: recall that listed minibond issues are exempt from the mandatory fiscal tax on the interest deriving from such securities when traded on the ExtraMotPro and held by qualified investors or by collective organisms for investment and saving (called OICR in Italian) when their investment in such securities is equal to at least 50% of the fund's total assets. On the other hand, as shown in a previous section, the listing has both direct and indirect costs, only some of which are proportional to the amount raised.

Private placement and the choice not to list minibonds used to avoid such costs but did not allow investors to avoid taxation on the interests gained.

In April 2018, the Italian Tax Agency (Agenzia delle Entrate) formally entered the debate on the fiscal regime applied to minibonds releasing an opinion (called *interpello* in Italian) in response to a formal request by a closed investment fund (Sviluppo Imprese Centro Italia SGR S.p.A.). Despite the fact that the minibond issue in question was not traded on the ExtraMotPro and the fund held less than 50% of its financial assets in debt securities, Agenzia delle Entrate ruled in favour of extending the exemption from the 26% tax on minibond interest also to Sviluppo Imprese Centro Italia SGR S.p.A. (JDSupra 2018; Orrick 2018). This *interpello* has legal validity only with respect to the case it applies to, but may represent an interesting precedent for other firms and further help the diffusion of minibonds also amongst firms and investment funds that previously did not qualify for tax exemption (Riccio 2018).

We believe that current studies risk that attempt to gauge the prospects of the minibond market focusing solely on the fate of the ExtraMotPro risk to underestimate the true potential impact of such new security.

The ExtraMotPro market remains a rather illiquid market, with very few secondary transactions, predominantly characterized by a buy-and-hold attitude (Minnetti 2015).

According to Thomadakis (2017), the key features that may lead to the success of initiatives like the minibonds lie in the lower costs involved, the less time-consuming and fewer informational and reporting requirements and the attractive risk/return trade-off. In light of these features, it seems relevant to address whether the listing of minibonds in the ExtraMotPro segment represents a necessary step to support further the expansion of this type of securities. In fact, issuing minibonds on the ExtraMotPro entails further costs compared to resorting to private placement, but also allows benefits from tax breaks.

As long as the listing costs are offset by a more lenient fiscal treatment, listing may still hold interesting prospects, but if the distinction between who qualifies for tax exemptions and who does not becomes more blurred (and independent from listing), the minibond market may further develop within the private placement segment rather than in a multilateral market.

Focusing on our database and comparing listed and non-listed emissions in the Veneto region since the inception of the new minibonds market, we can highlight some interesting differences. Limited responsibility

(SRL in Italian) represent 25% of the sample and emit 36% of non-traded minibonds but only 15% of listed ones.

Figure 10.3 shows the distribution of minibond new issues over time by legal form, distinguishing between unlisted and listed securities. While SRL companies have always preferred non-listed issues, the number of SPAs deciding to not list their debt securities fluctuates over time.

A Kruskal–Wallis test confirms that there is a statistical difference (p value = 0.0005) in the choice between listed and non-listed emission by SRLs and SPAs in Italian: this confirms that traded emissions are much more likely for the latter group.

There is also a statistically significant difference between listed and non-listed emission for what concerns the maturity of minibonds emitted (Kruskal–Wallis test, p value = 0.002) and a marginally significant difference with respect to the sectoral composition of the emitters (Kruskal–Wallis test, p value = 0.06) as also shown in Figs. 10.4 and 10.5.

Figure 10.4 shows the distribution of minibond new issues by face value, distinguishing between listed and non-listed bonds. Even if there is a significant concentration of non-listed bonds with a face value smaller than € 5 million, the distribution seems to be quite similar.

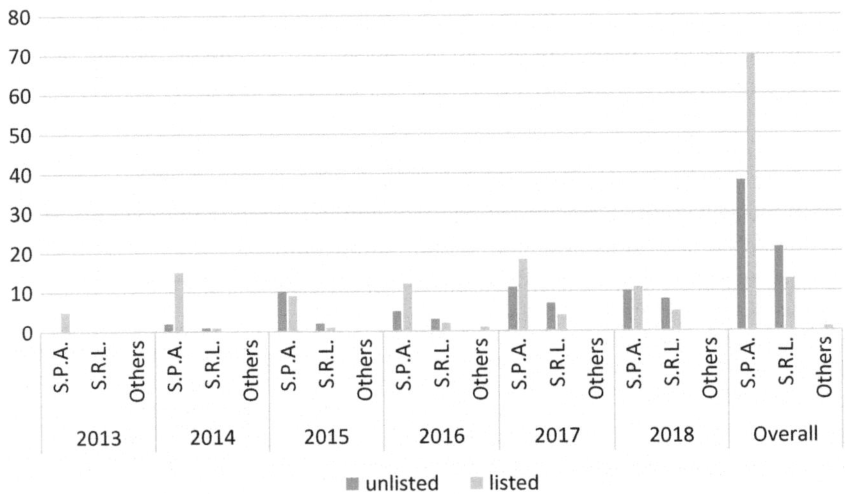

Fig. 10.3 Unlisted and listed minibond new issues by legal form over time

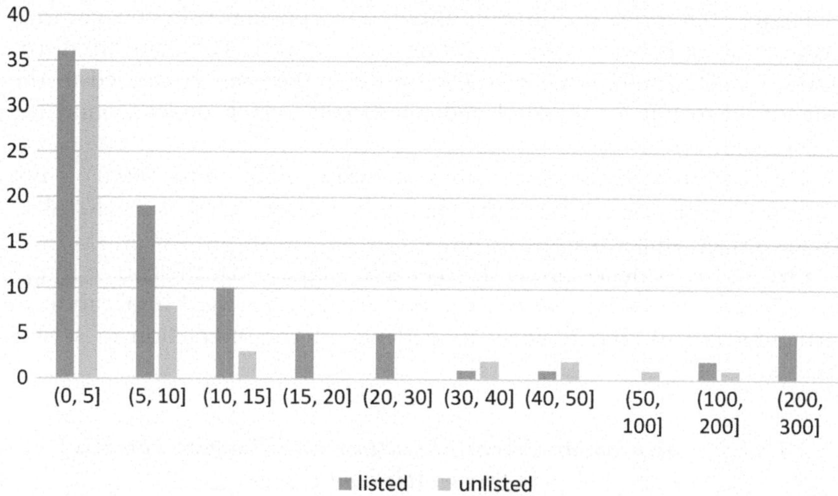

Fig. 10.4 Distribution of minibond new issues (unlisted and listed) by face value

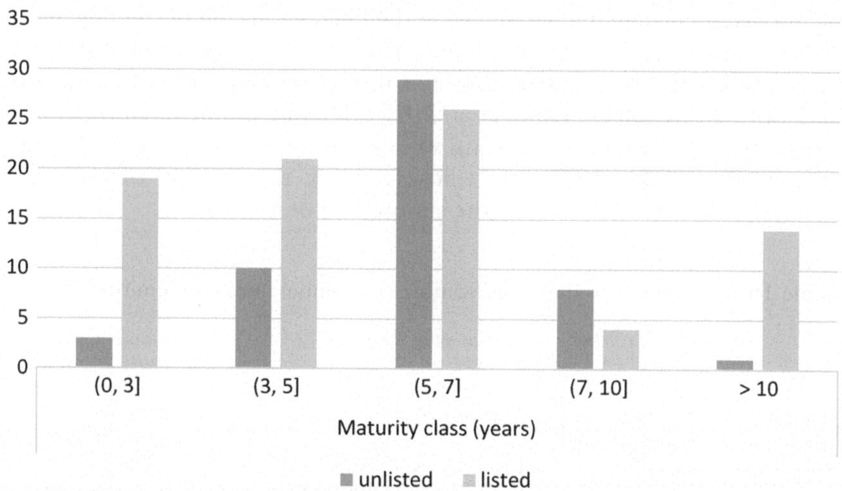

Fig. 10.5 Distribution of minibond new issues (unlisted and listed) by maturity class

Figure 10.5 shows the distribution of minibond new issues by maturity, distinguishing between listed and non-listed bonds. The maturity distribution of listed minibonds exhibits a positive skewness compared to the maturity distribution of non-listed minibonds, which peaks around the (5,7] category.

The pattern of emission volumes (in terms of amounts raised) is not statistically different when comparing listed and non-listed issues (Kruskal-Wallis test, p value = 0.17).

Overall the evidence presented seems to suggest that the choice to opt for a listed or a non-listed issue is not a straightforward implication of structural factors, but is likely to depend on the interaction of several factors.

10.3.3 Minibonds' Potential Outlook and Prospect: Potential Supply of Minibonds

Minibonds are a relatively novel tool in the financing landscape of SMEs whose success will be determined by their further diffusion and success stories. Thus, addressing whether the current structure of the Italian SMEs universe is being positively affected by the introduction of this new financing tool is a first step in understanding the likely evolution of this new tool.

Preliminary assessments of the potential supply side of the market tried to define criteria to identify potential minibond emitters (Cribis 2014; Piattaforma PMI 2017; Landi et al. 2017). Despite minor variations, such criteria include specific accounting values and ratios, as shown in the following table (Table 10.3), and allow gauging the number of potential emitters, and hence the size of the supply side of the market.

Table 10.3 Criteria for the identification of potential minibond emitters

	Cribis (2014)	*Piattaforma PMI (2017)*	*Landi et al. (2017)*
Annual turnover	Between €10–150 million	At least €10 million	Between €20–100 million
Profitability	EBITDA/turnover > 7%	EBITDA always positive in the last three years and EBITDA/turnover > 7% in the last year	EBITDA/turnover > 5%
Financial leverage	Debt/EBITDA < 5 times over	Debt/net assets < 3 times over Debt/EBITDA < 4 times over	Debt/net assets < 3 times over Debt/EBITDA < 4 times over

Table 10.4 Number of potential minibond issuers in the Triveneto region by geographical area, business activity and legal form

Geographical area	*Friuli-Venezia Giulia*	*Trentino-Alto Adige*	*Veneto*
	387	467	2166
Business activity	*Manufacturing*	*Services*	*Others*
	1622	238	1160
Legal form	*S.P.A.*	*S.R.L*	*Others*
	776	2156	88

Based on similar criteria,[5] we identify the number of potential emitters in the Triveneto Region for 2017, as reported in Table 10.4.

Recall that such criteria are considered a necessary but not sufficient condition to identify potential emitters (Piattaforma PMI 2017), thus risk heavily underestimating the potential supply of minibonds. Nevertheless, it is worth noting that the number of potential emitters is very large, even across different sets of criteria and studies.

A formal proof of this underestimation can be found by analysing in depth the database we constructed for the North-East. Using our own criteria and looking at a total of 143 emissions of minibonds in our dataset, we can observe that only 59 firms fulfilled all necessary conditions to emit when they did so (further referred to as *compliant firms*). A total of 45 firms did not fulfil all criteria at the time of minibond emission (*non-compliant firms*). This seems to suggest that the criteria used to identify potential emitters may be largely overlooked by firms, questioning their predictive power in determining the real potential supply of minibond issuers.

10.4 Conclusions and Further Work

This paper represents a preliminary assessment of the minibond market focused on a specific geographical area that represents a significant segment of the market so far—the North-East of Italy. We review the data currently available in other studies as well and complement the dataset with further information regarding non-listed issues, which have received

[5] The criteria we used to extract firms from the AIDA Database are regions = Veneto, Trentino-Alto Adige and Friuli-Venezia Giulia, annual turnover between 3 and 100 million, EBITDA/turnover ≥ 5, debt/EBITDA ≤ 5.

less attention by scholars so far but represent an interesting and growing subset of the minibond market.

Preliminary analyses show that different patterns underlie the issues of listed and non-listed securities in terms of maturity but not in amounts raised. Moreover, we also show that some features of the emitters are relevant in determining whether or not to list a minibond, finding that corporations (SPA) are over-represented in the set of issuers of listed securities compared to their frequency in the sample. We presented also a real-life instance of a minibond issue in which the difference between listed and non-listed securities in terms of the advantages for the investors has been erased by the Italian tax authority. This suggests that the potential demand for minibonds may be affected in important ways not originally foreseen by the legislators that are worthy of further monitoring and investigation.

Besides reflecting on how the tax legislation indirectly affects minibond demand and thus their current outlook, we attempted a preliminary assessment of how current criteria to determine potential emitters fare in terms of empirical evidence. Looking at real emitters, we find that 42% of our sample issuers did not respect these criteria at the time of the emission of minibonds, suggesting that these criteria are not used by firms in shaping the decision to emit minibonds. Thus, estimation of potential issuers using such criteria risks to largely underestimate the potential pool of emitters, besides missing out on the real determinants of the choice to issue minibonds (and the related choice of whether to list them on the ExtraMotPro or not).

This study is a preliminary study that still needs to disentangle important effects underlying these choices, for which further data need to be collected. For example, we are collecting accounting data of both emitters and potential emitters over a reasonable time frame (3–5 years prior to emission or to eligibility according to the criteria), in order to run more complex analyses on the interaction between structural factors already looked at so far (legal, form, sector, etc.) and accounting values and measures. Moreover, the finding that there may be different patterns underlying the choice between listed and non-listed issues across corporations and limited-partnership companies suggests that some corporate governance factors, such as the proprietory structure may be relevant in determining this financing choice.

References

Abdulsaleh, A.M., and A. Worthington. 2013. Small and Medium-Sized Enterprises Financing: A Review of Literature. *International Journal of Business and Management* 8 (14).

Accornero, M., P. Finaldi Russo, G. Guazzarotti, and V. Nigro. 2015. *First-Time Corporate Bond Issuers in Italy.* Occasional Papers (Questioni Di Economia e Finanza), Banca d'Italia, April (269).

Altman, E.I., M. Esentato, and G. Sabato. 2018. Assessing the Credit Worthiness of Italian SMEs and Mini-Bond Issuers. *Global Finance Journal.* no. 100450.

Angelini, M., A. Gennaro, and R. Giovannini. 2019. Financial Policy of Italian SMEs: The Impact of Mini-Bond. *Corporate Ownership and Control* 16 (3): 113–128.

Banca d'Italia. 2019a. L'economia Del Friuli Venezia Giulia. *Economie Regionali.*

———. 2019b. L'economia Del Veneto. *Economie Regionali.*

———. 2019c. L'economia Delle Province Autonome Di Trento e Bolzano. *Economie Regionali.*

Berger, A., and G. Udell. 1998. The Economics of Small Business Finance: The Roles of Private Equity and Debt Markets in the Financial Growth Cycle. *Journal of Banking and Finance* 22 (6): 613–673.

Broccardo, E., L. Erzegovesi, and M. Mazzuca. 2014. I Minibond e i Modelli Di Finanziamento Delle Imprese. *Bancaria* 7/8.

Caratelli, M., and L. Fattobene. 2018. Strumenti Alternativi Di Finanziamento per Le PMI: Mini-Bond, Crowdfunding e Business Lending. *Bancaria* 11.

Denis, D., and V. Mihov. 2003. The Choice among Bank Debt, Non-Bank Private Debt, and Public Debt: Evidence from New Corporate Borrowings. *Journal of Financial Economics* 70 (1): 3–28.

EC. 2019. 2018 SBA Fact Sheet Italy. *European Commission*, 1–19.

Feihle, P., and J. Lawrenz. 2017. The Issuance of German SME Bonds and Its Impact on Operating Performance. *Schmalenbach Business Review* 18 (3): 227–259.

Global Capital 2018. Private debt markets. USPPs, Schuldscheine, Euro PPs, Unitranche, Direct Lending, Unrated Bonds, MTNs, Regulation, April 2018, retrieved at https://www.globalcapital.com/special-reports?issueId=b181cj0xkk8p2v

Grasso, A., and F. Pattarin. 2019. Risk and Pricing on the Italian Minibond Market. In *Frontier Topics in Banking: Investigating New Trends and Recent Developments in the Financial Industry*, ed. E. Gualandri, V. Venturelli, and A. Sclip, 45–72. Springer International Publishing.

Johnson S. 1997. An Empirical Analysis of the Determinants of Corporate Debt Ownership Structure, *The Journal of Financial and Quantitative Analysis*, Vol. 32, No. 1 (Mar., 1997), pp. 47–69.

Kale, J., and C. Meneghetti. 2011. The Choice between Public and Private Debt: A Survey. *IIMB Management Review* 23 (1): 5–14.

Landi, G., D. Colantonio, and M. Soriani. 2017. Minibond Strumenti Di Debito Alternativi.

Minnetti, F. 2015. Minibond e Pmi: Le Condizioni per Un'affermazione Duratura. *Bancaria* 5.

Muller, P., A. Mattes, D. Klitou, O. Lonkeu, P. Ramada, F. Ruiz, and J. Farrenkopf. 2018. Annual Report on European SMEs The 10th Anniversary of the Small Business Act.

Osservatorio Mini-bond. 2018. Osservatorio Mini-Bond 5° Report Italiano Sui Mini-Bond.

Ou, C., and G. Haynes. 2006. Acquisition of Additional Equity Capital by Small Firms - Findings from the National Survey of Small Business Finances. *Small Business Economics* 27 (2–3): 157–168.

Riccio, G. 2016. Direct Access to the Debt Capital Market by Unlisted Companies in Italy and the Effects of Changes in Civil Law: An Empirical Investigation. In *Financial Crisis, Bank Behaviour and Credit Crunch*, ed. Stefania P.S. Rossi and Roberto Malavasi, 179–193. Springer International Publishing.

Riccio, S. 2018. Regime fiscale dei minibond non quotati, Forum Iuris website, retrieved at https://www.forumiuris.it/regime-fiscale-dei-minibond-non-quotati/

Rossi, E. 2014. Minibond Le Prime Esperienze Di Quotazione Sul Mercato Obbligazonarie ExtraMot Pro. *Bancaria* 12.

Schweizer, D., J. Proelss, and M. Mietzner. 2015. Hidden Champions or Black Sheep? Evidence from German Mini-Bonds. *SSRN*.

Thomadakis, A. 2017. Developing EU Capital Markets for SMEs: Mission Impossible? *ECMI Commentary* 46.

Thompson, J., K. Boschmans, and L. Pissareva. 2018. *Alternative Financing Instruments for SMEs and Entrepreneurs: The Case of Capital Market Finance*. OECD Papers on SMEs and Entrepreneurship.

Websites

Cribis. 2014. Quasi 8000 imprese potrebbero emettere un mini-bond. Accessed 12 August 2019. https://www.cribis.com/news/quasi-8000-imprese-italiane-potrebbero-emettere-un-mini-bond/.

JDSupra. 2018. L'Agenzia delle Entrate commenta il regime fiscale del private placement di MiniBond non quotati. Accessed 30 July 2019. https://www.jdsupra.com/legalnews/l-agenzia-delle-entrate-commenta-il-90423/.

Orrick. 2018. Tax Law Update. Accessed 30 July 2019. https://reaction.orrick.com/rs/vm.ashx?ct=24F76F1AD0E44FA9C6DF87A49E4FF377BB8B6CB7CD820ADD59E263747BC62.

Piattaforma PMI. 2017. Aggiornamento sul mercato dei Minibond. Accessed 12 August 2019. https://www.bvdinfo.com/BvD/media/General/IT/Analisi-mercato-Minibond-Febbraio-2017.pdf.

CHAPTER 11

Start-Ups Beyond the Crisis: A Survival Analysis

Giulia Baschieri, Giorgio S. Bertinetti, and Gloria Gardenal

11.1 Introduction

One of the reasons why entrepreneurs fail to enter the market and substitute old and unsuccessful firms through turnaround is the lack of financial resources. In a seminal work, Zingales (1998) shows how financial resources—in particular internal finance—play a fundamental role for young, private and small firms. The difficulties in accessing the capital market can determine the failure of a firm and the consequent exit from the market, despite its effective capability to innovate and be successful.

G. Baschieri
Department of Management, University of Bologna, Bologna, Italy
e-mail: giulia.baschieri@unibo.it

G. S. Bertinetti • G. Gardenal (✉)
Department of Management, Ca' Foscari University of Venice, Venice, Italy
e-mail: bertinet@unive.it; ggardenal@unive.it

C. Cruciani et al. (eds.), *Banking and Beyond*, Palgrave Macmillan Studies in Banking and Financial Institutions,
https://doi.org/10.1007/978-3-030-45752-5_11

In this paper, we analyse the post-entry performance of new Italian manufacturing companies and the role played by the initial capital structure and other firm/industry-specific factors in determining their survival in the market. Our analysis focuses on the firms incorporated in the database Aida Bureau van Dijk in 2009, right after the outbreak of the financial crisis, and investigates the relative importance of firm- and industry-specific factors in determining the duration of new entrants. As for firm-specific factors, we consider debt-to-asset ratio (as a proxy for leverage and thus the initial capital structure), labour productivity (as a proxy for quality) and employment (as a proxy for size) at the time of entry. Several studies have proven that start-ups typically encounter difficulties in raising capital and therefore rely heavily on internal finance and borrowing to sustain initial operations.

Financing burdens may affect productivity growth by reducing a new firm's survival chances. Given that, we contribute to the literature that investigates the role played by financing and quality in a new firm's success.

Previous studies by Baldwin et al. (2000) and Huynh et al. (2010, 2012a) analyse new firm survival in Canada. Huynh and Petrunia (2008) study entry penetration rates of new Canadian manufacturing companies. Dunne et al. (1989), Audretsch (1991) and Audretsch and Mahmood (1995) do the same for the US; Boeri and Bellmann (1995) for Germany; Mata and Portugal (1994) for Portugal; Fotopoulos and Louri (2000) for Greece; and Disney et al. (2003) and Bridges and Guariglia (2008) for UK companies. The studies that explicitly consider the role of financial resources on firm survival are those by Fotopoulos and Louri (2000), Bridges and Guariglia (2008) and Huynh et al. (2010, a). To our knowledge, there are no such studies on Italian manufacturing companies and our paper contributes to filling this gap. In this version of the paper, we do not consider several entry cohorts (as, for example, in Huynh et al. 2012b) but we focus on the individual entry cohort of 2009 and monitor entrants in the time span 2009–2016. To our purpose, we use the database Aida Bureau Van Dijk as the main data provider for employment and financial information. Our duration analysis relies on Huynh et al.'s (2012a) findings and methodology. Our findings are as follows: the relation between leverage and firm hazard is positive and significant for Italian manufacturing companies as well. We also find a weak evidence of a positive relation between the quintiles of the leverage distribution and the hazard ratio but this relation requires further investigation.

The rest of the paper is organized as follows. Section 11.2 presents a discussion of the literature about the role of financial resources on firm success. Section 11.3 describes the database used and the data. Section 11.4 discusses the methodology and the empirical specification. Section 11.5 discusses the results and highlights the limitations of this analysis. Section 11.6 concludes.

11.2 Firm Survival and the Role of Financial Resources

The literature has well demonstrated that firm-specific characteristics affect the choice of financial security (e.g., Jensen and Meckling 1976; Noe and Rebello 1996; Rajan and Zingales 1995). It has also been well established that the offer of different forms of finance attracts different types of entrepreneurial firms. In their seminal work about selection effects and capital structure, DeMeza and Webb (1987, 1992) and Stiglitz and Weiss (1981) focused on debt and common equity. Consistent with the seminal work of Akerlof (1970), Stiglitz (Stiglitz and Weiss 1981) and Spence (1973), the theoretical literature shows that equity attracts firms with low expected returns (*lemons*), debt finance attracts firms with high variability in returns (*nuts*) and convertible securities attract firms with low variability of returns (Brennan and Kraus 1987). Moreover, the presence of asymmetric information, which is particularly intense for small and medium enterprises (SMEs) (Binks and Ennew 1996; Berger and Udell 1998; Ferri and Murro 2015)[1] makes information opacity a defining characteristic of small business finance (see, for example, Berger and Udell 1998). The sharing of credit information is one of the possible mechanisms to reduce information asymmetries, where private credit bureaus and public credit registries facilitate this exchange (Kallberg and Udell 2003; Jappelli and Pagano 2002), thus solving information problems between SMEs and their external financiers (Kallberg and Udell 2003). It also serves to lower the cost of adverse selection and moral hazard (Zhang 2016). This determines SMEs' general preference for external debt over equity (under the Pecking Order Theory), which increases in presence of such information sharing, which results in more bank financing and in higher levels of leverage.

[1] SMEs are characterized by the privacy of contracts, limited accounting disclosure and the minimal presence in public markets.

If we look more deeply into the survival literature, a rich body of former empirical studies analyses the determinants of new-firm survival over time according to many different perspectives. Several elements explaining the survival chances of start-ups are indeed investigated, and can be roughly summarized considering three different categories: personal- (or entrepreneur-specific), firm-specific and environmental-specific factors (which in turn can be divided into local-, macroeconomic- or industry-specific factors).

Most of the studies focus in particular on the firm-specific determinants of survival. Within this approach, the start-up size appears as one of the key elements explaining the survival chances of new firms: small firms have disadvantages of scale compared to bigger companies; they face higher risk of insolvency and illiquidity due to restrictions on the access to capital markets; and they suffer in the competition for better labour force. The combination of these elements forces the smaller start-ups either to grow or to exit the market. Size can be measured considering the firm employment, the initial amount of capital or the first-year turnover. Overall, most of the empirical results univocally converge in evidencing the so-called liability of smallness (e.g., Lucas 1978; Audretsch and Mahmood 1995; Geroski 1992; Honjo 2000; Mata and Portugal 1994, 1999; Segarra and Callejon 2002). A second factor directly influencing the survival chances is the firm age (e.g., Sutton 1997; Caves 1998), despite some studies suggesting a non-monotonic relationship between age and survival probability (e.g., Wagner 1994). Finally, the most relevant firm-specific survival determinants are related to financial variables: a lower degree of financial leverage, higher collaterals or a higher amount of start-up capital decrease the risk of failure (Fotopoulos and Louri 2000; Bunn and Redwood 2003; Vartia 2004). Bridges and Guariglia (2008) deepen this relation and show that this effect is stronger for purely domestic than for globally engaged firms, which have access to both internal and international financial markets, diversify their financing and related risks, and benefit from lower sensitivity to financial variables than their domestic peers, resulting in higher performance. In addition, exporting firms are less affected by the domestic economic cycle, with a more stable cash flow and therefore less liquidity constraints and better performance (e.g., Guariglia and Garcia-Vega 2007).

Quite surprisingly, the effect of variables used in the rating methodology, which only partly considers some of the aforementioned financial variables, is largely ignored in the survival literature, and whether these variables have any effect on the likelihood of a start-up to default is still at issue.

A second interesting stream of literature also examines the impact of environmental-specific factors on the likelihood of survival. The probability of default decreases with the increase in the firm's industry growth rate and market dynamics (e.g., Mata and Portugal 1994). In addition, industry heterogeneity, which implies a continuous job creation and destruction, pushes firms to adjust to changing environmental conditions, and increases the survival rate for firms able to innovate and change fast while enhancing the failure rate for companies without these skills. Despite being little investigated, innovation therefore seems a key factor for survival. The local economic environment also seems to play a role: regional agglomeration economies suggest positive externalities in terms of availability suppliers, customers, cooperating firms and a network of local qualified employees and managers (e.g., Fotopoulos and Louri 2000).

Finally, only a few studies investigate founders' or entrepreneurs' personal skills that might affect start-up performances and therefore survival chances (e.g., Vivarelli 2004).

The role of financial resources on firm post-entry success and on firm dynamics overall has been extensively considered by scholars. Theoretical studies by Cooley and Quadrini (2001), and Albuquerque and Hopenhayn (2004) tackle this issue and find that highly productive firms choose to borrow more given their equity and have higher leverage levels. Cooley and Quadrini (2001) also show that size, leverage, productivity and age matter to firm survival. On the contrary, Lang et al. (1996) argue that promising entrants with good investment opportunities prefer to have lower initial leverage in order to benefit from financial slack, which allows taking advantage of the investment opportunities.

Empirical research on firm dynamics investigates the role of financial decisions on firm growth, innovation, export and distribution. As an example, Oliveira and Fortunato (2006) use the contributions of the literature about cash flow sensitivity (i.e., Fazzari et al. 1988; Kaplan and Zingales 1997; Cleary 1999) and combine them with the firm growth literature: their results show that Portuguese manufacturing companies' growth is positively affected by cash flows. Financing also plays a role in firm innovation. Hall (2002) finds evidence that new firms have higher financing costs for R&D. With respect to export, Bellone et al. (2010) show that less financially constrained companies are more likely to be exporters but export doesn't prevent them from accessing financial markets. Finally, Cabral and Mata (2003) find that financial constraints determine skewed size distributions for entrant Portuguese manufacturing companies but the skewness reduces with age and by lowering financial constraints.

A more recent stream of literature investigates the role of financial considerations on the entry and post-entry survival of new companies. Some studies follow the cash-flow sensitivity literature and separate firms into financially constrained and not constrained. This approach presents some difficulties because of limited information on new firms. Musso and Schiavo (2008) try to overcome this limitation by using more than one variable to identify financially constrained and non-constrained companies: their results show that hazard and productivity growth positively associate, while firm growth negatively associates, with the level of financial constraints. Their intuition is that companies become more financially efficient in order to survive.

On the other hand, other authors argue that high cash-flow sensitivity is not indicative of a financially constrained firm. In particular, a high level of cash-flow sensitivity normally characterizes companies facing the least constraints (Kaplan and Zingales 1997; Cleary 1999; Almeida et al. 2004). Cash flows can also be useful to detect information about an investment's quality (Gomes 2001; Alti 2003) and company growth. Jovanovic (1982) and Brito and Mello (1995) show that young and small firms with strong cash flows are successful and grow, whereas those with weak cash flows suffer and eventually fail. This relation is independent of whether a company is financially constrained or not.

The second approach focuses on leverage and its role in new firm survival. Leverage is more easily observable also for new entrants and provides a direct measure of a firm's financial state. In particular, a too high initial leverage (measured as debt-to-asset ratio) may create a future burden on a firm and undermine its probability of survival (Fotopoulos and Louri 2000). Thus, new firms with high initial debt-to-asset ratio may suffer from financial constraints that limit future opportunities. Moreover, they could also suffer from the debt-overhang problem (Myers 1977), that is investors unwilling to finance the company if future expected profits will be used to repay past borrowing. Beside this, other studies argue that the decision to get new debt balances two important aspects: on the one hand, the benefit of being large; on the other hand, increasing bankruptcy or default costs that could affect firm survival (Cooley and Quadrini 2001). These opposite arguments related to debt suggest a potential non-linear relationship between the optimal debt-to-asset ratio and future hazard rates, which is well documented by Huynh et al. (2012b). The present paper contributes to this stream of literature and analyses the role of initial leverage on post-entry survival.

11.3 Database and Data

11.3.1 Database

Central to our analysis is the firm-level Aida database. Aida is a commercial database provided by Bureau van Dijk. It contains financial information about nearly one million private and publicly owned Italian firms. The database includes up to ten years of information per company, with quite a good coverage. Aida is especially useful because it covers a large fraction of new and SME companies across all industries. It is created by collecting standardized data provided by the office of the Registrar of Companies and includes firm-level accounting data in standardized financial format. In addition to financial information, Aida also provides other firm-level information. We use information on the year of incorporation (2009) to calculate the age of the firm. Aida also assigns companies a three-digit NACE code—the European standard of industry classification—but it is also possible to use other industrial classifications. In our paper, we use the US SIC codes at a two-digit level so that we have a sufficient number of firms per industry. Moreover, we build macro-industrial groupings following Huynh et al. (2012b), in order not to introduce too many variables in our model.

11.3.1.1 Data and Variables

We clarify the definition of firm entry and exit as it is the primary focus of this paper by examining the post-entry performance through new entrants' survival patterns. The Aida database contains historical data for the last ten years. We are interested in analysing start-ups born in 2009. Therefore, we select companies "incorporated" in 2009, with no more than 50 employees in the first year: this prevents us from selecting companies already existing and deriving from an M&A operation. The criterion "status" allows us to determine if the company is still active in 2016 or not and, if not, in which year the company exited the market. It is notably important to recall that the possible statuses of a company in Aida are as follows:

1. Active
    (a) Active
    (b) Active (default of payment)
    (c) Active (insolvency proceedings)
    (d) Active (dormant)
    (e) Active (branch)
2. Inactive
    (a) In liquidation
    (b) Bankruptcy
    (c) Dissolved (merger or takeover)
    (d) Dissolved (demerger)
    (e) Dissolved (liquidation)
    (f) Dissolved (bankruptcy)
    (g) Dissolved
    (h) Inactive (no precision)
    (i) Inactive (branch)

We consider an "exit" for every status belonging to the "inactive" category. After the year of exit, the company is no more observed or recorded in our dataset. As for the active companies, we do not have dormant firms or branches.

Table 11.1 presents the number of entrants in 2009, divided by industry. We recall that we focused on the manufacturing companies and we grouped them according to the two-digit USSIC codes using the following criterion:

- Food and Kindred Products (USSIC 20)
- Textile Mill Products and Other Textile Products (USSIC 22–23)
- Wood, Furniture, Paper (USSIC 24–27)
- Chemical & Petroleum (USSIC 28–29)
- Rubber & Leather (USSIC 30–31)
- Stone, Clay, Glass & Metal (USSIC 32–34)
- Machinery, Electronic Equipment, Transportation, Instruments (USSIC 35–38)
- Other Manufacturing (USSIC 39)

Table 11.1 Description of two-digit industries in manufacturing

Industrial classification	*USSIC code*	*Number of entrants*
Food and kindred products	20	38
Textile mill products and other textile products	22–23	24
Wood, furniture & paper	24–27	41
Chemical & petroleum	28–29	9
Rubber & leather	30–31	30
Stone, clay, glass & metal	32–34	90
Machinery, electronic equipment, transportation, instruments	35–38	82
Other manufacturing	39	5
Total		319

Note: Tabulates the number of entrants in a particular industry for the year 2009

USSIC standard industry classification with ad hoc groupings

As in Huynh et al. (2012a) our variables of interest are only firm-specific and time-invariant. New firm duration is analysed for only one entry cohort.[2] The year 2009 is chosen because it is very close to the outbreak of the financial crisis in Italy, a particularly difficult moment for a start-up to be born and raise financial resources to operate in the market. Therefore, all these entrants face the same entry and post-entry business cycle conditions. A baseline hazard captures any impact on firm hazard from business cycle and other common time-varying conditions. We cover a time span of eight years, from 2009 to 2016.

The proportional time-invariant regressors are divided into two categories: (1) initial firm conditions and (2) industry conditions at year of entry.

Initial firm-specific variables include the following:

- Leverage
- Labour productivity
- Employment size

Initial industry-specific variables include the following:

- Entry rate (entry penetration)
- Entrant employment share
- Capital-to-labour ratio

[2] See note 4.

Leverage or a firm's debt-to-asset ratio is the key variable of this study and provides an indication of the financial position of a firm upon entry. It is measured in book value terms and can be greater than 1. In contrast, the market debt-to-asset ratio is restricted to between zero and 1. However, most of these firms are private, so market value of equity is unobserved. The relationship between leverage and firm hazard is not clear. On the one hand, high leverage may create a debt burden for a firm (Fotopoulos and Louri 2000), suggesting a positive relationship between firm hazard and initial leverage; on the other hand, firms balance the trade-off between the benefits of being large and the costs of increased bankruptcy risk when determining debt levels (Cooley and Quadrini 2001).

Another firm-specific variable is initial employment size, measured as the log of the number of employees at the year of entry. A firm's initial size provides an indication of its financial resources as it must raise substantial amounts of financial capital to become large. For example, Cooley and Quadrini (2001) demonstrate that firms with higher equity levels are larger, all else being equal. Larger initial size should indicate a firm has deep pockets (see Telser 1966; Zingales 1998). Deeper financial pockets smooth a firm's operations and allow the firm to survive any temporary negative hits to profits. In addition, financial resources provide a new firm the necessary time to develop into a fully functioning establishment. Therefore, we expect that firm survival is positively related to initial size.

To measure initial labour productivity, we use the ratio between the number of employees after one year from entry divided by the sales at the end of the same year (t + 1). We use the ratio at t + 1 in order to remove possible biases in the index due to the fact that some companies in the dataset are founded at the beginning of the year and others at the end. The sales-per-employee ratio provides a broad indication of how expensive a company is to run. It can be especially insightful when measuring the efficiency of businesses such as banks, retailers, consultants, software companies and media groups. A higher sales-per-employee ratio indicates that the company can operate on low overhead costs, and therefore do more with less employees, which often translates into healthy profits. Companies that concentrate on selling and distributing products will typically enjoy much higher sales-per-employee figures than firms that manufacture goods. Manufacturing is typically very labour-intensive, while sales and marketing activities rely on fewer people to generate the same sales numbers. Labour productivity may indicate firm quality. It may also provide an indirect measure of a firm's capital and sunk costs upon entry. Higher initial labour productivity suggests that a firm has a higher level of capital relative to labour. Higher capital levels likely means the firm has better access to financial resources, but also that a firm is more productive overall and/or operates in an industry with larger capital requirements. Further, more capital is also beneficial to firm survival because the firm can increase production in the future with greater ease by simply hiring more workers. Thus, initial labour productivity should associate negatively with firm hazard for all these reasons.

Moving to the initial industry variables, entry rate measures the logarithm of the number of entrants as a portion of the total number of firms within an industry at the year of entry (38,260 as reported by Aida database). Initial employment market share gives the portion of employment for an entry cohort as a portion of total employment within an industry at the year of entry (121,124 total employees as reported by Aida database); and capital-to-labour ratio is the ratio of total capital to total employment within an industry at the time of entry. Dunne et al. (1989) note that industry entry rates are highly correlated with industry exit rates. Caves (1998) documents entry rates and entrant survival across countries and finds this fact is robust. The positive correlation between entry and exit rates across industries suggests that some industries are subject to a greater amount of firm turnover. Jovanovic (1982) suggests entry is also about a firm learning its status within an industry. Thus, entry rate is expected to have a positive impact on firm hazard. Across industries, firms having a larger initial employment share indicate that the entrants are closer in size to incumbents after controlling for entry penetration rate. Thus, we expect a negative correlation between hazard rates and initial employment share within an industry. However, a larger employment share means that there is a greater demand for workers by new firms within an industry. This larger demand from new firms suggests that wages should rise within an industry. A rising wage increases the costs for firms, and may increase failure rates. The final industry proportional variable is industry capital-to-labour ratio at a firm's time of entry. This variable provides a measure of capital intensity with more capital-intensive industries having higher capital-to-labour ratios. Entry should be more difficult in more capital-intensive industries with high sunk capital costs. Firms entering highly capital-intensive industries are able to overcome the necessary capital requirements. Thus, hazard rates should have a negative relationship with industries' capital-to-labour ratio.

Table 11.2 provides descriptive statistics for the proportional time-invariant variables just described. Panel A contains summary statistics for the whole sample of 2009 entrants. Panel B presents summary statistics for

Table 11.2 Summary statistics

	Mean	*Median*	*Standard dev.*	*25th*	*75th*	*Number*
Panel A: all firms						
Leverage	50.02	0.82	186.42	0.60	0.92	319
Leverage—Q1	0.16	0.00	0.20	0.00	0.34	64
Leverage—Q2	0.66	0.67	0.07	0.61	0.73	64
Leverage—Q3	0.82	0.82	0.03	0.80	0.85	64
Leverage—Q4	0.91	0.91	0.02	0.88	0.92	64
Leverage—Q5	250.68	1.03	356.72	0.97	588.44	63
Employment size (log)	0.86	0.90	0.43	0.60	1.18	318
Labour productivity	194.06	125.22	230.86	63.75	222.05	242
Employment market share (log)	−2.41	−2.23	0.28	−2.60	−2.14	319
Panel B: survivors						
Leverage	39.33	0.80	164.42	0.55	0.91	215
Leverage—Q1	0.15	0.00	0.20	0.00	0.33	50
Leverage—Q2	0.66	0.67	0.07	0.59	0.72	46
Leverage—Q3	0.82	0.83	0.04	0.79	0.86	39
Leverage—Q4	0.90	0.90	0.02	0.88	0.92	46
Leverage—Q5	245.46	1.00	351.17	0.97	582.47	34
Employment size (log)	0.87	0.90	0.43	0.60	1.18	215
Labour productivity	199.36	132.20	211.71	72.59	239.71	165
Employment market share (log)	−2.42	−2.23	0.30	−2.60	−2.14	215
Panel C: exitors						
Leverage	72.11	0.84	224.47	0.73	0.96	104
Leverage—Q1	0.20	0.16	0.22	0.00	0.39	14
Leverage—Q2	0.67	0.69	0.07	0.61	0.74	18
Leverage—Q3	0.82	0.82	0.03	0.81	0.84	25
Leverage—Q4	0.91	0.92	0.02	0.90	0.93	18
Leverage—Q5	256.81	1.06	369.27	0.98	588.44	29
Employment size (log)	0.85	0.90	0.44	0.48	1.18	103
Labour productivity	182.68	97.17	268.49	52.17	185.17	77
Employment market share (log)	−2.39	−2.23	0.25	−2.60	−2.14	104

Some statistics are odd: labour productivity presents significantly higher levels with respect to Huynh et al. (2012a); leverage presents very high levels in Q5. This will require further analysis for authors on the final dataset those entrants surviving past 2016, whereas Panel C shows summary statistics for those entrants exiting the market prior to 2017. Generally, surviving entrants have more employees, are less productive and have a lower leverage ratio compared with exitors. Figure 11.1 provides survival rates, while Fig. 11.2 gives hazard rates for our entry cohort.

11.4 Methodology

11.4.1 Duration Analysis

The econometric technique used to study the exit probability of new firms is duration analysis. Unlike the standard logit models, duration models account for incompletely observed lifespans of firms surviving past the sample period. Duration models are used here to estimate the hazard rate for Italian manufacturing firms belonging to the 2009 entry cohort to assess their survival probability. The variables described in the previous paragraph are the initial conditions of manufacturing firms in the 2009

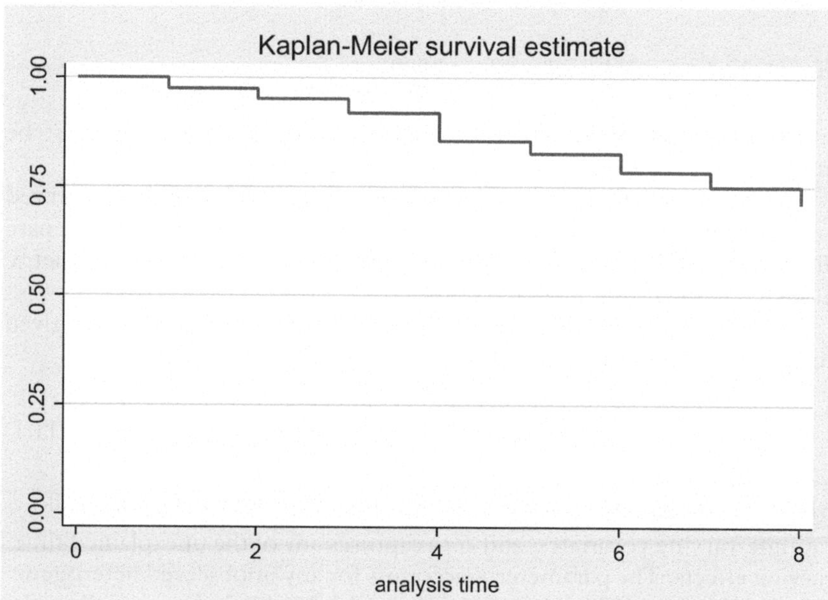

Fig. 11.1 Survivor function, cohort 2009

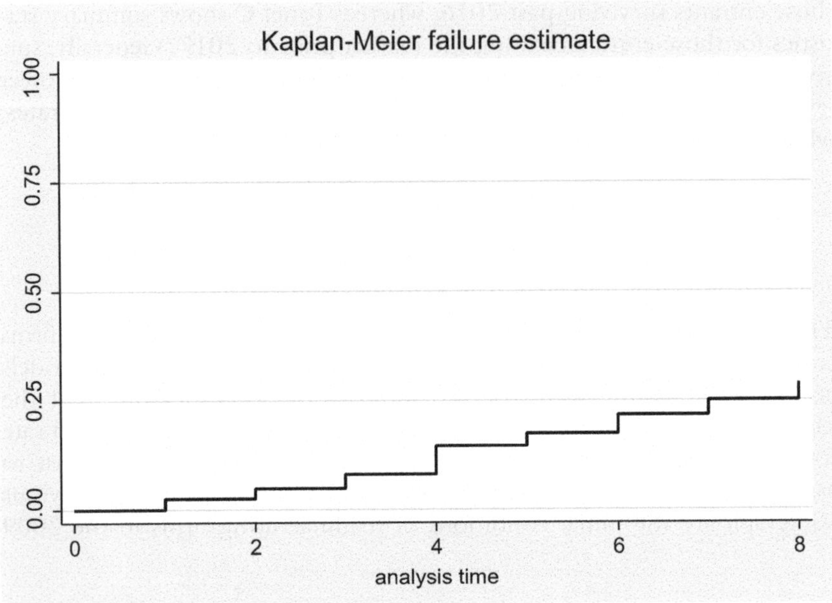

Fig. 11.2 Empirical hazards, cohort 2009

entry cohort. However, there are unobservable variables that must be modelled as firm-specific unobserved heterogeneity.

Huynh et al. (2012a) examine model misspecification and unobserved heterogeneity on firm duration for the 1985 entry cohort. They compare different possible estimation techniques (parametric versus semiparametric models), highlighting pros and cons.

In our paper, the exit probability, the proportion of deaths in a given year, is modelled using the Cox proportional hazard model:

$$\theta\left(t_i \middle| x_{it}, v_i\right) = v_i \phi\left(x_{it}\right) \lambda\left(t_i\right) \tag{11.1}$$

where t_i is the duration of the new firm i, $\phi\left(x_{it}\right) = exp\left(x_{it}^{'}\beta\right)$, which allows for time-varying covariates, and $\lambda(t_i)$ captures any of the unexplained time-varying effects. The parameter v_i accounts for any unobserved heterogeneity within a group. The limit of the Cox model is that it does not allow the unobserved heterogeneity to be modelled as a fixed effect. Therefore, distributional assumptions must be made when capturing v_i as a random effect. As in Huynh et al. (2012b), we use a Gamma distribution to account for this unobserved heterogeneity/shared-frailty with $g(v) = v^{\left(\frac{1}{\theta}\right)-1} e^{\left(-\frac{v}{\theta}\right)} / \Gamma\left(\frac{1}{\theta}\right)\theta^{1/\theta}$. These shared-frailty models allow for within-group correlation. The Gamma distribution has a positive support with a mean of 1 and finite variance θ. The semiparametric estimated hazard is robust to misspecification because of the flexibility of the non-parametric baseline hazard; therefore, the Cox proportional hazard estimator is consistent (see Cameron and Trivedi 2005 for further details on the Cox proportional hazard).

11.5 Results

In this section, we discuss results from the duration analysis. We investigate the determinants of entrant firm survival in the Italian manufacturing industry. All specifications include firm-specific variables as regressors (initial labour productivity and employment size) and industry-specific variables (entry penetration rate, employment market share size and capital-to-labour ratio). Our main objective is to assess whether the initial firm debt-to-asset ratio (leverage) is positively and significantly related to the survival of new firms.

Table 11.3 presents a summary of our results: Column 1 shows the output of our model without considering unobserved heterogeneity and the quintiles of the distribution for leverage; column 2 presents a model where unobserved heterogeneity is present; column 3 presents a model with leverage quintiles and unobserved heterogeneity. These specifications are performed in order to focus on the effects of initial debt-to-asset ratio on a firm's hazard rate.

In all the three model specifications considered, leverage positively affects firm hazard ratios, suggesting that companies that use higher initial levels of debt have a higher probability of failure, in coherence with the existing literature. However, none of the other firm-specific regressors is significant, meaning that our models are not well specified. This could be due to the small sample size together with the absence of several values. Moreover, we are not able to prove a non-linear relationship between leverage and firm hazard ratios, as in Huynh et al. (2012a, b). In fact, our Qleverage variable is a categorical variable assuming value from 1 to 5

Table 11.3 Duration of new firms

	(1)	(2)	(3)
Leverage	1.000925 (0.0003548)***	1.000925 (0.0003548)***	
Qleverage			1.361809 (0.1069216)***
Employment size (log)	0.7168954 (0.168467)	0.7168948 (0.168485)	0.7999238 (0.1869523)
Labour productivity	0.9987169 (0.0010968)	0.9987169 (0.0010969)	0.9982581 (0.0011905)
Entry rate	0.5197342 (1.074623)	0.5197302 (1.074737)	0.5585251 (1.138825)
Employment market share (log)	2.017478 (4.438812)	2.017419 (4.439191)	2.187916 (4.78936)
Capital-to-labour ratio	0.9998269 (0.0009279)	0.999827 (0.000928)	0.9999326 (0.0009416)
Heterogeneity (θ)	No	Yes	Yes
Log likelihood	−228.0567	−228.00887	−222.62646

Note: standard errors in parentheses

*Statistical significance at the 10% level

**Statistical significance at the 5% level

***Statistical significance at the 1% level

according to the quintile of the distribution of the leverage variable. It is significant at a 1% confidence level but if we discard this variable and introduce the corresponding values of each quintile (five different variables), none of them is significant, as in other studies.

11.6 Conclusions

This paper considers the life duration of entrant Italian manufacturing firms established in 2009, right after the outbreak of the financial crisis, using the comprehensive Aida Bureau van Dijk database. Data limitation is the cause of the difficulty in doing such research about young, small and private firms, especially about their financial state. Using financial and industrial data provided by Aida Bureau van Dijk, we study the relationship between initial leverage and firm hazard. Focusing only on the 2009 cohort—as a first step of a much broader research project—we cannot introduce in our model time-varying industry and macroeconomic factors; we have to focus only on time-invariant firm-specific regressors. We test for a common finding in the literature about financial resources and firm survival, that is a positive relation between firm hazard (probability of failure) and leverage, measured as debt-to-asset ratio. We also try to detect if such a relation is a non-monotonic one, as proved by Huynh et al. (2012b).

Our analysis confirms that the relation between leverage and firm hazard is positive and significant for the Italian manufacturing companies as well. We also find a weak evidence of a positive relation between the quintiles of the leverage distribution and the hazard ratio but this relation requires further investigation.

References

Akerlof, G. 1970. The Market for Lemons: Qualitative Uncertainty and the Market Mechanism. *Quarterly Journal of Economics* 84: 488–500.

Albuquerque, R., and H. Hopenhayn. 2004. Optimal Lending Contracts and Firm Dynamics. *Review of Economic Studies* 71 (2): 285–315.

Almeida, H., M. Campello, and M.S. Weisbach. 2004. The Cash Flow Sensitivity of Cash. *Journal of Finance* 59 (4): 1777–1804.

Alti, A. 2003. How Sensitive Is Investment to Cash Flow When Financing Is Frictionless? *The Journal of Finance* 58 (2): 707–722.

Audretsch, D. 1991. New Firm Survival and Technological Regime. *Review of Economics and Statistics* 68 (3): 441–450.

Audretsch, D., and T. Mahmood. 1995. New Firm Survival: New Results Using a Hazard Function. *Review of Economics and Statistics* 77 (1): 97–103.

Baldwin, J., L. Bian, R. Dupuy, G. Gellatly. 2000. *Failure Rates for New Canadian Firms: New Perspectives on Entry and Exit.* Occasional Papers 61-526-XPE, Statistics Canada.

Bellone, F., P. Musso, L. Nesta, and S. Schiavo. 2010. Financial Constraints and Firm Export Behaviour. *The World Economy* 33 (3): 347–373.

Berger, A., and G. F. Udell. 1998. The Economics of Small Business Finance: The Roles of Private Equity and Debt Markets in the Financial Growth Cycle. *Journal of Banking and Finance* 22: 613–73.

Berger, A.N., and G.F. Udell. 2006. A More Complete Conceptual Framework for SME Finance. *Journal of Banking and Finance* 30 (11): 2945–2966.

Binks, M.R., and C.T. Ennew. 1996. Growing Firms and the Credit Constraint. *Small Business Economics* 8 (1): 17–25.

Boeri, T., and L. Bellmann. 1995. Post-entry Behaviour and the Cycle: Evidence from Germany. *International Journal of Industrial Organization* 13: 483–500.

Brennan, M., and A. Kraus. 1987. Efficiency Financing under Asymmetric Information. *Journal of Finance* 42: 1225–1243.

Bridges, S., and A. Guariglia. 2008. Financial Constraints, Global Engagement, and Firm Survival in the United Kingdom: Evidence from Micro Data. *Scottish Journal of Political Economy* 55 (4): 444–464.

Brito, P. and A. Mello. 1995. Financial contraints and firm post-entry performance. *International Journal of Industrial Organization* 13 (4): 543–565.

Bunn, P. and V. Redwood. 2003. Company accounts based modelling of business failures and the implications for financial stability. Bank of England working papers. Bank of England. https://EconPapers.repec.org/RePEc:boe:boeewp:210

Cabral, L.M., and J. Mata. 2003. On the Evolution of the Firm Size Distribution: Facts and Theory. *American Economic Review* 93 (4): 1075–1090.

Cameron, A., and P.K. Trivedi. 2005. *Microeconometrics: Methods and Applications.* Cambridge University Press.

Caves, R.E. 1998. Industrial Organization and New Findings on the Turnover and Mobility of Firms. *Journal of Economic Literature* 36: 1947–1982.

Cleary, S. 1999. The Relationship between Firm Investment and Financial Status. *The Journal of Finance* 54 (2): 673–692.

Cooley, T.F., and V. Quadrini. 2001. Financial Markets and Firm Dynamics. *American Economic Review* 91 (5): 1286–1310.

DeMeza, D., and D.C. Webb. 1987. Too Much Investment: A Problem of Asymmetric Information. *Quarterly Journal of Economics* 102: 281–292.

———. 1992. Efficient Credit Rationing. *European Economic Review* 36: 1277–1290.

Disney, R., J. Haskel, and Y. Heden. 2003. Entry, Exit and Establishment Survival in UK Manufacturing. *Journal of Industrial Economics* 51 (1): 91–112.

Dunne, T., M. Roberts, and L. Samuelson. 1989. The Growth and Failure of U.S. Manufacturing Plants. *Quarterly Journal of Economics* 104: 671–698.

Fazzari, S., R.G. Hubbard, and B. Petersen. 1988. Finance Constraints and Corporate Investment. *Brookings Papers on Economic Activity* 1: 141–195.

Ferri, G., and P. Murro. 2015. Do Firm–Bank 'Odd Couples' Exacerbate Credit Rationing? *Journal of Financial Intermediation* 24 (2): 231–251.

Fotopoulos, G., and H. Louri. 2000. Determinants of Hazard Confronting New Entry: Does Financial Structure Matter. *Review of Industrial Organization* 17 (3): 285–300.

Geroski, P. A. 1992. Entry, Exit and Structural Adjustment in European Industry. In Karel Cool, J. Damien Neven and Ingo Walter (Eds.), *European Industrial Restructuring in the 1990s* (pp. 139–161). London: Macmillan.

Gomes, J.F. 2001. Financing Investment. *American Economic Review* 91 (5): 1263–1285.

Guariglia, A. and M. Garcia-Vega. 2007. Volatility, Financial Constraints, and Trade. U. of Nottingham Research Paper No. 2007/33. Available at SSRN: https://ssrn.com/abstract=1025447

Hall, B.H. 2002. The Financing of Research and Development. *Oxford Review of Economic Policy* 18 (1): 35–51.

Honjo, Y. 2000. Business Failure of New Firms: An Empirical Analysis Using a Multiplicative Hazards Model. *International Journal of Industrial Organization* 18: 557–574.

Huynh, K., and R. Petrunia. 2008. Entry Penetration in Canadian Manufacturing. *Economics Letters* 100 (1): 87–90.

Huynh, K.P., and R.J. Petrunia. 2010. Age Effects, Leverage, and Firm Growth. *Journal of Economic Dynamics and Control* 34 (5): 1003–1013.

Huynh, K.P., R.J. Petrunia, and M.C. Voia. 2010. The Impact of Initial Financial State on Firm Duration across Entry Cohorts. *Journal of Industrial Economics* 58 (3): 661–689.

Huynh, K.P., D.T. Jacho-Chávez, R. Petrunia, and M. Voia. 2011. Functional Principal Component Analysis of Density Families with Categorical and Continuous Data on Canadian Entrant Manufacturing Firms. *Journal of the American Statistical Association* 106 (495): 858–878.

Huynh, K.P., R. Petrunia, and M. Voia. 2012a. Initial Financial Conditions and the Survival of Nascent Canadian Manufacturing Firms. *Managerial and Decision Economics* 33 (2): 109–125.

———. 2012b. Duration of New Firms: The Role of Startup Financial Conditions, Industry and Aggregate Factors. *Structural Change and Economic Dynamics* 23: 354–362.

Jappelli, T., and M. Pagano. 2002. Information Sharing, Lending and Defaults: Cross-Country Evidence. *Journal of Banking and Finance* 26 (10): 2017–2045.

Jensen, M.C., and W. Meckling. 1976. Theory of the Firm: Managerial Behavior, Agency Costs, and Capital Structure. *Journal of Financial Economics* 3: 305–360.

Jovanovic, B. 1982. Selection and the Evolution of Industry. *Econometrica* 50 (3): 649–670.

Kallberg, J.G., and G.F. Udell. 2003. The Value of Private Sector Business Credit Information Sharing: The US Case. *Journal of Banking and Finance* 27 (3): 449–469.

Kaplan, S.N., and L. Zingales. 1997. Do Investment-Cash Flow Sensitivities Provide Useful Measures of Financing Constraints. *The Quarterly Journal of Economics* 112 (1): 169–215.

Lang, L., E. Ofek, and R. Stulz. 1996. Leverage, Investment and Growth. *Journal of Financial Economics* 40 (1): 3–29.

Lucas, R. E. 1978. On the Size Distribution of Business Firms. *The Bell Journal of Economics* 9 (2): 508–523.

Mata, J., and P. Portugal. 1994. Life Duration of New Firms. *Journal of Industrial Economics* 42 (3): 227–245.

Mata, J. and P. Portugal. 1999. Technology Intensity, Demand Conditions, and the Longevity of Firms. In D.B. Audretsch and A.R. Thurik (Eds.), *Innovation, Industry Evolution and Employment, Cambridge* (pp. 265–279). UK: Cambridge University Press.

Musso, P., and S. Schiavo. 2008. The Impact of Financial Constraints on Firm Survival and Growth. *Journal of Evolutionary Economics* 18 (2): 135–149.

Myers, S. 1977. Determinants of Corporate Borrowing. *Journal of Financial Economics* 5 (2): 147–175.

Noe, T.H., and M.J. Rebello. 1996. Asymmetric Information, Managerial Opportunism, Financing and Payout Policies. *Journal of Finance* 51: 637–660.

Oliveira, B., and A. Fortunato. 2006. Firm Growth and Liquidity Constraints: A Dynamic Analysis. *Small Business Economics* 27 (2): 139–156.

Rajan, R.G., and L. Zingales. 1995. What Do We Know about Capital Structure? Some Evidence from international data. *Journal of Finance* 50: 1421–1460.

Segarra, A. and M. Callejon. 2002. New Firms' Survival and Market Turbulence: New Evidence from Spain. *Review of Industrial Organization* 20: 1–14.

Spence, M. 1973. Job Market Signaling. *Quarterly Journal of Economics* 87: 355–374.

Stiglitz, J., and A. Weiss. 1981. Credit Rationing in Markets with Imperfect Information. *American Economic Review* 73: 393–409.

Sutton, J. 1997. Gibrat's Legacy. *Journal of Economic Literature* 35: 40–59.

Telser, L.G. 1966. Cutthroat competition and the long purse. *Journal of Law and Economics* 9: 259–277.

Vartia, L. 2004. Assessing Plant Entry and Exit Dynamics and Survival–Does Firms' Financial Status Matter?. Mimeograph, European University Institute.

Vivarelli, M. 2004. Are All the Potential Entrepreneurs So Good?. *Small Business Economics* 23: 41–49.

Wagner, J. 1994. The Post-Entry Performance of New Small Firms in German Manufacturing Industries. *Journal of Industrial Economics* 42 (2): 141–154.

Zhang, S. 2016. Institutional Arrangements and Debt Financing. *Research in International Business and Finance* 36: 362–372.

Zingales, L. 1998. Survival of the Fittest or the Fattest? Exit and Financing in the Trucking Industry. *Journal of Finance* 53 (3): 905–938.

Index[1]

[1] Note: Page numbers followed by ‘n’ refer to notes.

C. Cruciani et al. (eds.), *Banking and Beyond*, Palgrave Macmillan Studies in Banking and Financial Institutions,
https://doi.org/10.1007/978-3-030-45752-5

The manufacturer's authorised representative in the EU is Springer Nature Customer Service Centre GmbH, Europaplatz 3, 69115 Heidelberg, Germany. If you have any concerns regarding our products, please contact ProductSafety@springernature.com

Printed and bound by CPI Group (UK) Ltd, Croydon, CR0 4YY
22/09/2026
02221061-0002